OXFORD COMPARATIVE CONSTITUTIONALISM

Ex-Ministers as Constitutional Judges

OXFORD COMPARATIVE CONSTITUTIONALISM

Comparative constitutional law has a long and distinguished history in intellectual thought and in the construction of public law. As political actors and the people who create or modify their constitutional orders, they often wish to learn from the experience and learning of others. This cross- fertilization and mutual interaction has only accelerated with the onset of globalization, which has transformed the world into an interconnected web that facilitates dialogue and linkages across international and regional structures. Oxford Comparative Constitutionalism seeks to publish scholarship of the highest quality in constitutional law that deepens our knowledge of local, national, regional, and global phenomena through the lens of comparative public law.

ALSO PUBLISHED IN THIS SERIES

Redefining Comparative Constitutional Law
Essays for Mark Tushnet
Edited by Madhav Khosla and Vicki C. Jackson

Foreign Relations Federalism
The EU in Comparative Perspective
Thomas Verellen

Responsive Judicial Review
Democracy and Dysfunction in the Modern Age
Rosalind Dixon

Outsourcing Rulemaking Powers
Constitutional limits and national safeguards
Cedric Jenart

Abusive Constitutional Borrowing
Legal globalization and the subversion of liberal democracy
Rosalind Dixon and David Landau

A Theory of African Constitutionalism
Berihun Adugna Gebeye

Eternity Clauses In Democratic Constitutionalism
Silvia Suteu

Deliberative Peace Referendums
Ron Levy, Ian O'Flynn, Hoi L. Kong

Scales of Memory Constitutional Justice and Historical Evil
Justin Collings

The Global South and Comparative Constitutional Law
Edited by Philipp Dann, Michael Riegner, and Maxim Bönnemann

Ex-Ministers as Constitutional Judges

MATHIAS MÖSCHEL, *PHD, LLM*
Head of the Legal Studies Department,
Central European University, Austria

OXFORD
UNIVERSITY PRESS

OXFORD
UNIVERSITY PRESS

Great Clarendon Street, Oxford, OX2 6DP,
United Kingdom

Oxford University Press is a department of the University of Oxford.
It furthers the University's objective of excellence in research, scholarship,
and education by publishing worldwide. Oxford is a registered trade mark of
Oxford University Press in the UK and in certain other countries

Published in the United States of America by Oxford University Press
198 Madison Avenue, New York, NY 10016, United States of America

British Library Cataloguing in Publication Data
Data available

Library of Congress Control Number: 2024948922

ISBN 9780198930198

DOI: 10.1093/9780198930228.001.0001

Printed and bound by
CPI Group (UK) Ltd, Croydon, CR0 4YY

MIX
Paper | Supporting
responsible forestry
FSC® C013604
FSC
www.fsc.org

The manufacturer's authorised representative in the EU for product safety is Oxford University Press España S.A. of El Parque Empresarial San Fernando de Henares, Avenida de Castilla, 2 – 28830 Madrid (www.oup.es/en or product.safety@oup.com). OUP España S.A. also acts as importer into Spain of products made by the manufacturer.

To my late father, Günther Möschel, whose even-mindedness, balance, profound humanity, and sense of humour accompany us every day

Acknowledgements

I have always believed and written that research is a collective endeavour, even when one is the sole author. The current work has not only confirmed but reinforced this belief. This book would not exist in its current form if each and all of the individuals nominated here below had not contributed to it.

First, my deep gratitude goes to all the individuals who have to remain anonymous and who—despite their busy schedules—have kindly agreed to take their time with me and to patiently answer my questions. These interviews will remain forever with me as wonderful intellectual and human experiences.

Second, I would like to thank Central European University (CEU) for providing the institutional backing and framework within which to write this book. I also benefited from research stays at the Ecole de droit of Sciences-Po in Paris and at the European University Institute (EUI) in Florence. As crucial as such institutional affiliations and backings may be, they are made up of persons and I would like to specially thank a few who are affiliated with the above-mentioned institutions for providing intellectual and material help to develop and sharpen my thoughts further: Markus Böckenförde, Horatia Muir-Watt, Xymena Kurowska, Sébastien Pimont, Valentina Spiga, Guillaume Tusseau, and Inga Winkler.

Many other colleagues outside of those specific institutions have also contributed to this book, each in their own way. I have learnt enormously and received helpful and invaluable information and feedback from conversations and exchanges with Maria Bertl, Giacomo Delledonne, Muriel Fabre-Magnan, Barbara Havelkova, Aurore Gaillet, Konrad Lachmayer, Elisabetta Lamarque, Giuseppe Martinico, Andreas Müller, Nicoletta Perlo, Thomas Perroud, Antoine Vauchez, and Ulrich Wagrandl.

In a much more material way, I would also like to thank the editors of OUP and especially Paulina dos Santos Major for guiding me patiently through the book production process, as well as Mirella Benes for designing the wonderful book cover. Moreover, special thanks go to various junior colleagues who have helped me with background research, technological support, proof-reading, and similar issues. I hope that Joshua Haynes Mannering, Sophie Raehme, Darren Seiffert, and Arnisa Tepelja as well as the other PhD researchers who took a doctoral workshop on this book learnt a lot while reading and helping me with drafts of this book. I wish all of them a successful academic career.

Apart from intellectual and material support, emotional stability is key when embarking on the writing path. The initial thoughts of this book were developed at a difficult time, when CEU had to move from Budapest to Vienna and when

Covid-19 had its grip over the world. Without friends and family, I would not have had the stamina to move on.

In this sense, my heartfelt thanks go out to my husband, Laurent Laforest, who has not only been my emotional but also intellectual pillar. Of course, my siblings, Katarina and Rupert as well as my mother, Lilo, have been there all the way. Last but not least, a special mention to Sebastiano Midolo and Edurne Iraizoz for both their friendship and linguistic help during the early stages of the book.

Contents

Figures

Tables

Table of Cases

INTERNATIONAL AND REGIONAL

African Court on Human and People's Rights (ACtHR)

Court of Justice of the European Union (CJEU)

European Court of Human Rights (ECtHR)

NATIONAL

Austria

France

Germany

Italy

Spain

UK

US

Abbreviations

ACtHR	African Court of Human and People's Rights
AfD	Alternative für Deutschland
AG	Advocate General
BAG	Bundesarbeitsgericht (German Supreme Labour Court)
BCC	Benin Constitutional Court
BFH	Bundesfinanzhof (German Supreme Finance Court)
BGBl	Bundesgesetzblatt (Austrian and German Federal Law Gazette)
BGH	Bundesgerichtshof (German Supreme Court)
BSG	Bundessozialgericht (German Supreme Social Court)
BVerfG	Bundesverfassungsgericht (German Federal Constitutional Court)
BVerfGG	Bundesverfassungsgerichtsgesetz (Statute on the German Federal Constitutional Court)
BVerwG	Bundesverwaltungsgericht (German Supreme Administrative Court)
B-VG	Bundesverfassungsgesetz (Austrian Constitution)
Cass	Corte di cassazione (Italian Supreme Court)
CC	Conseil constitutionnel (French Constitutional Court)
C Cass	Cour de cassation (French Supreme Court)
CCC	Ustavni sud Republike Hrvatske (Croatian Constitutional Court)
C conti	Corte dei conti (Italian Court of Accounts)
C cost	Corte costituzionale (Italian Constitutional Court)
CCR	Curtea Constituțională a României (Romanian Constitutional Court)
CE	Conseil d'Etat (French Supreme Administrative Court)
CEE	Central and Eastern Europe
CJEU	Court of Justice of the European Union
Cons St	Consiglio di Stato (Italian Supreme Administrative Court)
DVBl	Deutsches Verwaltungsblatt
EC	European Commission
ECHR	European Convention on Human Rights
ECtHR	European Court of Human Rights
ENA	Ecole nationale d'administration (National School of Administration)
EP	European Parliament
EU	European Union
GG	Grundgesetz (German Federal Constitution)
NJW	Neue Juristische Wochenschrift
NPD	Nationaldemokratische Partei Deutschland
NVwZ	Neue Zeitschrift für Verwaltungsrecht
OGH	Oberster Gerichtshof (Austrian Supreme Court)
PiS	Prawo i Sprawiedliwość (Law and Justice Party)

QPC	*question prioritaire de constitutionnalité* (priority question of constitutionality)
SCC	Ústavný súd Slovenskej republiky (Slovak Constitutional Court)
Snr	Senior
TC	Tribunal constitucional (Spanish Constitutional Court)
TEU	Treaty on the European Union
TFEU	Treaty on the Functioning of the European Union
TK	Trybunał Konstytucyjny (Polish Constitutional Court)
UN	United Nations
USSC	United States Supreme Court
VfGG	Verfassungsgerichtshofgesetz (Statute on the Austrian Constitutional Court)
VfGH	Verfassungsgerichtshof (Austrian Constitutional Court)
VwGH	Verwaltungsgerichtshof (Austrian Supreme Administrative Court)

1
Introduction

A Justice Minister introduces a new code of criminal procedure which is named after him. Shortly after its promulgation he becomes constitutional judge and (potentially) decides on the constitutionality of this reform. A Prime Minister who has been active in a given political party becomes constitutional judge and finds himself (potentially) judging an electoral dispute involving one of his friends from the same party. Another minister is part of a government and, in accordance with internal constitutional practice, legislation is presumed to be adopted unanimously by the cabinet. He becomes a constitutional judge and, according to that practice, he was in favour of such legislation. Yet another minister intervenes in public debates about a legislative reform, expressing him or herself in favour or against it. These are only a few situations involving ex-ministers that really occurred and that give a sense of the type of issues this book intends to shed light on.

Puzzlingly, so far, the issue of what happens when former members of government become constitutional judges has not raised much academic-comparative debate, at least in established constitutional democracies, where there is a longer track record and history of constitutional courts. One reason for this silence could be that it simply was not worth discussing because, so far, the participation of ex-ministers as constitutional judges did not lead to profound troubles that could shake the foundations of such institutions. But the political-legal context is changing. Against a backdrop of backsliding constitutional democracies and illiberal constitutionalism, is this seemingly anodyne practice and reality still so irrelevant? Did we overlook something so far that takes on a different flavour even in the established constitutional democracies which this book looks at? These are some more issues which this book intends to raise.

It is not unheard of that, around the Globe, ex-ministers join constitutional courts as judges. The world's first constitutional court in Austria had four judges with such a political past. Since then, one can identify—to a larger or lesser extent, depending on the legal system—former high-level executive politicians becoming constitutional judges. The same observation is true for supreme courts, where ex-ministers have also joined the highest judicial ranks. The passage from highest executive functions to highest judicial ones is what this book intends to provide an in-depth and contextualized analysis of. So far, there is a surprising dearth of literature looking into what such a change of hats means from a theoretical, epistemological, empirical, and practical perspective for constitutional law and understandings of constitutional courts. Put briefly and differently, this book intends to

Ex-Ministers as Constitutional Judges. Mathias Möschel, Oxford University Press. © Mathias Möschel 2025.
DOI: 10.1093/9780198930228.003.0001

look into what happens to constitutional courts when ex-ministers become constitutional judges, and thus guardians of the constitution.

This main research question will be broken down into a set of sub-questions that will guide the analysis and reader and that will be organized in two separate, yet related levels. On a first, more theoretical plane, the questions that such participation raises are many. How, if at all, is this participation linked to the phenomenon of judicialization of politics? Is there an increase or decrease over time? What consequences does the participation of ex-ministers as constitutional judges have with regard to contemporary understandings of separation of powers, rule of law, independence, and impartiality of constitutional courts, as well as of constitutional justice? What advantages and risks do ex-ministers bring to constitutional courts? What, if any, are the legal limits to their participation at the national and international level? If such risks are deemed to prevail, how can they be minimized?

A second set of questions relates to a more temporal and contextual plane that has arisen with regard to more recent developments in (comparative) constitutional law and practice: the rise of illiberalism or constitutional/democratic backsliding. One could surmise that the reason for the absence from academic literature of any in-depth analysis of the practice and reality of nominating ex-ministers as constitutional judges is that, so far, it has caused no reasons for serious concern. The constitutional and democratic traditions, practices, and real-life experiences have functioned well-enough to implicitly or explicitly limit any potential risks that could, in theory, come with such a consecutive mixing of functions. Can we presume that this will remain the case if and when such traditions and practices are eroding at the hands of illiberal political forces that are emerging in Europe and elsewhere? Or does the participation of ex-ministers look slightly more worrying against such a backdrop?

Without directly and exhaustively answering all these questions, this book intends to provide some initial reflection points via a comparative constitutional analysis of four established constitutional systems in Western Europe.

1.1 Defining the Scope; or What this Book is About

So far, an in-depth comparative, academic analysis of the questions and issues raised above is lacking. Previous publications have either been limited to a single jurisdiction[1] or—when comparative—have focused on doctrinal descriptions and

[1] See eg for Austria: Kurt Heller, *Der Verfassungsgerichtshof* (Verlag Österreich 2010); for Italy: Gustavo Zagrebelsky and Valeria Marcenò, *Giustizia costituzionale, I. Storia, principi, interpretazione* (2nd edn, il Mulino 2018); for Germany: Uwe Kranenpohl, *Hinter dem Schleier des Beratungsgeheimnisses. Der Willensbildungs- und Entscheidungsprozess beim BVerfG* (Verlag für Sozialwissenschaften 2010); for France: Dominique Schnapper, *Une sociologue au Conseil constitutionnel* (Gallimard 2010).

analyses of the composition and qualification requirements of constitutional court judges, independence and impartiality standards, or the rules pertaining to abstentions and recusals.[2] The personal, political, or institutional experience and/or identities of actual nominees have been less relevant in such academic publications. This is where newspaper articles on single nominations sometimes provide useful and interesting details that describe the political logics and drama surrounding such nominations or failed nominations. However, such articles are rarely comparative or academic in nature. They remain anecdotal, ephemeral. Moreover, one may wonder if they are driven by political biases. This book will combine the readings of such different sources which will allow for a more in-depth comparative, contextualized, and academic analysis of the consequences the presence of ex-ministers has on such institutions.

More broadly, the relative silence of (comparative) constitutional and academic literature on the question of what ex-ministers bring to constitutional courts as judges is puzzling because it is directly related to the famous and now almost 100-year-old theoretical debate between Carl Schmitt and Hans Kelsen on who should act as the 'Guardian of the Constitution' (*Hüter der Verfassung*). The debate developed between 1928 and 1932 in various fora and successive publications.[3] It highlighted the different understandings these two men had of the state, separation of powers, and of the role constitutional courts can and should play in the context of that dynamic.[4] In essence, for Schmitt and his understanding of power in the political order, the best-placed institution for the protection of the Constitution was the President. In opposition to Schmitt's view, Kelsen proposed a constitutional court as the ideal guardian of the constitution, believing such an institution to be more neutral and less political than the President.

Schmitt's main objection to Kelsen's proposition of a constitutional court as such a guardian was that the interpretation of the open-ended norms and principles of constitutional and international law does not allow judges to neatly apply a formalist method of 'subsumption' by characterizing the facts of a case according to sufficiently clear legal rules.[5] Instead, the interpretation of such norms and

[2] For comparative law publications touching upon some of the issues discussed in this book, see: Guillaume Tusseau, *Contentieux constitutionnel comparé* (LGDJ 2021); Maartje de Visser, *Constitutional Review in Europe. A Comparative Analysis* (Hart 2014); Marcel Kau, *United States Supreme Court und Bundesverfassungsgericht: Die Bedeutung des United States Supreme Court für die Errichtung und Fortentwicklung des Bundesverfassungsgerichts* (Springer 2007).

[3] For a good overview of these various sides of this debate see: Gustavo Zagrebelsky and Valeria Marcenò, *Giustizia costituzionale, I. Storia, principi, interpretazione* (2nd edn, il Mulino 2018) 49, fn 92.

[4] For recent summaries of these different understandings, see in English: Lars Vinx, *The Guardian of the Constitution. Hans Kelsen and Carl Schmitt on the Limits of Constitutional Law* (CUP 2015) 1–21; in German: Robert Chr. van Ooyen, 'Die Funktion der Verfassungsgerichtsbarkeit in der pluralistischen Demokratie und die Kontroverse um den '"Hüter der "Verfassung"' in Robert Chr. van Ooyen (ed) and Hans Kelsen, *Wer soll der Hüter der Verfassung sein?* (2nd edn, Mohr Siebeck 2019) vi–xxiii; and Dieter Grimm, *Verfassungsgerichtsbarkeit* (Suhrkamp 2021) 105–22.

[5] The irony that it was Schmitt who raised the issue of neatly separable legal and political spheres—when it is often Kelsen and his legal positivism which are associated with such arguments—has not escaped the literature: Robert Chr. van Ooyen, 'Die Funktion der Verfassungsgerichtsbarkeit in der

principles (which Schmitt considers non-justiciable) damage adjudication by politicizing it (*Politisierung der Justiz*) to a far greater extent than politics can hope to be judicialized (*Judizialisierung der Politik*).[6]

Kelsen also understood the (risk of) politicizing constitutional courts, but he proposed ways to rein politics in. First, his approach was predicated on a narrow understanding of what a constitutional court's role should be, ie that its mission ought to be confined to the determination of vertical and horizontal conflicts of powers in which open-ended principles such as equity, justice, freedom, equality, and/or morality would and should have little room. In that sense, Kelsen's idea of a constitutional court was concerned not so much with the substantive protection of individual rights but rather with the procedural arbitration of constitutional conflicts amongst and between organs of state and political actors.[7]

Secondly, he agreed with Schmitt that a certain degree of politicization was unavoidable. To avoid throwing the baby out with the bathwater, he advocated for making the court's political nature and any political influence on it more explicit, through the design of the nomination procedure for its judges:

> However desirable it would be to keep all party-political influences away from the judicature of the constitutional court, it is particularly difficult to achieve the realization of this postulate. One cannot close one's eyes to the fact that even experts—consciously or unconsciously—are motivated by political concerns. Whenever this danger is especially large, it is almost better to accept the legitimate participation of political parties in the formation of the court, instead of having to deal with non-official and uncontrollable party-political influence. This could take place, for instance, by filling a part of the seats on the court through election in parliament and to organize this election in a way that takes account of the relative strength of the parties. If the other positions are filled with experts the latter will have much greater freedom to give consideration to purely juristic matters, since their political conscience will then be relieved by the participation of those who are appointed to protect political interest.[8]

One could say that, in a rather pragmatic and realistic way, Kelsen saw the involvement of politics and political parties in the formation of constitutional courts as a necessary evil. At the same time, further recommendations on the composition

pluralistischen Demokratie und die Kontroverse um den "Hüter der Verfassung"' in Robert Chr. van Ooyen (ed) and Hans Kelsen, *Wer soll der Hüter der Verfassung sein?* (2nd edn, Mohr Siebeck 2019) xix–xx.

[6] Lars Vinx, *The Guardian of the Constitution. Hans Kelsen and Carl Schmitt on the Limits of Constitutional Law* (CUP 2015) 90–91.

[7] ibid 27–56.

[8] ibid 48.

and qualifications of the future members of such courts indicate how he tried to minimize such political influence. Indeed, in his own words, '[i]t is of the utmost importance that legal experts be given due consideration in the composition of the court. ... It is also important to exclude from membership in the constitutional court members of parliament or of government, because their acts are the acts that are to be controlled by the court.'[9] He further reiterated that: '[w]ith regard to the composition of the constitutional court, which is a collegial organ, one has to take care, above all, to eliminate party-political influence and to attract legal expertise, in particular, in constitutional law.'[10]

With the benefit of hindsight, we know that the institutional aspect of Kelsen's vision and solutions prevailed over Schmitt's in the modern design of constitutionality review.[11] Constitutional courts and not presidents have become the arbiters of constitutional disputes and the guardians of constitutions. Nevertheless, the observations gleaned from the famous *disputatio* between Schmitt and Kelsen are of relevance for this book's analyses. Indeed, Kelsen's early indications on the composition, nomination procedures, and the political and/or legal natures of constitutional courts are directedly linked with the object of this book and the question: what happens when ex-ministers join constitutional courts as judges? Would the degree of politicization in constitutional courts today be acceptable to the likes of Kelsen?

As we have already seen, Kelsen 'only' refers to this issue indirectly by advocating the principle that a parliamentarian or a member of government should not be eligible to sit simultaneously on the bench of a constitutional court. This principle derives from the cardinal rule of natural justice that no one should act as a judge in their own cause (*nemo iudex causa sua*). Ironically, the Austrian Constitutional Court of 1920, the Verfassungsgerichtshof (VfGH),[12] did not respect this basic principle, given that some of the sitting judges in the early days of the court were simultaneously members of the government and/or parliament.[13] This initial incongruence of the design of the VfGH's with Kelsen's teachings can (also) be

[9] ibid.

[10] ibid 76.

[11] This does not mean that the role of courts in exercising the function of constitutionality review has not remained uncontested, especially by authors in English-speaking academia. See for all: Jeremy Waldron, *The Dignity of Legislation* (CUP 1999); Mark Tushnet, *Taking the Constitution Away from the Courts* (Princeton University Press 1999); Larry D Kramer, *Popular Constitutionalism and Judicial Review* (OUP 2004); and Martin Loughlin, *Against Constitutionalism* (Harvard University Press 2022).

[12] Throughout this book, where possible, I shall use abbreviations based on these institutions' names in their original language, rather than the English translations thereof. See the list of abbreviations provided. As to the translations, unless indicated otherwise, they are those of the author.

[13] See the tables in Chapter 3. Art 122 of the 1931 Spanish Constitution also permitted members of parliament to simultaneously sit as constitutional court judges on the short-lived first Spanish constitutional court. For a critique of this practice, see: Francisco Fernández Segado, *La justicia constitucional en América Latina y España* (vol III, Dykinson 2009) 561–69.

explained by the fact that Kelsen developed its intellectual foundations and justifications *after* its establishment.[14]

Kelsen seemingly failed to consider temporal factors in his normative observations on the minimization of the political influence upon—or the political nature of—constitutional courts; today one cannot (or should not) be a constitutional court judge and a member of parliament or government simultaneously. But ought the participation of *ex*-ministers in such courts be seen as a politicization of a constitutional court's judicial functions? In this sense, this book can be read as adding to those early debates.[15]

Simultaneously, this book also enters into a dialogue with more contemporary academic discussions and developments in comparative constitutional law and comparative politics that are on occasion subsumed under the umbrella term 'judicialization of politics' and also what Hirschl (and Schmitt earlier) called the 'flip side of the judicialization of politics', namely, the 'politicization of the judiciary'.[16] Especially in the writings of Alec Stone Sweet and Ran Hirschl, these old Schmittian expressions have taken a modern turn. According to them, since the late twentieth century, politics and politicians have, for a variety of reasons, relied increasingly on courts and judicial means to consider and address key moral, public policy, and political issues.[17] Other related terms, such as 'juridicization',[18] 'juristocracy',[19] 'jurocracy',[20] or 'courtocracy',[21] have been developed, in part by the authors mentioned above. However, I will use the terms *judicialization of politics* and *politicization of the judiciary*, which have emerged as the most common in the literature.

In particular with regard to the former expression, the focus on constitutional court judges who were ex-ministers sheds light upon the personified links between the law and politics. Does the increase of 'judicialization of politics' also lead to an

[14] See: Guillaume Tusseau, *Contentieux constitutionnel comparé* (LGDJ 2021) 153.

[15] The fact that the judicial review of the constitutionality of statutes remains controversial due to the 'counter-majoritarian difficulty' (on this term: Alexander Bickel, *The Least Dangerous Branch. The Supreme Court at the Bar of Politics* (Yale University Press 1986)) is a different debate that will not be considered in-depth here. However, see on this: Jeremy Waldron, 'The Core of the Case Against Judicial Review' (2006) 115 Yale LJ 1346.

[16] Ran Hirschl, 'Judicialization of Politics' in Gregory A Caldeira, R Daniel Kelemen, and Keith E Whittington (eds), *The Oxford Handbook of Law and Politics* (OUP 2008) 120.

[17] See eg: Alec Stone Sweet, *Governing with Judges. Constitutional Politics in Europe* (OUP 2000); John Ferejohn, 'Judicializing Politics, Politicizing Law' (2002) 65 Law & Contemporary Problems 41; and Ran Hirschl, 'Judicialization of Politics' in Gregory A Caldeira, R Daniel Kelemen, and Keith E Whittington (eds), *The Oxford Handbook of Law and Politics* (OUP 2008) 119–41.

[18] Alec Stone, *The Birth of Judicial Politics. The Constitutional Council in Comparative Perspective* (OUP 1992) 8–10.

[19] Ran Hirschl, *Towards Juristocracy. The Origins and Consequences of the New Constitutionalism* (Harvard University Press 2004).

[20] Donald Horowitz, *Courts and Social Policy* (The Brooking Institution 1977).

[21] Kim Lane Scheppele, 'Democracy by Judiciary (or why can courts be sometimes more democratic than Parliaments)' in Adam Czarnota, Martin Krygier, and Wojciech Sadurski (eds), *Rethinking the Rule of Law in Post-Communist Europe* (CEU Press 2003) 25.

increased 'politicization of the judiciary', via nominating more such political personalities to constitutional courts? As to the latter expression, I use it in somewhat particular ways here.

The first term, *politicization*, could be understood in various ways, though it mostly bears a negative connotation. In the legal context, the expression often refers to the idea that there is a legal sphere separate from the political. Politicization therefore implies the contamination of the former by the latter. As we have already seen in the Kelsen-Schmitt debate, according to Schmitt, assigning the power to conduct constitutionality review to the courts generally or to a constitutional court specifically has the potential to transform the neutral and objective legal nature of such institutions into something more contentious and political. In other domains of social sciences, the term is used to identify a process whereby a previously unpolitical matter becomes a subject of public discussion with consequent effects—usually negative—upon the quality of political decision-making.[22] For the purposes of this book, I will use the term in a literal or rather in the embodied/bodily sense, namely to refer to when ex-ministers become constitutional judges, and politics physically joins the judicial decision-making process via the personae and high-level political past of some of its members.[23]

With regard to the term *judiciary*, for this book's purposes I will also adopt a specific definition. I consider constitutional courts to be part of the judiciary in a broader sense. This may be seen as more or less problematic, depending on the legal system one is looking at. In Germany, this inclusion seems to be more conventional, given that Article 92 of the German Constitution (*Grundgesetz*—GG) places the Federal Constitutional Court (*Bundesverfassungsgericht*—BVerfG) amongst the bodies that belong to the judicial power. In other systems, such as in Italy, the Constitution regulates the Constitutional Court (*Corte costituzionale*—C cost) in a separate section from the one regulating the judiciary, leading to discussions on whether that court ought to be considered part of the judiciary.[24] The inclusion of constitutional courts as part of the judiciary is probably most problematic in France, where the term 'Constitutional Council' (*Conseil constitutionnel*—CC) and the body's origins indicate that it ought not be considered a court. Moreover, the individuals sitting on the CC are not officially referred to as judges, but as members who—on top of that—are not required to have any legal education.

However, apart from internal developments, especially with regard to France, several transnational and external changes have arguably strengthened the judicial nature of constitutional courts over the years, very much to the detriment

[22] See eg in international relations: Michael Zürn, 'The Politicisation of World Politics and Its Effects: Eight Propositions' (2014) 6 European Political Science Review 47.

[23] As I am clarifying my terminology here, I will at times also use the term 'minister' to refer to former members of government or of the executive. In no way is this intended to refer to members of the clergy.

[24] For a summary of these discussions, see Elisabetta Lamarque, *Corte costituzionale e giudici nell'Italia repubblicana* (Laterza 2017) 20–29.

of their political nature in two major ways. On the one hand, over the past few years, constitutional courts have themselves started referring cases to the Court of Justice of the European Union (CJEU) under the preliminary reference procedure.[25] The CJEU has recognized that these courts are indeed courts or tribunals of a member state for the purposes of Article 267 of the Treaty on the Functioning of the European Union (TFEU). Not only has this—so to speak—judicialized these bodies and strengthened their legal profile vis-à-vis their political one, but it has also led to them engaging in an active judicial dialogue with the highest courts of the European Union (EU).

On the other hand, constitutional courts are increasingly 'forced' into framing things judicially rather than politically, due to the rulings and interpretations of the European Court of Human Rights (ECtHR), which has applied the right to fair trial enshrined in Article 6 of the European Convention on Human Rights (ECHR) to certain constitutional proceedings, especially those which relate to the determination of civil rights and obligations or to criminal charges.[26] In broader terms, constitutional courts are expected to respect the right to a fair trial in the same manner as most other courts are required to. For these reasons and due to these developments, I include these constitutional courts as part of the judiciary, not necessarily in formal terms, but certainly in functional ones. As a consequence, I consider the issue of political participation on constitutional courts to be a question of the politicization of a particular type of judicial body.

Linking back to Stone Sweet's and Hirschl's analyses of the judicialization of politics, one hypothetical consequence of this increased judicialization of politics is that politicians in turn attempt to control the judiciary by nominating close friends and (former) politicians/colleagues to constitutional courts at an increased rate. Put differently, if constitutional courts were previously less relevant to political actors and legislative work, now that these activities are being judicialized/constitutionalized, and are thereby placing hitherto unheard-of constraints upon political actors, one might expect that politicians would try to find ways of removing such constraints by controlling the judiciary. One such possible control method would be to place former politicians onto constitutional courts.[27] Therefore, contemporary discussions and analyses that have developed in comparative judicial politics and comparative constitutional law are certainly relevant for this book's purposes.

Apart from drawing on the insights and conversing with the scientific fields of comparative constitutional law and comparative politics, this book also engages with political sociology, wherein an awakening of interest in constitutional courts

[25] In chronological order this happened: for Austria, with decisions B 2251/97-24 and B 2594/97-15 of 10 March 1999; for Italy, with decision no 103 of 13 February 2008; for Germany, with decision 2 BvR 2728/13 of 14 January 2014; and for France, with the CC, decision 2013-314P QPC of 4 April 2013.

[26] See especially below Chapter 5.

[27] An answer to this question will be provided at the end of Chapter 3.

as actors located between law and politics is taking place. Indeed, according to such literature, the judicialization of modern societies and the emergence of a relatively uniform legal constitutional model in many jurisdictions has increasingly legalized social and political interaction, leading to relatively similar institutional results.[28] A particular Bourdieusian strand of these political-sociological approaches[29] is of interest to my own work here. In fact, the notion of the 'juridical field' developed by Bourdieu has led to several publications on courts and/or the role of lawyers in constructing this juridical field,[30] a strand of literature which incorporates ethnographical,[31] socio-historical,[32] and/or biographical methods of studying individual lawyers and judges in these institutions or constitutional spaces.[33] On such biographical methods and approaches to studying and understanding especially apex courts, one can also find recent comparative constitutional studies that focus on or are structured around single judges' biographies. However, in most cases these focus on judges from common law countries[34] and only rarely on civil law countries and their apex court judges.[35] The ultimate outcome and result is a Geertzian 'thicker'[36] comparative constitutional ethnographical description and analysis[37] of the phenomenon in these four jurisdictions that may help by providing broader

[28] Paul Blokker, 'Sociology of constitutional law and politics' in Jiří Přibáň (ed), *Research Handbook on Sociology of the Law* (Edward Elgar 2020) 230–31. From the same author, see also: Paul Blokker, 'Politics and the Political in Sociological Constitutionalism' in Paul Blokker and Chris Thornhill (eds), *Sociological Constitutionalism* (CUP 2017) 178.

[29] Other approaches in this domain that are mentioned are Luhmannian perspectives, critical-theoretical works, conflict-theoretical analyses, and cultural approaches: ibid. 231–36.

[30] See eg for the EU context: Antoine Vauchez and Bruno De Witte (eds), *Lawyering Europe: European Law as a Transnational Field* (Hart 2013); closer to the object of this book, see eg: Antonin Cohen, 'Legal Professionals or Political Entrepreneurs? Constitution Making as a Process of Social Construction and Political Mobilization' (2010) 4 International Political Sociology 107, or on the French CC: Nicolas Bau and Liora Israël, 'Quelques éclairages sociologiques sur la composition du Conseil constitutionnel' in Elina Lemaire and Thomas Perroud (eds), *Le Conseil constitutionnel à l'épreuve de la déontologie et de la transparence* (IFJD 2022) 61.

[31] See eg: Bruno Latour, *The Making of Law. An Ethnography of the Conseil d'Etat* (Polity Press 2010) and even more directly applicable to this book: Dominique Schnapper, *Une sociologue au Conseil constitutionnel* (Gallimard 2010).

[32] See eg: Antoine Vauchez, 'Judicialization: A sociohistorical perspective (lessons and questions from the French Fifth Republic)' in Mikael Rask Madsen and Chris Thornhill (eds), *Law and the Formation of Modern Europe. Perspectives from the Historical Sociology of Law* (CUP 2014) 96.

[33] See eg: Vera Fritz, 'Judge Biographies as a Methodology to Grasp the Dynamics inside the CJEU and its Relationship with EU Member States' in Mikael Rask Madsen, Fernanda Nicola, and Antoine Vauchez (eds), *Researching the European Court of Justice* (CUP 2022) 209.

[34] See eg: Rosalind Dixon and George Williams (eds), *The High Court, the Constitution and Australian Politics* (CUP 2015), esp chs 5–16 and Rehan Abeyratne and Iddo Porat (eds), *Towering Judges. A Comparative Study of Constitutional Judges* (CUP 2021).

[35] Rolf Lamprecht's history of the BVerfG, which is structured in chapters according to its individual presidencies, is one of the exceptions: *Ich gehe bis nach Karlsruhe. Eine Geschichte des Bundesverfassungsgerichts* (Spiegel Buchverlag 2011). See also chs 11, 13, 14, and 15 in the previously cited volume, Rehan Abeyratne and Iddo Porat (eds), *Towering Judges. A Comparative Study of Constitutional Judges* (CUP 2021).

[36] Clifford Geertz, *The Interpretation of Cultures* (Basic Books 1973) esp 310–23.

[37] See: Kim Lane Scheppele, 'Constitutional Ethnography: An Introduction' (2004) 38 Law & Society Review 389.

thoughts about the participation of ex-ministers or politicians in apex courts in a given socio-legal context.

Having outlined the terminology and fields with which this book engages directly or indirectly, some additional explanations and observations as to the overall scope in relation to the choice of jurisdictions, reference materials, and methodology are necessary. With regard to the first aspect, the focus of this analysis will be on four established European constitutional courts, namely those of Austria, Italy, Germany, and France, even though I will occasionally refer to other constitutional or supreme courts in Europe and around the world.

The case selection is not random and falls into what Ran Hirschl identified as the third kind of comparative inquiry. In such endeavour, the goal is to:

> generate concepts and analytical frameworks for thinking critically about constitutional norms and practices ... involves a quest for a detailed understanding of how people living in different cultural, social, and political contexts deal with constitutional dilemmas that are assumed to be common to most modern political systems [and focuses] not on a single jurisdiction, but on a single practice (or a set of closely related practices) as carried out in or encountered by different jurisdictions.[38]

The single practice analysed in this book is that of ex-ministers who become constitutional court judges and the varying constitutional dilemmas this may raise over time and jurisdictional space.

The choice of these four jurisdictions is informed by two distinct factors. The first, substantial one, is that the constitutional courts of these jurisdictions are amongst the oldest and most established constitutional courts in the world. Their relatively long history and arguably longer constitutional tradition(s) allow for long-term observations and a clearer diachronic analysis. The second one is more methodological and practical: I speak the languages of these countries and know their legal systems. This allows for an in-depth contextualization via the analysis of the literature on these bodies in the national languages of each relevant jurisdiction. Moreover, it allows for the surveys and interviews with members and former members of those courts to be conducted in their native language, rather than in English.

When previously referring to the term 'literature', I read this rather broadly to include primary sources like constitutional, legislative, and regulatory texts, as well as secondary literature from the domains of comparative constitutional law, comparative politics, national constitutional law, and the political sciences. In addition, somewhat less usual for legal doctrine, I also include newspaper articles or

[38] Ran Hirschl, *Comparative Matters. The Renaissance of Comparative Constitutional Law* (OUP 2014) 238.

blogs, which are sometimes a valuable source of information for politically sensitive nominations of constitutional court judges that are at times overlooked in academic analyses because they have not passed peer-review processes or because they are deemed to be too partial or political.

Another rather unusual secondary source of information for understanding what happens behind the scenes of constitutional courts in an institutional sense is the personal memoirs or writings of former constitutional court judges.[39] Especially in France, there exists a 'cottage industry' of such publications which provides a whole treasure trove of information.[40] In the other countries under examination, these kinds of (autobiographical) accounts by former judges are rare,[41] are only a (small) part of broader memoirs of a professional or political life,[42] and/or are short/deal with a specific aspect of a judge's life or thoughts.[43]

[39] On the value of judicial (auto)biography to social sciences and beyond, see eg: J Woodford Howard Jr, 'Judicial Biography and the Behavioral Persuasion' (1971) 65 American Political Science Review 704; and Laura Krugman Ray, 'Lives of the Justices: Supreme Court Autobiographies' (2004) 37 Connecticut L Rev 233.

[40] The most scientific of such memoirs is the already mentioned study by sociologist and former member of the CC, Dominique Schnapper, *Une sociologue au Conseil constitutionnel* (Gallimard 2010). In terms of detail and exclusive focus on the experience at the CC, it is followed by Jean-Louis Debré, *Ce que je ne pouvais pas dire* (Robert Laffont 2016) and by Jacques Robert, *La garde de la République. Le Conseil constitutionnel raconté par l'un de ses membres* (Plon 2000). The other books used are mostly comprised of the memoirs of former politicians where the role at the CC covers 'only' a smaller part of the publication. See: Léon Noël, *De Gaulle et les débuts de la Ve République* (Plon 1976) 118–31, 199–241, and 267–71; Gaston Palewski, *Mémoires d'action* (Plon 1988), esp 288–94; Yves Guéna, *Ecrits et discours III (1997–2007)* (La Lauze 2008) 11–75; Pierre Joxe, *Cas de conscience* (Labor et Fides 2010) 159–223; and Alain Juppé, *Une histoire française* (Tallandier 2023). Other smaller publications in the form of articles by—or interviews with—former members of the CC reminiscing about their experience have also been published: Georges Vedel, 'Neuf ans au Conseil constitutionnel' (1989) 55 Le Débat 48 <https://www.conseil-constitutionnel.fr/les-membres/neuf-ans-au-conseil-constitutionnel> accessed 17 November 2022; Monique Pelletier, 'Quatre années trop courtes' (2008) 25 Les cahiers du Conseil constitutionnel 37 <https://www.conseil-constitutionnel.fr/nouveaux-cahiers-du-conseil-constitutionnel/quatre-annees-trop-courtes> accessed 17 November 2022; and Noëlle Lenoir, '1992–2001. Souvenirs d'une femme au Conseil constitutionnel' (2008) 25 Les cahiers du Conseil constitutionnel 15.

[41] See eg for Italy: Sabino Cassese, *Dentro la Corte. Diario di un giudice costituzionale* (il Mulino 2015).

[42] See eg for Germany: Roman Herzog, *Jahre der Politik* (Siedler Verlag 2007) 115–48; Thomas Dieterich, *Ein Richterleben im Arbeits- und Verfassungsrecht* (Berliner Wissenschaftsverlag 2016) 165–213; and Peter Becker and Heike Simon (eds), *Helmut Simon. Leben zwischen den Zeiten* (Nomos 2020) 111–73; for Austria one could mention the collected autobiographical accounts of Austrian public law professors that include former members of the VfGH, like Ludwig Adamovich, Ernst Durig, Godehard Josef Ebers, and Karl Wolff. See: Nikolaus Grass (ed), *Österreichische Rechts- und Staatswissenschaften der Gegenwart in Selbstdarstellungen* (Universitätsverlag Wagner 1952), respectively 10, 41, 83, and 231 and Ludwig Adamovich, *Erinnerungen eines Nonkonformisten* (Seifert Verlag 2011) 74–119.

[43] See eg, for Italy: Giuliano Vassalli, 'Testimonianza' (2006) 11 Giornale di storia costituzionale 55, 61–64; and Ugo de Siervo, 'Riflessioni su un'esperienza di lavoro alla Corte costituzionale' (2006) 11 Giornale di storia costituzionale 81; for Germany: Theodor Ritterspach, 'Erinnerungen an die Anfänge des Bundesverfassungsgerichts' in Eckart Klein (ed), *Grundrechte, soziale Ordnung und Verfassungsgerichtsbarkeit. Festschrift für Ernst Benda zum 70. Geburtstag* (CF Müller 1995) 201–07; and Ernst-Wolfgang Böckenförde, 'A Christian in the Office of Constitutional Judge [1999]' in Mirjam Künkler and Tine Stein (eds), *Religion, Law, and Democracy. Selected Writings. Ernst-Wolfgang Böckenförde* (OUP 2020) 280.

One plausible explanation of the predominance of such memoirs in the French context is that many members of the CC are—or were—high-level politicians, and that it is not unusual for politicians to publish memoirs of this kind.[44] Whatever the reasons for this difference may be, these autobiographical accounts can provide interesting 'insider' information that would otherwise be overlooked or simply unavailable. Interviews with former constitutional judges that are published either in newspaper articles or in books are also a potential source of information and lie somewhere between an autobiographical account and an externally written publication. Such interviews are particularly known in Germany.[45]

My methodology combines sources from primary and secondary literature with surveys and semi-structured interviews of current judges, former judges, and high-level staff working at these constitutional courts. Surveys and interviews are increasingly used in legal scholarship and projects, especially in order to better understand how judges reason and how courts function.[46]

The rationale for resorting to both surveys and interviews was to ensure that I do not overlook important aspects in my analyses, to help better understanding what the participation of ex-ministers means for constitutional courts from the inside, and to see if this is perceived to be an issue at all by the concerned actors. The use of surveys and interviews also explains an additional practical justification for limiting my primary focus to four countries: time and languages. Extending this study to other constitutional courts might simply have become unmanageable, especially because the idea was to run these surveys and interviews in the relevant countries' respective national languages, rather than in English.

The combined use of surveys *and* interviews had a slightly different purpose. The surveys were thought of as providing a first contact that would serve as a discussion basis for the follow-up interviews. Especially for the initial interviews, this last purpose was relevant, but as the number of interviews grew, there was sufficient comparative material that could be referred to without resorting to the survey results. Moreover, the thought was that surveys do not require a lot of

[44] For some tentative explanations on why and how former high-level politicians write their memoirs, see: Hans-Peter Schwarz, 'Memoirenfron und Memoirenlust, oder: Warum und wie schreiben unsere Spitzenpolitiker ihre Erinnerungen? Beobachtungen eines geneigten Lesers' in Mathias Herdegen and others (eds), *Festschrift für Roman Herzog zum 75. Geburtstag* (Beck 2009) 485.

[45] As an example, see: Alec Stone Sweet and Giacinto della Cananea, 'Interview with Dieter Grimm' (2021) 21 German LJ 1541; or Alec Stone Sweet and Giacinto della Cananea, 'Biographical Interview with Ernst-Wolfgang Böckenförde [2011]' in Mirjam Künkler and Tine Stein (eds), *Constitutional and Political Theory: Selected Writings. Volume I* (OUP 2016) 369.

[46] For some recent examples on such empirical legal studies as well as the benefits and dangers of such research, see: Urszula Jaremba and Elaine Mak, 'Interviewing Judges in the Transnational Context' (2014) 5 Law and Method, <https://www.lawandmethod.nl/tijdschrift/lawandmethod/2014/05/RENM-D-13-00002.pdf> accessed 10 November 2023; Esther Nir, 'Approaching the Bench: Accessing Elites on the Judiciary for Qualitative Interviews' (2018) 21 International Journal of Social Research Methodology 77; and Hanna Emilia Korkea-aho and Païvi Sirkku Maria Leino-Sandberg, 'Interviewing Lawyers: A Critical Self-reflection on Expert Interviews as a Method of EU Legal Research' (2019) 12 European Journal of Legal Studies 17.

time-investment by the people contacted and that therefore I might obtain higher numbers and more answers to the questions asked. This last point did not materialize, because somewhat surprisingly people were more ready to be interviewed than to complete the survey. As to the surveys, these asked the same questions, with some minor linguistic adaptations needed to reflect different institutional names.[47] In total, 33 individuals responded to the surveys: six for Austria, 13 for Italy, six for Germany, and eight for France.

The interviews (then) allowed for a more in-depth conversation and exchange during which I could probe the interviewees on some issues. They consisted of four set questions. Three were the same for each legal system and a fourth question zoomed in more specifically on national particularities.[48] These four questions constituted the cornerstones of the interviews which then followed the flow of the discussion with each single interviewee. After the interviews, a transcription of the full conversation was sent to the interviewees, asking for their approval and indications if there were things they did not want to see cited or published. Quite a few did cancel or integrate certain passages, despite the guaranteed anonymity. Moreover, some interviewees also wanted to see 'their' cited passages for final approval.

As to the interviews, I spoke with 37 people. Thirty-two of those interviews were in person and five were online. They took place in a timespan of roughly a year, namely from January 2023 to February 2024. Two interviewees did not want to be recorded or cited at all; a third withdrew his consent to be cited at a later stage. In overall terms, 22 of the interviewees were constitutional judges at the time of the interviews, ten were former judges, and five were high-level personnel. Eight of the interviewees had been ex-ministers who had gone on to become constitutional judges, and thereby the direct subject of study for this book. As to the gender subdivision, 25 were male and 12 were female. The lower female number can be explained by the underrepresentation of women in these constitutional courts. Subdivided per legal system, the interviews concerned ten individuals for France, 11 for Italy; seven for Austria where—to the best of my knowledge—this is the first time that interviews had been used in a scientific study for constitutional judges; and nine for Germany. To provide some perspective to these numbers, there are 9 constitutional judges in France, 15 in Italy, 14 in Austria, and 16 in Germany.

In terms of how the interviewees were identified, I relied on the snowballing method. At the same time, I tried to also identify interviewees by direct contact either because they seemed to belong to a group or category that I had not talked to yet (eg women, or certain professional origins, on a given constitutional court) or because I wanted to ensure I was not only speaking to the same group of colleagues

[47] The surveys were formulated in French, German, and Italian. The English translation of the questions is included in Annex 1.

[48] The English version of the questions can be found in Annex 2.

with similar ideas or views. While the overall numbers cannot be statistically representative, they are quite high, given the obstacles one faces in accessing these types of personalities. In addition, the fact of including former constitutional judges and high-level staff working in these institutions also increased the overall numbers.

Apart from the numerical aspect, there were other reasons for not limiting these surveys and interviews to current judges, but instead extending them to these other categories as well. Judges may have little time to dedicate to surveys and/or to interviews. Moreover, they may feel bound by the secrecy of deliberation and by loyalty to their institution. Former judges instead might have more time, greater direct experience at a given constitutional court, and may even speak more freely. With regard to the inclusion of high-level staff in the surveys and interviews, there are several justifications. For example, some law clerks (*assistenti di studio*) of constitutional judges at the Italian C cost serve simultaneously as judges or law professors, and some have spent more than 20 years at the institution, far exceeding the nine years of a judge's mandate.[49] Others, like the General Secretary (*Secrétaire général*) of the CC, are not officially judges but are of crucial importance to the institution.[50] They provide additional perspectives on the various issues that the presence of a former member of government on a constitutional court may engender. Moreover, including them ensures that the survey- and interview-based research is done in a somewhat more numerically representative fashion.

Even though this book engages with literature and methods that fall outside the traditional approach of legal academia, it ultimately remains anchored in the legal arena. The analysis of how the participation of ex-ministers might be assessed and constrained from a supranational perspective, especially under EU and ECHR law, combined with the normative approach and angle I take in Chapter 6, re-focuses on the legal aspects. In fact, while the idea is to analyse a phenomenon that has gone relatively unnoticed so far in established constitutional democracies, in this chapter, I will also provide some legal/normative ideas to address and minimize the potential risks stemming from ex-ministers becoming constitutional judges.

Finally, this book is meant to be read as providing guidance on how to strengthen these bodies and their fundamental role in constitutional democracies, especially with regard to their legitimacy, their impartiality, and their perception by the public. Such strengthening might be particularly needed in view of possible political changes that could lead to democratic and constitutional backsliding also in

[49] At times these are full-time judges on secondment to the C cost, as opposed to young, brilliant law students just graduated from law school, as would be the case at the USSC, for example. On the Italian law clerks, see: Elisabetta Lamarque, 'Chi sono gli assistenti di studio dei giudici costituzionali' in *Alle frontiere del diritto costituzionale. Scritti in onore di Valerio Onida* (Giuffrè 2011) 1065.

[50] On the importance of this figure for the CC, see: Alexandre Ciaudo, 'Un acteur spécifique du procès constitutionnel: le secrétaire général du Conseil constitutionnel' (2008) 73 Revue française de droit constitutionnel 17, and more recently: Alexandre Ciaudo, 'La place du secrétaire général du Conseil constitutionnel dans le procès constitutionnel' in Elina Lemaire and Thomas Perroud (eds), *Le Conseil constitutionnel à l'épreuve de la déontologie et de la transparence* (IFJD 2022) 281.

established constitutional democracies. The current trends of court capture, court packing, and other such phenomena in both illiberal and liberal democracies re-centres the fundamental role of checks on arbitrary executive and legislative power that these fragile bodies are designed to play. If one agrees that it is desirable to carry out certain reforms to limit the participation of former high-level politicians on these courts in order to avoid political court capture, it may be preferable to get them done before the political climate becomes too tense. Such reforms may be seen as neutral in relatively stable political environments, but as highly political and controversial when instability or democratic backsliding starts or is already ongoing.[51] In this rather loose sense, the book can and should be seen as an engagement with the vast literature on illiberal democracies.

1.2 Narrowing the Scope; or What this Book is Not About

The description provided above also gives some indication as to what I will not be doing and/or looking into with this book. So as not to disappoint the readers, several provisos should be made from the start.

First and foremost, this book will not look into discussions concerning the politicization of courts understood as linking specific political opinions associated with individual judges with particular judicial outcomes and/or judicial attitudes. These debates have been particularly visible and discussed in the United States since the 1920s and 1930s when legal realists developed analyses of judicial work which noted that judging was not always as rule-bound as previously assumed, and thus many doors were left wide open for judicial discretion and therefore politics.[52] One consequence of these realist analyses was that nomination procedures were seen as increasingly important and were therefore followed more closely by the media and academia alike. Since at least the 1960s, the idea of hoping to influence decisions of the United States Supreme Court (USSC) by nominating judges on one end of the political spectrum or 'driven by similar criteria' has become increasingly commonplace.[53] These debates have become more acrimonious since Robert Bork's judicial nomination in the late 1980s. Apart from the fact that judicial

[51] See eg the attempt to introduce a separate administrative court system in Hungary under Viktor Orbán would not have been seen as particularly problematic in less politically fraught times, as many European countries have a separate court system for administrative matters. However, in the political context of democratic backsliding and illiberal constitutionalism, it has raised concerns; see the opinion by the Venice Commission, *Opinion on the law on administrative courts and on the law on the entry into force of the law on administrative courts and certain transitional rules* adopted by the Venice Commission at its 118th Plenary Session (Venice, 19 March 2019), Opinion no 943/2018, CDL-AD(2019)004 <https://www.venice.coe.int/webforms/documents/default.aspx?pdffile = CDL-AD(2019)004-e> accessed 17 November 2022.

[52] See on this: Brian Z Tamanaha, 'Understanding Legal Realism' (2009) 87 Texas L Rev 731.

[53] Mark Tushnet, *The Constitution of the United States of America. A Contextual Analysis* (Hart 2009) 133–34.

politics which is—at least in theory—limited by precedent and standards of judicial interpretation is not necessarily the same as ordinary politics that is much less constrained by such judicial concerns,[54] the former type of politicization is more difficult to track and is less visible in European constitutional courts.

This is not to say that politics is not visible or present in nomination procedures; quite the contrary. In Austria, Germany, and Italy, there are, more or less, open agreements amongst major political parties that determine who has the right to nominate the next constitutional court judge based on the proportional political representativity achieved at the latest elections.[55] This has been referred to using the German term *Parteienproporz* (party proportional representation)[56] or the Italian term of *lottizzazione* (allotment).[57]

What is less visible is how these political nominations translate into judicial decision-making because, unlike in the United States, many European constitutional courts do not allow dissenting opinions. Debates about their introduction divide even judges on these courts.[58] This absence makes it more difficult to verify the influence of judges' personal and political opinions on the judgments they write, and many systems make it extremely difficult to track how individual judges

[54] Michel Rosenfeld, 'Judicial Politics versus Ordinary Politics. Is the Constitutional Judge Caught in the Middle?' in Christine Landfried (ed), *Judicial Power: How Constitutional Courts Affect Political Transformations* (CUP 2018) 36–65.

[55] This becomes evident in the tables of judges provided in various publications in these three countries, and where party affiliation or sympathies are attached to individual judges' names. See eg for Germany: Georg Vanberg, *The Politics of Constitutional Review in Germany* (CUP 2005) esp Tables 3.2 and 3.3 at 84 and 86; for Italy: Patrizia Pederzoli, 'I giudici della Corte costituzionale' (*discrimen*, 23 November 2018), Tables 1 and 2 at 31–34 <https://discrimen.it/i-giudici-della-corte-costituzionale/> accessed 8 November 2022.

[56] See eg on this term and its effect on the election of BVerfG judges: Christine Landfried, 'Die Wahl der Bundesverfassungsrichter und ihre Folgen für die Legitimität der Verfassungsgerichtsbarkeit' in Robert Chr. van Ooyen and Martin HW Möllers, *Das Bundesverfassungsgericht im politischen System* (Verlag für Sozialwissenschaften 2006) 229.

[57] See for a use of this term in comparative constitutional law literature: Guillaume Tusseau, *Contentieux constitutionnel comparé* (LGDJ 2021) 514–17.

[58] For example, former judges Noëlle Lenoir (France), Pierre Joxe (France), Sabino Cassese (Italy), Nicolò Zanon (Italy) as well as former substitute judge Hans R Klecatsky (Austria) are in favour of the practice: Noëlle Lenoir, '1992–2001: Souvenirs d'une femme au Conseil constitutionnel' (2008) 25 Cahiers du conseil constitutionnel 15; Pierre Joxe, *Cas de conscience* (Labor et Fides 2010) 159–223; Sabino Cassese, *Dentro la Corte. Diario di un giudice costituzionale* (il Mulino 2015); Nicolò Zanon, *Le opinioni dissenzienti in Corte costituzionale* (Zanichelli Editore 2024); and Hans R Klecatsky, 'Über die Notwendigkeit einer grundlegenden Reform der österreichischen Verfassungsgerichtsbarkeit' in Gerhard Leibholz and others (eds), *Menschenwürde und freiheitliche Rechtsordnung. Festschrift für Willi Geiger zum 65. Geburtstag* (Mohr Siebeck 1974) 925, 942. Those who oppose the practice include: Gustavo Zagrebelsky (Italy), Jean-Claude Colliard (France), Jean-Louis Debré (France), Gebhard Müller (Germany) and also Christoph Grabenwarter (Austria). See: Gustavo Zagrebelsky, *Principî e voti* (Einaudi 2005) 69–72; Jean-Louis Debré, *Ce que je ne pouvais pas dire* (Robert Laffont 2016) 23; for Colliard, the passages in Pierre Joxe, *Cas de conscience* (Labor et Fides 2010) 184–85 and for Müller and Grabenwarter: Matthias K Klatt, 'Österreich auf dem Weg zum Sondervotum? Beobachtungen aus deutscher Perspektive' (*JuWiss-Blog*, 21 April 2021) <https://www.juwiss.de/34-2021/> accessed 14 April 2023.

decide in a given case;[59] the public only sees the allegedly unanimous 'majority' opinion. Yet, more difficult does not mean impossible. In recent years there have been studies—mainly by political scientists—which look into whether and when European constitutional court judges make their rulings in accordance with their political preferences.[60] Where the literature seems to be more inclined to finding alignments between political spectrum and judicial outcome, practically all the interviewees talked with for this book denied any correlation. One of them put it very directly by stating that 'pre-established political positions in the judicial activity due to past experiences are generally wrong'.[61]

Something else that needs to be considered in conjunction with the idea that judges might vote according to their political preferences or the politics of those who nominated them is the concept developed in French political science literature that has become known as the 'Becket effect',[62] or also in English language as the 'Becket complex'.[63] The Becket effect refers to the process whereby a new-found identification with an institution leads someone to renounce any previous personal or political allegiances that would compromise their loyalty to said institution. The phenomenon is named after Thomas Becket (1118–70), who after being a loyal Lord Chancellor (and friend) to King Henry II was appointed by the latter to become Archbishop of Canterbury, whereby Henry II hoped to hold both secular and clerical power. However, Becket did not play the expected role and became the King's main opponent as the Head of the Church, for which he was eventually murdered in Canterbury Cathedral.

According to some, this effect can also be observed in much less dramatic ways in constitutional courts,[64] in the sense that judges' previous personal/political allegiances do not, or only very marginally, influence judicial outcomes. Three former judges of constitutional courts in France, Germany, and Italy refer to this

[59] For this early explanation on the absence of studies on the politics of constitutional courts see eg: Alec Stone Sweet, *Governing with Judges* (OUP 2000) 49 and Mary Volcansek, *Constitutional Politics in Italy* (Macmillan Press 2000) 7.

[60] See eg: Raphaël Franck, 'Judicial Independence Under a Divided Polity: A Study of the Rulings of the French Constitutional Court, 1959–2006' (2009) 25 Journal of Law, Economics, & Organization 262; Christoph Hönnige, 'The Electoral Connection: How the Pivotal Judge Affects Oppositional Success at European Constitutional Courts' (2009) 32 West European Politics 963 (comparison between Germany and France); Monika Glavina, 'From a Potentially Powerful to a Polarised Court: The emergence of Dissenting Opinions on the Croatian Constitutional Court' (2024) 25 European Politics and Society 518; and also the references made to other studies on Spain, Portugal, France, and Germany by Arthur Dyevre, 'Unifying the Field of Comparative Judicial Politics: Towards a Theory of Judicial Behavior' (2010) 2 European Political Science Review 297, 301–02.

[61] Interviewee no 18, 3 July 2023.

[62] See: Bastien François, 'Le juge, le droit et la politique: éléments d'une analyse politiste' (1990) 1 Revue française de droit constitutionnel 49, 54–55. A less academic and old-style German saying provides that 'the office shapes the man' (*Das Amt prägt den Mann*).

[63] Marcel Storme, 'Reflections on Judicial Independence', in Shimon Shetreet and Wayne McCormack (eds) *The Culture of Judicial Independence in a Globalised World* (Brill 2016) 45, 47.

[64] See most explicitly on this: Jacques Chevallier, 'Le juge constitutionnel et l'effet Becket' in *Renouveau du droit constitutionnel. Mélanges en l'honneur de Louis Favoreu* (Dalloz 2007) 83.

experience in their writings[65] and how these institutions mould different personalities into a collegial body, facilitated by all sorts of rules, including the absence of dissenting opinions. This institutional environment reduces any pre-existing differences between the various judges. Examples of judges whose work on constitutional courts defied expectations derived from their political experience and nominating institutions are also known in Germany[66] and the United States.[67] The Becket effect is sometimes also referred to as 'due ingratitude' or 'obligation of ingratitude' which judges owe toward the politicians who nominated them.[68]

It is a different story to assess whether the strength of the Becket effect or obligation of ingratitude is the exception, the rule, or an idealized vision of a judge's role on the part of those who would prefer to believe in the independence and impartiality of constitutional court judges. However, the Becket effect seems to influence the thinking of some judges and former judges on these institutions, as the interviews confirm. One judge mentioned that he experienced the Becket effect when confronted with an ethical doubt about whether he should be the judge rapporteur on a matter on which he had previously published a critique of the constitutional court's jurisprudence. When approaching the constitutional court's president with that concern, he was told that being a constitutional court judge changes people and that he would adapt himself to the role in order to guarantee coherence, stability, and predictability. Eventually, the judge in question left behind his doctrinal opinions and instead chose the institutional role.[69]

Another interviewee described the Becket effect as follows:

> I would say that it [the Becket effect] definitely exists and that it depends very much on the existing rituals, strength of the internal socialization and other socialization-promoting elements that a court brings with it. And these are quite present at the BVerfG: the small number, the secrecy of deliberations etc. Everything that I described as a consensus-oriented culture earlier naturally has an extremely high socialization pressure. If you do not follow that

65 See: Dominique Schnapper, *Une sociologue au Conseil constitutionnel* (Gallimard 2010) 145–201; Roman Herzog, *Jahre der Politik* (Siedler Verlag 2007) 118–19; and Gustavo Zagrebelsky, *Principî e voti* (Einaudi 2005) 59–79.

66 With a particular focus on the two BVerfG Presidents, Roman Herzog and Hans-Jürgen Papier, see: Rolf Lamprecht, *Ich gehe bis nach Karlsruhe. Eine Geschichte des Bundesverfassungsgerichts* (Spiegel Buchverlag 2011) 202–03 and 268, respectively.

67 See briefly on this: Guillaume Tusseau, *Contentieux constitutionnel comparé* (LGDJ 2021) 513–14.

68 For Italy, see the mention of '*doverosa ingratitudine*' by Gustavo Zagrebelsky, *Principî e voti* (Einaudi 2005) 53; for France, Dominique Schnapper attributes the expression to Robert Badinter who claimed that there is a '*devoir d'ingratitude*' (Dominique Schnapper, *Une sociologue au Conseil constitutionnel* (Gallimard 2010) 194). See also the Opinion by the Venice Commission on the Constitutional Tribunal of Poland's reference to this 'duty of ingratitude': Venice Commission, *Opinion on Amendments to the Act of 25 June 2015 on the Constitutional Tribunal of Poland* adopted by the Venice Commission at its 106th Plenary Session (Venice, 11–12 March 2016), Opinion no 833/2015, CDL-AD(2016)001 para 119.

69 Interviewee no 2, 1 February 2023.

> consensus-orientated culture you put yourself on the sidelines, but if you do join it, then you are absorbed into it to a considerable extent. ... Hence, I believe that the BVerfG has a strong effect. The only nuance is possibly that the two-thirds majority [for nomination to the BVerfG] means that people do not have to switch from such radical positions to new radical positions, but instead tend to belong to the moderate spectrum from the outset.[70]

While the issue of dissenting opinions and the existence of a Becket effect at constitutional courts are absolutely relevant and fascinating topics, this book will not focus upon these elements that link to a specific inquiry of the field of judicial politics. Whether or not an ex-minister becomes a constitutional court judge and whether that has some bearing on the(ir) judicial output is not the main inquiry here. The main questions are rather of comparative-institutional nature and are primarily focused on the benefits and risks that such participation brings, and what can be done to mitigate any (potential) risks.

Another limitation of this book relates to its geographical scope. Under this aspect, I will not look at supreme courts and/or bodies that do both constitutionality review and legality review, as is the case for example in Canada, India, or the United States. I would argue that these institutions function somewhat differently, and that their judicial-court character is not as much in question compared to that of constitutional courts where the political element is even more visible.

This is not to say that parts of this book's analysis would not be interesting and relevant for those institutions as well. Indeed, the form of politicization I discuss here is certainly not unheard of in the United States. Most famously, Chief Justice John Marshall served as the Secretary of State under President John Adams. William Howard Taft became Chief Justice in 1921 after having served as President of the United States. Charles Evans Hughes had been Governor of the State of New York, a presidential candidate, and a Secretary of State before becoming Chief Justice in 1930.[71] Without wanting to state that the participation of former politicians and members of state or federal governments as USSC Justices was formerly the rule in the United States, it was certainly a more prominent practice in the past.[72] From the late 1950s onward, the frequency of former politician justices began waning. Earl Warren, formerly Attorney General and Governor of

[70] Interviewee no 34, 22 February 2024.

[71] For an overview of USSC nominations from their inception to today's Roberts' court, see: Henry J Abraham, *Justices, Presidents and Senators* (5th edn, Rowman and Littlefield Publishers 2008).

[72] The participation of former members of the legislative branch at various levels declined from 80.6% between 1789 and 1850 to 12.5% from 1953 onward. Similarly, previous executive experience either at federal, state, or local level was at 40% between 1789 and 1952, while it is practically non-existent today. For more detail on these numbers, see: Laura Fabiano, 'Legittimità e indipendenza della Corte suprema statunitense nella procedura di nomina dei suoi giudici' in Marina Calamo Specchia (ed), *Le Corti costituzionali. Composizione, Indipendenza, Legittimazione* (Giappichelli 2011) 63, 71 at fnn 38 and 39.

California, became Chief Justice in 1953. In 1962, Arthur Joseph Goldberg, the former Secretary of Labour, was nominated as Associate Justice but resigned only three years later to become the United States' Ambassador to the United Nations (UN).[73] Since that time, nominations to the USSC have been predominantly members of the bench, if one considers that former Solicitors General, like Thurgood Marshall or Elena Kagan, are not nominations of (former) politicians. The last minister to be considered as a potential nominee was in 2010 in the person of Janet Napolitano, the former Governor of Arizona and Secretary for Homeland Security under President Obama. A similar trend in the reduction of former politicians joining supreme courts has also been observed in Canada and Australia, and is explained as being due to a combination of changes in the legal profession, changes within politics, and changes in public perception.[74] Israel also seems to be observing such a trend in reduction of political nominees, even though here the cause seems to be more related to the practice of the Judicial Appointments Committee than to anything else.[75]

I will also not focus upon constitutional courts that emerged in the aftermath of authoritarian regimes in the late 1970s and early 1980s such as those in Spain, Portugal, and Greece, nor those established after the fall of Communism in Central and Eastern Europe (CEE) in the 1990s, nor those outside of Europe. Although interesting examples exist in such jurisdictions and will occasionally be mentioned to add to my analysis, the book's focus will revolve around the previously mentioned Western European constitutional courts. That does not mean that the constitutional or supreme courts of those other legal systems are irrelevant for this book. On the contrary, especially the events and reforms in Hungary, Poland but also in Israel and other countries where apex courts are under fire from illiberal or constitutional backsliding governments constitute to some extent the backdrop of some of the thoughts motivating this book. They will be referred to more explicitly when discussing the issue of (over- or mono-)politicization of constitutional courts and in the concluding thoughts to this book.

Third, with regard to the selected jurisdictions, for Germany I will not look at the state (*Länder*) constitutional courts, even though a cursory reading of the literature reveals interesting examples and observations at that level, too.[76]

[73] Much more detailed information on the background of USSC Justices can be found at: Lee Epstein and others, *The Supreme Court Compendium* (6th edn, Sage 2015) 293–550.

[74] Douglas MacDonald, 'Worlds Apart. The Appointment of Former Politicians as Judges' (2016) 41 Alternative LJ 17.

[75] Itzhak Gaalnor and Dana Blander, *The Handbook of Israel's Political System* (CUP 2018) 219.

[76] See, most recently the so-called 'Thuringia Project': Maximilian Steinbeis, 'The Thuringia Project' (*VerfBlog* 16 June 2023) https://verfassungsblog.de/the-thuringia-project/ accessed 28 August 2024. Older references can also be found at: Astrid Lorenz, 'Das Verfassungsgericht des Landes Brandenburg als politisiertes Organ? Möglichkeiten und Grenzen politischer Einflussnahme' in Werner Reuter (ed), *Landesverfassungsgerichte. Entwicklung—Aufbau—Funktionen* (Springer, 2017) 105 and Maria Daniela Poli, 'Le Corti costituzionali dei *Länder* in Germania: assetti strutturali e problemi aperti' in Marina Calamo Specchia (ed), *Le Corti costituzionali. Composizione, Indipendenza, Legittimazione* (Giappichelli 2011) 23.

A further narrowing down of the object of this study is that I limit my focus to ex-ministers. For France, I shall not include in my analysis the constitutionally authorized participation of past Presidents of the Republic as *de iure* members of the CC.[77] This issue has been discussed and critiqued sufficiently as an anachronism in the literature, and needs no further engagement here.[78] However, the potential presence of such personalities coupled with the great number of other former high-level politicians on the French CC further reinforces some of the arguments that I will be making in this book.

More broadly, I shall not be looking at former members of parliament having joined the constitutional court. This exclusion does not weaken the points made in this book. On the contrary, if one included such members in the count, then the constitutional courts analysed here might look even more 'political'. Arguably, the issue of former parliamentarians becoming constitutional court members raises similar issues in terms of the independence and impartiality of former government members, given that they come from a different state power which constitutional courts are supposed to control.[79]

One major justification for this choice is that many, if not most, of the important pieces of legislation and major legislative reforms which have the potential to raise important issues of constitutionality are drafted and presented by governments and not by single members of parliament. The latter category may occasionally initiate minor legislative proposals and some of these may end up becoming law. Nevertheless, the primary driver behind legislative proposals nowadays is the executive power. Of course, there are slight variations in terms of numbers amongst the four systems examined. But overall, the numbers speak clearly: in Germany between 1949 and 2021 the legislative proposals made by the government amounted to 74% of the total;[80] in Italy the numbers between 2018 and 2022 look roughly the same and if one considers the practice of decree laws (*decreti legge*—government decrees that are adopted under certain emergency conditions and then ratified by parliament into law) or legislative decrees (*decreti legislativi*—delegated legislation), the government's control over bills might be even higher;[81]

[77] Art 56, para 2 of the French Constitution.

[78] In practice, today former Presidents Nicolas Sarkozy and François Hollande do not participate in the work of the CC, and current President Emmanuel Macron, has publicly indicated that he will not sit on the CC once his presidency is over. As to the critiques and suggestions to abolish former Presidents on the CC, see: Antoine Chopplet, 'Les membres de droit à vie du Conseil constitutionnel: inutile réforme ou abrogation nécessaire?' in Elina Lemaire and Thomas Perroud (eds), *Le Conseil constitutionnel à l'épreuve de la déontologie et de la transparence* (IFJD 2022) 123.

[79] See for instance in Poland, where the nomination of former members of Parliament to the constitutional court without any cooling-off period leads to many abstentions: Piotr Tuleja, 'Der polnische Verfassungsgerichtshof' in Armin von Bogdandy, Christoph Grabenwarter, and Peter Huber (eds), *Handbuch Ius Publicum Europaeum. Band VI, Verfassungsgerichtsbarkeit in Europa: Institutionen* (CF Müller 2016) 483.

[80] <https://www.bundesrat.de/DE/dokumente/statistik/statistik-node.html> accessed 20 December 2022.

[81] <https://www.senato.it/leg/18/BGT/Schede/Statistiche/Leggi/DDLLeggiApprovatePerIniziativa.html> accessed 20 December 2022.

in France, governmental bills constituted over 80% of total legislative proposals, even though those numbers may have improved pursuant to the 2008 constitutional reform;[82] in Austria it also seems that most bills are presented by the government.[83] It is beyond the scope of this book to provide detailed explanations on why this may be so. It suffices to say that the increase of emergency legislation since World War I,[84] a phenomenon exacerbated by terrorism and Covid-19, has contributed to a status quo where the executive is firmly in the driving seat. Moreover, the rise of the administrative (welfare) state combined with an increasingly legalistic approach to the regulation of technical issues has shifted legislative action away from parliaments and towards governments even in times that are not overshadowed by emergencies of various kinds.[85] Whether or not one could claim that the executive power is becoming or has become the most dangerous branch is—yet again—a matter for an another book to tackle.[86] For the narrower purposes of this one, I have hopefully convinced the reader that limiting the scope of my analysis to former members of government is justified by the fact that they are the likely source of the legislative proposals whose constitutionality might be challenged at some point and with which, inter alia, issues of impartiality may arise.

A minor justification is that in many cases, those individuals who had been ministers also had been parliamentarians during their political career. That is the case of many of the French examples but also some Italian personalities, like Giuliano Amato, Giuliano Vassalli, Paolo Rossi, or Oronzo Reale, who had been members of parliament.[87] Of course, the restriction of my analyses to ex-ministers may exclude quite high-standing personalities. The best example is Stephan Harbarth, the BVerfG's current President. As a former parliamentary group leader of the federal parliament, he certainly played a key political role for some time. Similarly in Italy, Bucciarelli Ducci probably stood out from ordinary parliamentarians as the President of the Lower House of parliament from 1963 to 1968. For France, one might need to mention Gaston Monnerville who was President of the Senate from

[82] On these (admittedly outdated) figures, see the analysis by: Pierre Avril, 'Qui fait la loi?' (2005) 114 Pouvoirs 89.

[83] <https://www.parlament.gv.at/PERK/GES/WEG/INITIATIVE/index.shtml> accessed 20 December 2022.

[84] See in this sense: Giorgio Agamben, *State of Exception* (Kevin Attell tr, University of Chicago Press 2005) 11–22.

[85] See eg for the United States: Gary S Lawson, 'The Rise and Rise of the Administrative State' (1994) 107 Harvard L Rev 1231.

[86] Especially in the United States at the time of the Federalist Papers, it was thought the most dangerous branch of government was the legislative branch (James Madison), while the judiciary was deemed the least dangerous (Alexander Hamilton). On this, see: Martin S Flaherty, 'The Most Dangerous Branch' (1996) 105 Yale LJ 1725. However, with contemporary developments pursuant to President Trump's nominations to the USSC, others have argued the judiciary is in fact the *most* dangerous; see: David A Kaplan, *The Most Dangerous Branch: Inside the Supreme Court in the Age of Trump* (Crown 2018).

[87] See below Table 3.2.

1946 to 1968 and during that time became one of the General de Gaulle's fiercest political opponents.[88]

However, in most cases, those who were 'only' former parliamentarians without government experience or broad public exposure are probably little known today. As examples, one could cite Ercole Rocchetti, Leonetto Amadei, Enzo Capalozza, Alberto Malagugini, and Ugo Spagnoli for Italy,[89] Jean-Michard Pellissier, Victor Chatenay, Louis Pasteur-Vallery-Radot, Léon Jozeau-Marigné, Marcel Rudloff, or Etienne Dailly for France, or Martin Hirsch for Germany. This somewhat tempers the downsides of excluding former parliamentarians in this book, knowing that in any case many, if not all, of the arguments raised in this book will probably apply to them as well.

As a final justification for the exclusion of former parliamentarians, the truth is that numerically they played some role in France and Italy only, whereas in Austria or Germany, they have been almost non-existent. That does not mean that in absolute terms, the situation may not be different elsewhere and that in other socio-historical-constitutional realities, former parliamentarians as constitutional judges play an important role that is worth analysing. For instance, one can well imagine that in systems like Belgium, where some former parliamentarians even have to constitutionally be part of the constitutional court, the picture might look different.[90] The hope is that this book may nevertheless provide interesting and relevant food for thought also for such systems and realities.

In terms of methodology, even though I will draw on qualitative methods from social sciences, I will not engage in quantitative or regression analyses. Moreover, an informed reader will realize that I neither directly nor methodologically engage more in-depth with the literature and findings from the field of comparative politics and the subfield of comparative judicial politics.[91] This literature provides interesting and helpful material, examples, thoughts, and inspiration for my work that cannot be found in traditional legal analyses of constitutional courts and their decisions. Of particular interest is the strand of literature that developed since the late 1990s that has zoomed in on the particularities of judicial politics in (European) constitutional courts,[92] and more specifically on lawyers and

[88] On that time, see his autobiographical account: Gaston Monnerville, *Vingt-deux ans de présidence* (le cherche midi 1980).

[89] On these bios see: Patrizia Pederzoli, 'I giudici della Corte costituzionale' (*discrimen*, 23 November 2018), Table 3 at 35–48 <https://discrimen.it/i-giudici-della-corte-costituzionale/> accessed 8 November 2022.

[90] Art 34, para 2 of the Loi spéciale on the Cour d'arbitrage of 6 January 1989.

[91] See eg: Theodore L Becker, *Comparative Judicial Politics. The Political Functionings of Courts* (Rand McNally 1970); Martin Shapiro, *Courts. A Comparative and Political Analysis* (Chicago University Press 1980); Martin Shapiro and Alec Stone Sweet, *On Law, Politics, & Judicialization* (OUP 2002); Carlo Guarnieri and Patrizia Pederzoli, *The Power of Judges. A Comparative Study of Courts and Democracy* (OUP 2002); and Mary L Volcansek, Comparative Judicial Politics (Rowman 2019).

[92] Arthur Dyevre, 'Unifying the Field of Comparative Judicial Politics: Towards a Theory of Judicial Behavior' (2010) 2 European Political Science Review 297.

(constitutional) judges as special political actors,[93] as veto players,[94] and/or literature which attempts a quantitative assessment of the correlation between judges' political backgrounds and judicial outcomes.[95]

However, the questions and methodologies employed by some of these authors are not the ones that I am raising or trying to answer. In this sense, I am not claiming that this book can address any of the challenges identified in the comparative political study of constitutional courts.[96] Nevertheless, I do hope that this book can provide some interesting information and food for thought for authors in the field of comparative judicial politics and that it can offer reflections which could form the basis of even more nuanced attitudinal or institutional approaches to these courts. For example, one could ask whether former judges, politicians, civil servants, attorneys, or law professors are more inclined to rule in one way than another, or whether courts with a relatively large number of ex-ministers or former politicians on the bench are more or less inclined to strike down legislation as unconstitutional.

Finally, I shall not look into the separate yet related issue of constitutional judges taking on a high-level political role *after* serving on the constitutional court. The potential problem here, as far as impartiality is concerned, is that the possibility of judges attaining desirable political positions at the end of their term may influence their independence and impartiality during their time in office. Examples of this practice exist in all four systems that form the core of this book's analysis. This phenomenon is rare in Austria, Germany, and France, but happens quite frequently in Italy.

For Austria, one could mention Brigitte Bierlein, the first female President of the VfGH (2018–19), who sat on that court from 2003 to 2019. She also became the first female Chancellor between 2019 and 2020, when a previous government collapsed in the aftermath of a political scandal. Less visible was Hans Klecatsky, who joined the VfGH as a substitute member in 1965 before becoming Justice Minister between 1966 and 1970.[97] In Germany, the most prominent example was Roman Herzog, who became President of Germany in 1994 after having served as a constitutional court judge from 1983 to 1994.[98] Even in France, it is not unheard of

[93] See eg: Tommaso Pavone, 'Lawyers, Judges, and the Obstinate State: The French Case and an Agenda for Comparative Politics' (2020) 18 French Politics 416.

[94] See eg: Nicos C Alivizatos, 'Judges as Veto Players' in Herbert Döring (ed), *Parliaments and Majority Rule in Western Europe* (Campus Verlag/Saint Martin's Press 1995) 566–89 and Sylvain Brouard and Christoph Hönnige, 'Constitutional Courts as Veto Players: Lessons from the United States, France and Germany' (2017) 56 European Journal of Political Research 529.

[95] Benjamin G Engst and others, 'Zum Einfluss der Parteinähe auf das Abstimmungsverhalten der Bundesverfassungsrichter—eine quantitative Untersuchung' (2017) 72 Juristen Zeitung 816.

[96] Christoph Hönnige, 'Beyond Judicialization: Why We Need More Comparative Research about Constitutional Courts' (2011) 10 European Political Science 346.

[97] Kurt Heller, *Der Verfassungsgerichtshof* (Verlag Österreich 2010) 365.

[98] For a recent analysis on post-judgeship activities in Italy, see: Patrizia Pederzoli, 'I giudici della Corte costituzionale' (*discrimen*, 23 November 2018) 22–25. <https://discrimen.it/i-giudici-della-corte-costituzionale/> accessed 8 November 2022.

for former members of the CC to move on to high positions with a high degree of public visibility.[99] This is somewhat surprising, given that this body was referred to as a government by retired politicians,[100] a place of semi-retirement for ex-ministers,[101] and somewhat more sarcastically as the 'Supreme Court of the Musée Grevin',[102] France's equivalent to Madame Tussaud's wax figure celebrity museum. Interestingly, in one of the questionnaires, the answer that was given to the question of which are the biggest risks for the independence for the CC was: 'Mixing with private interests; for members from the political world, a lack of understanding of the ethics of the judge; collusion; *pursuit of a career after leaving office*'.[103] This was then confirmed in a couple of interviews, demonstrating that even in France this risk cannot be wholly excluded.

A first interviewee located the issue somewhere in the future:

> As far as independence is concerned, risks could arise from the fact that, after their time on the CC, former members could be sensitive to professional ambitions or perspectives that would entice them to take positions that are not totally independent. For the moment, this risk has not occurred yet, because the members of the CC are all appointed at the end of their careers and therefore have no future career prospects ... but that could change in the future.[104]

A second one, instead, already saw the issue as a current one:

> The problem is not someone who retires at seventy and who is no longer considered to be active. The problem is someone who is still considered to have an economic or professional need to do something or to hold a position.[105]

In Italy, the phenomenon of constitutional judges moving to political or institutional positions that are based on government nomination following their

[99] The most famous example is Georges Pompidou, who spent three years at the CC between 1959 and 1962, only to become Prime Minister immediately after quitting the CC and eventually being elected President of the Republic. Other examples include Edmond Michelet, who resigned from the CC after having been elected to parliament in 1967, and who thereafter also presided over various ministries. More recently, Noëlle Lenoir became the Minister of European Affairs between 2002 and 2004 after completing her mandate at the CC, while Nicole Belloubet quit the CC in 2017 four years into her term in order to take up a post as Justice Minister.

[100] See the debates during the drafting of the 1958 Constitution in *Travaux préparatoires de la Constitution du 4 octobre 1958. Avis et débats du Comité consultatif constitutionnel*, cited by Alec Stone, *The Birth of Judicial Politics in France. The Constitutional Council in Comparative Perspective* (OUP 1992) 53.

[101] Dominique Schnapper, *Une sociologue au Conseil constitutionnel* (Gallimard 2010) 157.

[102] François Mitterrand, *Le coup d'État permanent* (Les Belles Lettres 2010 [1964]) 130.

[103] Questionnaire in French, Answer no 1 to question 6, 23 January 2023.

[104] Interviewee no 31, 14 December 2023.

[105] Interviewee no 1, 23 January 2023.

judgeship happens quite often.[106] One could thus mention Livio Paladin, who acted as Minister for Regional Affairs several times after having served on the C cost from 1977 to 1986; Leopoldo Elia who became senator as well as interim Foreign Affairs Minister in 1994 and went on to be Minister for Electoral and Institutional Reforms between 1993 and 1994 after having served on the C cost from 1976 to 1985; Giovanni Conso who served as Justice Minister between 1993 and 1994 after having served on the C cost from 1982 to 1991; Antonio La Pergola who became Minister for the Coordination of European Community Policies between 1987 and 1989 and acted as judge and Advocate General (AG) at the European Court of Justice between 1994 and 2006 after having served on the C cost from 1978 to 1987; Vincenzo Caianello who was Justice Minister for a brief period in 1996 after having served on the C cost between 1986 and 1995; Sergio Mattarella who became President of the Republic in 2015 after having served on the C cost from 2011 to 2015; or most recently Marta Cartabia, the first female President of the C cost, who became Justice Minister from 2020 to 2022 after having served on the C cost from 2011 to 2020. Not surprisingly, this practice was seen as problematic by some interviewees.[107]

Italy is not unique in facing the issue of constitutional or supreme court judges regularly obtaining government-nominated political or lucrative positions after the end of their judgeship. Analogous practices have been heavily critiqued in India[108] and have also been noted in Bulgaria and Ukraine.[109]

At the same time, at least for this book's purposes, I would argue that this issue is less directly problematic for such courts. Any image of constitutional courts' impartiality and neutrality is only impacted hypothetically, as it cannot be known a priori whether newly appointed judges will end up in a high-level political position after the end of their terms. This is not to deny the potential risk of impartiality, in the sense that a constitutional court judge with political ambitions may be more cautious in striking down legislation than one without.[110] In stark contrast, however, what judges did prior to joining constitutional courts may have very concrete

[106] See for an earlier analysis on this issue and how to address it: Giovanni Andrea Sacco, 'I giudici emeriti e l'indipendenza della Corte costituzionale' in Pasquale Costanzo (ed), *L'organizzazione e il funzionamento della Corte costituzionale* (Giappichelli 1996) 157.

[107] Interviewees no 12, 27 April 2023 and no 18, 3 July 2023.

[108] For some recent critiques of this practice, see: Madhav S Aney, Shubhankar Dam, and Giovanni Ko, 'Jobs for Justice(s): Corruption in the Supreme Court of India' (2021) 64 Journal of Law and Economics 479; and Shubhankar Dam, 'Active After Sunset: The Politics of Judicial Retirements in India' (2023) 51 Federal L Rev 31.

[109] See: Wojciech Sadurski, *Rights Before Courts* (Springer 2005) 15.

[110] The ECtHR weighed in on a related question concerning the French Supreme Administrative Court. In its judgment in *Sacilor Lormines v France*, no 65411/01, 9 February 2007, the ECtHR found a violation of Art 6 (right to fair trial) on the grounds of objective impartiality, because a judge in that institution had participated in a judgment involving the legitimacy of a government decree while amid negotiations for a successive high-level civil servant position at a ministry. While this does not concern a constitutional court, it nonetheless indicates in which ways the appearance of independence and impartiality can be affected.

and less hypothetical impacts on these courts, especially if the very same personalities were involved in drafting legislation whose constitutionality is now subject to review, or if the drafters of such legislation were their political allies or opponents.

1.3 Main Points and Structure of the Book

The main comparative argument which emerges from this book is that, whereas ex-ministers bring certain benefits, such as political and legislative experience, substantive knowledge as well as status to constitutional courts, and that current and former judges of these institutions welcome them to varying degrees, their participation poses certain risks that are not necessarily outweighed by the advantages of such participation. These risks range from broader theoretical ones, which are mostly to do with politicization, the appearance of independence and impartiality, to very practical risks such as the organization of case allocation and doubts about certain practices' compatibility with the right to a fair trial as developed by international (human rights) law. Therefore, I propose concrete proposals through which the downsides of ex-ministers' participation on such bodies could be addressed or minimized.

The argument will be structured as follows. In Chapter 2, I will lay out how these constitutional courts function in a diachronic manner and what the institutional frameworks of them is insofar as is relevant for the purposes of this book. Aside from the similarity of centralizing the constitutionality review of legislation, there are vast differences in the operation of these bodies. This is not supposed to be a long overview into each detail of these constitutional courts' differences, but it is important to understand the differences between their institutional frameworks because they have a bearing on how and why ex-ministers are nominated to constitutional courts and how they operate differently within that framework.

Chapter 3 will then describe who the concerned individuals are. Their names, former governmental functions, and a quantitative and descriptive assessment of the phenomenon will provide the basis for the qualitative and comparative analysis that adds context to the bare names and numbers. Moreover, I will already be able to answer some questions raised here in the Introduction. Rather than revealing an increase in the phenomenon over time as the flip side of the judicialization of politics, the analysis instead reveals path-dependency per system: the numbers remain the same and rather stable over time. Where many ex-ministers have been named in the past, as in France, that trend continues. Where occasionally some were named in the past, like in Germany and Italy, that also did not change, despite the increased judicialization of politics.

In Chapter 4, I will analyse what benefits and risks the participation of ex-ministers brings to constitutional courts. In the first part of the chapter, I consider the benefits of having these personalities on board, which can be summarized as the possession of specific expertise and knowledge regarding the political machinery of the country, something that a law professor or judge might not necessarily have. Moreover, such personalities may bring a certain diversity of viewpoints and socio-professional background as well as a certain prestige and a standing to an institution that an unknown or anonymous judge or law professor—who in Europe are generally deemed to be civil servants—may not have.

The second part of this chapter considers the attendant risks that will be described ranging from more theoretical aspects which touch upon broad issues such as the politicization, separation of powers, independence, and impartiality, and the public perception of these bodies to more practical risks, ie the concrete and operative issues that may arise from the allocation of cases to abstentions and recusals.

It is predominantly, albeit not exclusively, in this part of the book that I will reference newspaper articles, blogs, and scientific papers written in the four jurisdictions analysed, and I shall thereby highlight some of the main concerns. It is also mostly here that I will integrate the outcome of the interviews conducted, given that the viewpoint of judges, former judges, and high-level staff are all helpful tools for obtaining a fuller picture that takes into account the experience from within those institutions.

Chapter 5 brings the supranational level into the picture in two different ways. On the one hand, especially with regard to the issue of (over- or mono-)politicization, EU law may increasingly have a say, especially if former politicians are the result of rule of law backsliding which makes constitutional courts look increasingly (over- or mono-)politicized, captured, and dependent.

On the other hand, international human rights law demonstrates how the potential risks are not just theoretical or practical, but may amount to a violation of both binding and non-binding supranational requirements, the former mostly via the case law of the ECtHR on Article 6 (right to fair trial). This part will therefore assess how far certain rules and practices concerning in particular abstentions and recusals in the four systems under consideration conform to international (human rights) standards.

This chapter concludes that the participation of ex-ministers on constitutional courts further problematizes certain issues, thus strengthening the idea that some reforms or adjustments may be necessary also from the supranational law perspective.

Concrete steps towards the minimization of the risks attendant to such participation are then laid out in Chapter 6. Here I propose some possible solutions from a constitutional or legislative design perspective ranging from the least radical to the most radical. The least radical option is to require a previous legal education and/or a certain length of legal-professional experience as a prerequisite to being nominated as a constitutional court judge. As a next step, some interventions in the nomination procedures and practices, where for example the required presence of judges might somewhat reduce a too visibly political constitutional court. The next least invasive step would be to introduce a cooling-off period between one's time as a government member and one's nomination to the post of constitutional judge. Another key dimension of the problem worth considering is the establishment of clear and transparent rules on abstentions and recusals. The most 'extreme' solution would be to introduce an incompatibility for former ministers and also former parliamentarians *tout court*. Depending on the specific system, the adopted mechanisms may vary. For instance, proposing the introduction of a legal education as a prerequisite for nomination to a constitutional court is only relevant for France, as the other jurisdictions analysed already stipulate such requirements. The idea is simply to provide various *à la carte* options that can be adapted depending on the institutional context; they ought not to be seen as one-size-fits-all suggestions.

The concluding thoughts of this book in Chapter 7 will look at past and present reform proposals that could impact some of the thoughts provided here as well as situate the somewhat detailed analyses in a broader context. Moreover, in particular in this chapter a few forward-looking points of how the issues discussed in this book may become more relevant, especially in a climate and trend of illiberalism and constitutional backsliding.

This book hopefully provides useful analyses and thoughts regarding some of the issues that (may) arise if and when former ministers join constitutional courts. Whereas I focus on four specific legal systems, the analyses offered here are extendable *mutatis mutandis* to other constitutional and supreme courts around the world. Moreover, most of the insights offered and concerns raised apply not only to former members of government but by imperfect analogy also to former members of parliament or other types of politicians such as high-level civil servants of political nomination and experience. I conclude by positing that—against the backdrop of growing illiberalism—such bodies ought to be strengthened through the devising of clearer rules which could help avoid and prevent the all too easy political capture of such bodies via the appointment of one's political friends as guardians of the constitution.

2
A Diachronic Comparison of Constitutional Courts

Comparative constitutional law literature often refers to the 'European model of constitutional review',[1] in which constitutional courts exercise centralized constitutionality review of statutes alongside a whole set of other functions. From that perspective, these courts resemble each other to some extent, which justifies grouping and analysing them together.

Nevertheless, within that European model there exists considerable variation in terms of their origins, functioning, nomination procedures, and competences. It has thus already been written that 'there is no archetypal European constitutional court'.[2] For this reason, it is important to provide an overview of the relevant elements and characteristics of the four constitutional courts analysed here, how they function today (section 2.1), and the evolutions they have gone through since their creation (section 2.2). These descriptive elements will help better situate the different impact ex-ministers may have (had) as constitutional judges.

2.1 Main Characteristics Today

It is crucial to first shortly describe the main functional mechanisms of the constitutional courts under analysis here, because this will provide the normative and institutional backdrop and framework in which constitutional judges operate. I will briefly describe them in order of their creation and within each section refer to: (a) basic operational elements such as date of creation, starting date of functioning; (b) how many judges and for how long they are nominated; (c) what requirements they must fulfil; (d) who nominates and how they are nominated; (e) the rules on incompatibilities; (f) the rules on abstention and recusal; (g) organizational aspects, such as the role of President, Senates, substitutes, minimum quorum for decisions, dissenting opinions; (h) operational information relating to budget, personnel, or similar issues; (i) how constitutionality control of legislation

[1] See Victor Ferreres Comella, 'The European Model of Constitutional Review of Legislation: Toward Decentralization?' (2004) 2 ICON 461.

[2] Maartje de Visser, *Constitutional Review in Europe. A Comparative Analysis* (Hart 2014) 189.

Ex-Ministers as Constitutional Judges. Mathias Möschel, Oxford University Press.
DOI: 10.1093/9780198930228.003.0002

functions and the various other functions performed by these courts; and (j) how these constitutional courts operate in the broader court system.

As to the second-last point (i), in literature four purposes of constitutional adjudication have been identified, and depending on which purposes are allocated to constitutional courts, the participation of ex-ministers as constitutional judges may be more or less problematic. These purposes are broadly classified as 'keeping the legislature in check; protecting the fundamental rights of individuals in specific cases; resolving institutional disputes between different organs or levels of the State; and ensuring the integrity of political office and related processes'.[3]

In the short descriptions, I will roughly follow the order of the above-mentioned letters but every now and then, due to the particularities of the system described, I allow myself some smaller departures. At the end of this section, Table 2.1 summarizes these elements and facilitates an overview.

2.1.1 Austria

Starting with the oldest constitutional court of the ones analysed here, Austria's Constitutional Court (Verfassungsgerichtshof—VfGH) was created in 1920 and started functioning in the same year.[4] That first experience was short-lived. Pursuant to the resignation of seven of its judges in the politically charged climate of May 1933, the VfGH became inoperative and was revived again only in 1945.[5] Article 147 of the Austrian Constitution (the *Bundesverfassungsgesetz*—B-VG)[6] provides that the VfGH is composed of a President, a Vice-President, 12 permanent judges, and six substitute judges.[7] All judges are nominated to serve until 31 December of the year in which they turn 70 years old.[8] They must have a law degree and at least ten years' professional experience in a domain requiring a law degree for its exercise.[9] Nominations and verifications of whether the formal eligibility requirements for the nominees exist are made by the President of the

[3] ibid, 10. On these functions in more detail see ibid, ch 4, 93–203.

[4] It was preceded by a short-lived Austro-German Constitutional Court. For this section, I rely on the chapter by the current President of the VfGH, Christoph Grabenwarter, 'The Austrian Constitutional Court' in Armin von Bogdandy, Peter M Huber, and Christoph Grabenwarter (eds), *The Max Planck Handbooks in European Public Law* (3rd edn, OUP 2020) 19–70.

[5] On the detailed history of this, see: Kurt Heller, *Der Verfassungsgerichtshof* (Verlag Österreich 2010) 260–71.

[6] Under Austrian constitutional law, single statutory provisions may also have constitutional rank. See: Christoph Grabenwarter, 'The Austrian Constitutional Court' in Armin von Bogdandy, Peter M Huber, and Christoph Grabenwarter (eds), *The Max Planck Handbooks in European Public Law* (3rd edn, OUP 2020) 31, fn 67.

[7] Art 147, para 1 B-VG.

[8] Art 147, para 6 B-VG.

[9] Art 147, para 3 B-VG.

Republic,[10] upon proposal from different political bodies. The President, Vice-President, six permanent judges, and three substitute judges are proposed by the government. These nominees must be judges, civil servants, or professors of a legal subject at a university. Three permanent judges and two substitute judges are nominated upon proposal by the National Council (the *Nationalrat*, Austria's lower house of parliament) and three permanent judges and one substitute judge upon proposal by the Federal Council (the *Bundesrat*, Austria's upper house of parliament). Three members and two substitute members must have their permanent residence outside the federal capital Vienna.[11]

There are some incompatibilities. For instance, constitutional judges can neither be part of the government or parliament, nor can they hold an elected position at any level (federal, state, or European), nor be employees or officials of a political party.[12] A specific incompatibility concerns the function of President and Vice-President of the VfGH and for whom a cooling-off period prior to entering the VfGH is foreseen: if they were in any of the functions or positions for which the just mentioned incompatibilities are established, at least five years must have passed.[13] One particularity of the Austrian system is that being a constitutional court judge is not deemed to be a full-time position, which is why they can be, for example, a university professor or practising lawyer on the side. Only members who are civil servants are released from their functions and thus become full-time judges.[14] This may also explain why the VfGH operates in sessions and every three years elects in a secret ballot a number of permanent judge rapporteurs who are in charge of preparing the single decisions. In October 2020, there were 12 such rapporteurs as well as the Vice-President.[15] Another particularity of the VfGH is that the President has no vote, except when there is a tie.[16]

[10] See the explicit mention of this competence on the official website of the Federal Presidency: <https://www.bundespraesident.at/aktuelles/detail/aufgaben-und-rechte> accessed 31 May 2023.

[11] Art 147, para 2 B-VG.

[12] Art 147, para 4 B-VG.

[13] Art 147, para 5 B-VG.

[14] This part-time/full-time exercise of Austrian constitutional judges results from the formulation of Art 147 paras 2 and 4 B-VG. The reasons for their positions being part-time seem connected to the historical precedent of the Austrian Imperial Court, when judges were also not full-time, and also the need to guarantee a diversity of viewpoints and professions. In this sense: Michael Holoubek and Ulrich Wagrandl, 'A Model for the World: The Austrian Constitutional Court Turns 100' (2023) 17 ICL Journal 251, 263–66. The fact that the part-time requirement ensures that certain professions like attorneys would otherwise not be represented on the VfGH was also confirmed during some interviews: interviewee no 22, 12 September 2023, who added that for some professions, one might not get the most qualified people if they had to come full-time to the VfGH.

[15] <https://www.vfgh.gv.at/verfassungsgerichtshof/organisation/richterbank_und_rechtsprechende_taetigkeit.de.html#:~:text=Der%20Verfassungsgerichtshof%20w%C3%A4hlt%20aus%20seiner,und%20wird%20auch%20regelm%C3%A4%C3%9Fig%20vorgenommen> accessed 18 January 2023.

[16] Art 31 VfGG.

In terms of abstentions and recusals, the Statute on the VfGH (*Verfassungsgerichtshofgesetz*—VfGG) prohibits recusals by parties in underlying litigation.[17] However, there are grounds for exclusion based on which a judge or substitute judge must either abstain or can be excluded by the VfGH. These grounds are: when they would be excluded according to ordinary rules applicable to the judiciary; if they have already participated in lower-level litigation of the same case; and if there exist other important reasons that could raise doubts as to their full impartiality.[18] Moreover, they can be excluded from any hearing and decision regarding a decision of an election authority if they participated in the decision of such authority.[19] Most importantly for the purposes of this book, judges or substitute judges can also be excluded when they have to examine the constitutionality of statutes or the legality of regulations if they were members at the time of adoption of the respective body which adopted the instrument before them. This exclusion goes so far as to include the mere re-publication (*Wiederverlautbarung*) of such instruments, if they were members of the federal government or the respective state-level government.[20]

Whether or not such a ground for abstention/exclusion exists is determined by the VfGH itself in a non-public hearing.[21] In practice, concerned judges signal their potential conflict of interest to the VfGH's President and, if indeed a conflict is established, a substitute judge is invited to sit on the case.[22]

From the surveys conducted, one can note in Figure 2.1 how on a scale from 0–10 there is a relative dissatisfaction with the existing mechanisms of protection of the VfGH's independence and impartiality and in particular, incompatibilities, abstentions, and recusals, as well as the cooling-off period for the President and Vice-President.

The VfGH decides in a single bench. The minimum quorum needed for decisions is eight judges and a chairperson, with a small bench of four judges and a chairperson being sufficient in some other proceedings.[23] Dissenting opinions are not permitted.

Operationally, the budget for 2023 was 18.78 million euro.[24] In terms of personnel, in 2021 there were 105 non-judicial positions. Forty of those served as law clerks (*verfassungsrechtliche MitarbeiterInnen*) who work with the permanent

[17] Art 12, para 1 VfGG.
[18] Art 12, para 2 VfGG.
[19] Art 12, para 3 VfGG.
[20] Art 12, para 4 VfGG.
[21] Art 12, para 6 VfGG.
[22] <https://www.vfgh.gv.at/verfassungsgerichtshof/organisation/richterbank_und_rechtsprechende_taetigkeit.de.html> accessed 11 October 2022.
[23] See Art 7, paras 1–2 VfGG.
[24] <https://service.bmf.gv.at/Budget/Budgets/VBB/de/2021/Home/Treemap?type=EV&houseHold=1&currency=MioEuro&showTable=false&showGrafic=true&filter=0301> accessed 10 January 2023.

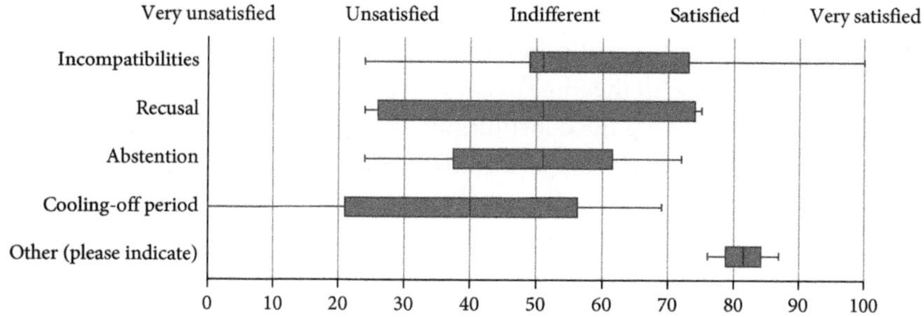

Figure 2.1 Survey answers to question 3 for Austria

judge rapporteurs, meaning that each has about three law clerks.[25] In terms of approval ratings in an annual opinion poll run by the Austrian Press Agency, 41% of people surveyed in 2022 indicated they trusted the VfGH.[26] This put it in fifth position amongst other public institutions, behind the police (55%), the army (52%), the employee's representative chamber (*Arbeiterkammer*) (50%), and universities (42%). In the previous poll, the VfGH had ranked second, with 45% approval just behind the police.[27]

In Austria the constitutionality review function for legislation can generally only occur once a legislative act has entered into force.[28] State or federal legislation can be declared unconstitutional pursuant to the initiative of a number of actors, ranging from state or federal legislators or governments,[29] courts,[30] or individuals raising the issue directly in certain situations,[31] or incidentally in a court procedure.[32] A limited individual constitutional complaint procedure (*Entscheidungsbeschwerde*) exists against judgments by administrative courts.[33] The VfGH can ex officio raise the issue of constitutionality of legislation if a statute needs to be applied in a case already pending before it.[34] A similar logic and

[25] See the VfGH's official annual report for 2021, 18 <https://www.vfgh.gv.at/downloads/taetigkeitsberichte/VFGH_Taetigkeitsbericht_2021.pdf> accessed 18 January 2023.

[26] OGM, 'APA Vertrauensindex Institutionen Juli 2022', 29 July 2022 <https://www.ogm.at/2022/07/29/ogm-apa-vertrauensindex-institutionen-juli-2022/> accessed 4 October 2023.

[27] OGM, 'APA Vertrauensindex Institutionen Juli 2021', 30 July 2021 <https://www.ogm.at/2021/07/30/ogm-vertrauensindex-institutionen-juli-2021/> accessed 4 October 2023.

[28] Christoph Grabenwarter, 'The Austrian Constitutional Court' in Armin von Bogdandy, Peter M Huber, and Christoph Grabenwarter (eds), *The Max Planck Handbooks in European Public Law* (3rd edn, OUP 2020) 36.

[29] Art 140 B-VG, paras 2–3. The action can be triggered by the federal government, state governments, one-third of the members of the National or Federal Council with regard to federal laws and by the federal government and one-third of the members of a state parliament, if such power is established by state constitutions, with regard to state laws.

[30] Art 140 B-VG, para 1a.

[31] Art 140 B-VG, para 1c.

[32] Art 140, para 1d B-VG.

[33] Art 144 B-VG.

[34] Art 140, para 1b B-VG.

intervention by actors as described above for the review of legislation is extended, with some adaptations, to constitutional challenges to ordinances (*Verordnungnen*, ie administrative acts with the force of law) by federal or state authorities.[35]

Apart from determining the constitutionality of legislation in the various ways described above, the VfGH also performs a few other tasks.[36] In particular, it decides on competence conflicts between various federal and state authorities;[37] reviews individual judicial acts in adjudicating on appeals against decisions and orders by lower administrative courts;[38] decides on challenges to various elections as well as results of popular initiatives, plebiscites, referenda, or citizens' initiatives at various levels;[39] judges on the lawfulness of international treaties;[40] overviews litigation involving parliamentary inquiry committees;[41] and is in charge of the impeachment of various state representatives.[42] One can see that the 'other' functions of this constitutional court are quite broad.

As a last point, the VfGH sits atop a judicial pyramid that is composed of a Supreme Court, the Oberster Gerichtshof (OGH) which is in charge of criminal and civil matters, and an Administrative Supreme Court, the Verwaltungsgerichtshof (VwGH) in charge of administrative matters.

2.1.2 Italy

The Italian Corte costituzionale (C cost) was created in 1948 but started operating only in 1956.[43] Article 135 of the Italian Constitution provides that the C cost shall be composed of 15 judges who are nominated for nine years without a possibility to be reappointed. As to their qualifications, they must be judges or retired judges of the ordinary and administrative supreme courts, university law professors, or attorneys who have practised law at least for 20 years. The nomination procedure is a mixed one: one-third are nominated by the President of the Republic; one-third by parliament in a joint session in which successful nominees require a two-thirds majority within two rounds of a secret vote (reduced to three-fifths in the third round); and one-third by the ordinary and administrative supreme courts.[44]

35 Art 139 B-VG.

36 The list is partly drawn from the website of the VfGH: <https://www.vfgh.gv.at/kompetenzen-und-verfahren/functions.en.html> accessed 13 October 2022.

37 Art 138 B-VG.

38 Art 144, para 1 B-VG.

39 Art 141 B-VG.

40 Art 140a B-VG.

41 Art 138b B-VG.

42 Arts 142 and 143 B-VG.

43 A concise overview of the institutional functioning of the C cost can be found in: Gustavo Zagrebelsky and Valeria Marcenò, *Giustizia costituzionale, II. Oggetti, procedimenti, decisioni* (2nd edn, il Mulino 2018) 13–47.

44 Art 135, para 1 of the Italian Constitution; for the majorities to be reached in parliament, see: Art 3, Legge costituzionale 22 November 1967, no 2.

A statute then specifies that from the five court-named judges, three should come from the Supreme Court (Corte di cassazione—Cass), one from the Supreme Administrative Court (Consiglio di Stato—Cons St), and one from the Court of Accounts (Corte dei conti—C conti).[45]

The Italian Constitution also indicates some incompatibilities of being constitutional judge, namely that of being a member of parliament, of a regional parliament, the practice of the legal profession, and with every appointment and office indicated by statute.[46] These are that judges of the C cost may not hold any other public or private office or employment; they may not engage in any professional, commercial, or industrial activity, or act as a director or auditor in profit-oriented companies; they may not sit on competition selection boards or hold university posts and may not be candidates in local or political elections;[47] and they may not engage in any activity pertaining to a political association or party.[48] Constitutional judges who used to be ordinary judges and university professors may not continue in those functions for the duration of their mandate.[49] One last incompatibility for members of the national governing body for judges, the Higher Council of the Judiciary (*Consiglio superiore della magistratura*—CSM) was established later.[50] The C cost itself checks whether the nominees have the required subjective eligibility criteria to become constitutional court judges by deciding with absolute majority.[51]

Regarding abstentions and recusals, the Italian system is interesting because it excludes both, except for impeachment procedures. The internal procedural rules adopted by the C cost provide that '[i]n judgments regulated by the current supplementary rules, the causes for abstention or recusal of judges do not apply'.[52]

From the surveys conducted, the Italian constitutional judges seem rather dissatisfied with the various mechanisms of incompatibilities, abstentions, recusals, and/or cooling-off periods. This may not come as a surprise given that—apart from incompatibilities, no such mechanisms exist in positive law. What is more surprising is that as Figure 2.2 shows—a few of the respondents answered the question about cooling-off periods, even though these do not exist in the Italian system.

[45] See Art 2, Legge 11 March 1953, no 87.
[46] Art 135, para 6.
[47] Art 7, Legge 11 March 1953, no 87.
[48] Art 8, Legge 11 March 1953, no 87.
[49] Art 7, Legge 11 March 1953, no 87. This limitation was considered too harsh by some of the interviewees. See eg interviewee no 7, 3 March 2023.
[50] Art 33, para 1, Legge 24 March 1958, no 195.
[51] Art 2, Legge costituzionale 22 November 1967, no 2.
[52] See: Art 32 of the latest version of the *Norme integrative per i giudizi davanti alla Corte costituzionale* <https://www.cortecostituzionale.it/documenti/comunicatistampa/CC_CS_20220601145710.pdf> accessed 13 October 2022. Approving of this choice, see: Gustavo Zagrebelsky, *Principî e voti* (Einaudi 2005) 64.

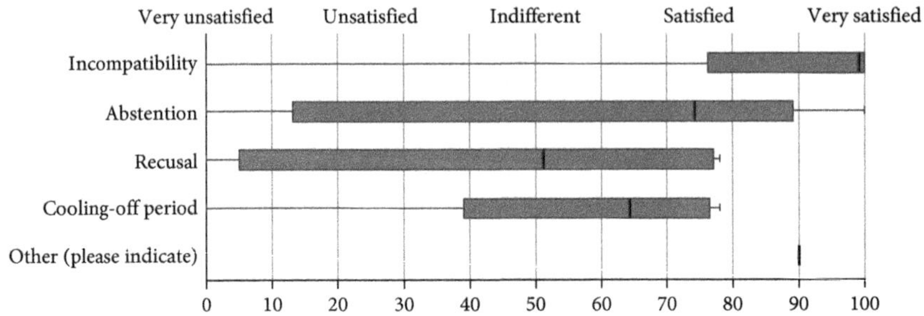

Figure 2.2 Survey answers to question 3 for Italy

The C cost decides in a single bench and judicial decisions require a minimum quorum of 11 judges to be valid.[53] Dissenting opinions are not allowed.

Another noteworthy institutional characteristic of the C cost is that the President is elected by colleagues at the court and shall remain in office for three years and can be re-elected.[54] (S)he is considered *primus inter pares*, as a sign of the strong collegial aspect and functioning of this institution, and has in that sense ceremonial rather than other functions. The rather timid role of the President is compounded by the reality and practice that presidents of the C cost are often in office only for a few months, shortly before their mandate ends.[55] This has been critiqued for various reasons, including that it prevents presidents from having any real leading and shaping function for the institution.[56]

In terms of budget, the C cost had 65,496,500 euro for 2023.[57] Without entering into the details of the personnel, each judge can have up to a maximum of three law clerks. The President is allowed to have four.[58] For the C cost, it is difficult to obtain separate indications of public trust in the C cost, given that official statistics are provided only for the court system as a whole.[59]

[53] Art 16, Legge 11 March 1953, no 87. This quorum is reduced to nine or eight for non-judicial decisions by Art 6, para 2 of the C cost's internal general regulations (*Regolamento generale della Corte costituzionale*), adopted on 20 January 1966 and amended at various points. See: <https://www.cortecostituzionale.it/documenti/download/pdf/CC_Fonti_REGGENluglio_2009_05032011.pdf> accessed 8 November 2022.

[54] Art 135 of the Italian Constitution.

[55] See on this information the website of the C cost: <https://www.cortecostituzionale.it/jsp/consulta/istituzioni/la_struttura.do> accessed 13 October 2022.

[56] In clear terms on this see: Sabino Cassese, *Dentro la Corte. Diario di un giudice costituzionale* (il Mulino 2015) 207, 228, 234–35, 240–42, and 256–58.

[57] <https://www.cortecostituzionale.it/documenti/composizione/bilancio/bilancio_2023.pdf> accessed on 25 July December 2024.

[58] Elisabetta Lamarque, 'Chi sono gli assistenti di studio dei giudici costituzionali' in *Alle frontiere del diritto costituzionale. Scritti in onore di Valerio Onida* (Giuffrè 2011) 1065, 1077.

[59] ISTAT, 'La fiducia nelle istituzioni del Paese', 16 May 2021, <https://www.istat.it/it/files/2022/05/Fiducia-cittadini-istituzioni2021.pdf> accessed 4 October 2023.

As to the functioning of constitutionality review of legislation, the Italian system only knows constitutionality review of state or regional statutes or acts having force of statute.[60] One procedurally not irrelevant point is that such litigation is only incidental in the sense that citizens or individuals do not have direct access to the C cost and can only raise the issue of constitutionality of a statute during an ongoing, underlying trial. If the judge does not find the question manifestly unfounded, (s) he stays the proceedings and refers the issue to the C cost.[61] Another consequence of this formulation and procedure is that the constitutionality control of any other legal regulation, administrative or court decision is not possible under Italian constitutional law.

Besides judging on the constitutionality of statutes and acts having the force of statutes of both state and regional level, the C cost also decides on competence conflicts between different powers of the state, between the state and the regions, as well as infra-regional conflicts.[62] It also judges charges brought against the President of the Republic.[63] In such impeachment procedures the C cost sits as a broader body, in the sense that another 16 members are chosen from a list of citizens who would be eligible to be elected to the Senate and which parliament elects every nine years by using the same procedures as those followed in appointing ordinary judges. Moreover, the C cost also decides on the admissibility of referenda that have the goal to abrogate legislation under Article 75 of the Italian Constitution.[64] Compared with the other constitutional courts analysed here, the additional functions of the C cost remain fairly limited.

As a last point, the C cost sits atop a judicial pyramid that is composed of three separate institutions: the Supreme Court (Cass), the Supreme Administrative Court (Cons St), and the Court of Accounts (C conti).

2.1.3 Germany

The German Federal Constitutional Court (Bundesverfassungsgericht—BVerfG) was created in 1949 and started operating in 1951. Article 94 of the German Federal Constitution (*Grundgesetz*—GG) provides that the BVerfG is composed of federal judges and other members, and that half of the members are elected by the lower house of parliament, the Federal Assembly (*Bundestag*), and half of them

[60] Art 134, para 1 of the Italian Constitution.
[61] Art 1 of legge costituzionale no 1, 9 February 1948.
[62] Art 134, para 2 of the Italian Constitution.
[63] Art 134, para 3 of the Italian Constitution.
[64] Art 2 of legge costituzionale no 1, 11 March 1953.

by the upper house of parliament, the German Federal Council (*Bundesrat*). These general rules are then integrated by more specific ones in a statute on the BVerfG (*Gesetz über das Bundesverfassungsgericht*—BVerfGG).[65] A particularity of the BVerfG is that it is structured in two separate Senates, composed of eight judges each. Three judges of each Senate must come from one of the five apex courts, where they need to have had at least three years of experience.[66] Moreover, this statute specifies that all judges must have turned 40 years old; must be qualified to become judges;[67] are named for a duration of 12 years or until they turn 68; and cannot be re-elected.[68]

The details of the nomination and election procedure by the two houses of parliament are laid out in Articles 5–9 of the BVerfGG. The Federal Council elects the future judges with a two-thirds majority.[69] At the Federal Assembly, the procedure is a little bit more complex: it elects the constitutional judges in a secret ballot and by qualified majority (eight out of 12), based on a recommendation made by a small committee of 12 members of parliament who themselves deliberate behind closed doors.[70] The President and Vice-President are nominated alternately by the Federal Assembly and the Federal Council and they each preside over one of the two respective Senates.[71]

As to the incompatibilities, the GG provides that a constitutional judge can neither be part of either federal or state chambers of parliament, nor of any federal or state government.[72] Moreover, the BVerfGG adds that any professional activity other than that of law professor is incompatible with that of constitutional judge.[73]

The specific two-Senate structure also has consequences on the subdivision of competences. The First Senate is mostly responsible for fundamental rights issues, whereas the Second Senate deals predominantly with institutional conflicts, even though some departures from this principle are authorized by statute and each year in a plenary session, the BVerfG can further depart from that allocation of competences.[74]

With regard to abstentions and recusals, the applicable provisions in the BVerfGG distinguish between (mandatory) exclusion (*Ausschluss*)[75] and

[65] Gesetz über das Bundesverfassungsgericht of 12 March 1951.
[66] Art 2 BVerfGG.
[67] Art 3 BVerfGG, paras 1 and 2.
[68] Art 4 BVerfGG, paras 1–3.
[69] Art 7 BVerfGG.
[70] Art 6 BVerfGG.
[71] Art 9 BVerfGG.
[72] Art 94, para 1 GG.
[73] Art 3, para 4 BVerfGG.
[74] See Art 14 BVerfGG and <https://www.bundesverfassungsgericht.de/DE/Verfahren/Geschaeftsverteilung/geschaeftsverteilung_node.html> accessed 6 January 2023.
[75] Art 18 BVerfGG.

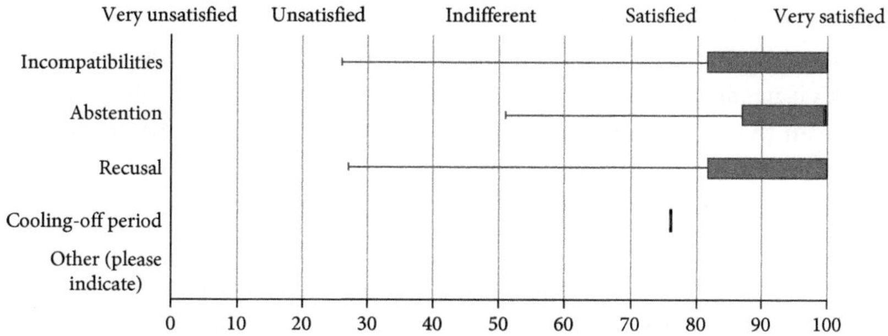

Figure 2.3 Survey answers to question 3 for Germany

abstentions and recusals ((*Selbst-*)*Ablehnung*).[76] As to the former, the BVerfGG specifies that constitutional judges are excluded from judging if they had previously been active in the same underlying matter functionally or due to their profession.[77] Importantly for the purposes of this book, participation in a legislative procedure, and the expression of a scientific opinion on a legal issue that might be relevant in a pending case, are not deemed to be such grounds for exclusion.[78]

As to the latter two, this includes both voluntary abstentions that are initiated by the constitutional judges themselves whenever they have doubts about their own impartiality in a given matter. Recusals instead are commenced by third parties who would like to challenge a judge's impartiality. Common to both is that the BVerfG issues publicly available and motivated decisions that form a certain jurisprudence, in which it has held that both provisions need to be construed narrowly.[79] Recusal requests are decided without the concerned judge being present[80] who must nevertheless be allowed to express him or herself.[81] If an abstention or recusal is accepted, a substitute judge, who cannot be one of the Senate Presidents, is appointed from the other Senate.[82]

Unlike their Austrian and Italian colleagues, the German survey participants seemed to be quite satisfied with their various rules on incompatibilities, abstentions, and recusals, as Figure 2.3 shows.

[76] Art 19 BVerfGG.
[77] Art 18, para 1, point 2 BVerfGG.
[78] Art 18, para 3 BVerfGG.
[79] For an overview of the doctrinal and jurisprudential interpretation of the BVerfGG of these two provisions, see one of the typical German article-by-article statutory commentaries on the BVerfGG: Hans Lechner and Rüdiger Zuck, *Bundesverfassungsgerichtsgesetz. Kommentar* (5th edn, CH Beck, 2006) 113–25. See also the more recent overview by: Kai Zähle, 'Die Ausschließung und Ablehnung eines Richters nach §§ 18, 19 BVerfGG in der Rechtsprechung des Bundesverfassungsgerichts' (2012) 37 Archiv des öffentlichen Rechts 173.
[80] Art 19, para 1 BVerfGG.
[81] Art 19, para 2 BVerfGG.
[82] Art 19, para 4 BVerfGG.

In terms of decision-making, judgments are adopted by a simple majority, with some exceptions where a two-third majority is required.[83] A minimum quorum of six judges is needed to take a valid decision, with the possibility of substitutes to be drawn from the other Senate in urgent cases.[84] Separate opinions are possible,[85] but are resorted to rather exceptionally.

Operationally, the budget of the BVerfG for 2023 was established at 40 million euro.[86] In terms of personnel, one should mention the presence of four law clerks per judge.[87] Approval ratings of the BVerfG in opinion polls are generally high and reached 70% at the turn of the year 2022/23, putting it in fourth place behind doctors (81%), the police (79%), and universities (74%).[88]

As to the actual competences, those are mostly listed in Article 93 of the GG.[89] In terms of constitutionality review of legislation, the BVerfG does both abstract and concrete review.[90] It also decides on horizontal disputes between high federal organs (*Organstreit*)[91] as well as on vertical federal–state conflicts.[92] Certainly, the best-known and most important feature—also in terms of docket number—is the individual constitutional complaint procedure (*Verfassungsbeschwerde*) which is formulated broadly, in the sense that any person may raise such a complaint if one of their substantive or procedural fundamental constitutional rights has been violated by a public authority, including court rulings. Such a complaint must be brought after having exhausted all judicial remedies. But the BVerfG decides also on other matters, such as the prohibition of political parties,[93] election disputes of

[83] Art 15, para 4 BVerfGG

[84] Art 15, para 2 BVerfGG.

[85] Art 30, para 2 BVerfGG.

[86] See the BVerfG annual report for 2022: <https://www.bundesverfassungsgericht.de/SharedDocs/Downloads/DE/Jahresbericht/jahresbericht_2023.pdf?__blob=publicationFile&v=4> accessed 25 July 2024, 6.

[87] <https://www.bundesverfassungsgericht.de/DE/Das-Gericht/Organisation/organisation_node.html> accessed 17 January 2023. See in the literature on these clerks: Otwin Massing, 'Legal Assistants at the German Federal Constitutional Court. A "Black Box" of Research?' in Ralf Rogowski and Thomas Gavron (eds), *Constitutional Courts in Comparison: The US Supreme Court and the German Federal Constitutional Court* (Berghahn Books 2002) 180.

[88] RTL/ntv-Trendbarometer, 'Vertrauen in Institutionen' <https://www.n-tv.de/politik/Vertrauen-in-Institutionen-sinkt-weiter-article23849698.html> accessed 4 October 2023. This rating had decreased by three points from the previous poll and in Eastern Germany the approval was only at 58%, down by 15 points.

[89] For an overview of these also in terms of docket numbers, see: Donald P Kommers, *The Constitutional Jurisprudence of the Federal Republic of Germany* (Duke University Press 1989) 12 and Donald P Kommers and Russell A Miller, *The Constitutional Jurisprudence of the Federal Republic of Germany* (3rd edn, Duke University Press 2012) 11. For more up-to-date and detailed numbers, until 2020 the BVerfG published an overview of its decisional statistics each year:
<https://www.bundesverfassungsgericht.de/EN/Verfahren/Jahresstatistiken/Archiv/Archiv.html> accessed 19 February 2024. Since then, they are published in the BVerfG's annual report.

[90] Respectively Art 93, para (1), 2 and 2A, and Art 100, para (1) GG.

[91] Art 93, para (1), point 1.

[92] Art 93, para (1), point 3.

[93] Art 21, para 2 GG.

the Federal Assembly,[94] impeachment of judges[95] or the federal President,[96] forfeiture of basic rights,[97] international law disputes,[98] and in more recent years increasingly also requests for temporary injunctions.[99] Again, one can see that the functions here go well beyond the 'mere' constitutionality control of legislation and involve the BVerfG in quite political affairs.

As a last point, the BVerfG sits atop a judicial pyramid that is composed of five different supreme courts: the Supreme Court (Bundesgerichtshof—BGH) which deals with civil and criminal matters, the Supreme Administrative Court (Bundesverwaltungsgericht—BVerwG), the Supreme Labour Court (Bundesarbeitsgericht—BAG), the Supreme Finance Court (Bundesfinanzhof—BFH), and the Supreme Social Court (Bundessozialgericht—BSG).

2.1.4 France

The French CC was created in 1958 and started operating in 1959. Article 56 of the French Constitution is the main provision on this institution and provides that:

> The Constitutional Council shall comprise nine members, each of whom shall hold office for a non-renewable term of nine years. One third of the membership of the Constitutional Council shall be renewed every three years. Three of its members shall be appointed by the President of the Republic, three by the President of the National Assembly and three by the President of the Senate. The procedure provided for in the last paragraph of article 13 shall apply to these appointments. The appointments made by the President of each House shall be submitted for the opinion solely of the relevant standing committee in that House.
>
> In addition to the nine members provided for above, former Presidents of the Republic shall be *ex officio* life members of the Constitutional Council.
>
> The President shall be appointed by the President of the Republic. He shall have a casting vote in the event of a tie.[100]

No constitutional, legislative or regulatory text indicates any age or educational requirements to become members of the CC, the presumption being that members

94 Art 41, para 2 of the GG.
95 Art 98, para 2 of the GG.
96 Art 61 of the GG.
97 Art 18 of the GG.
98 Art 100, para 2 of the GG.
99 Art 32 of the BVerfGG.
100 Art 56 of the French Constitution.

shall be citizens in possession of their civil and political rights. That means non-lawyers are also eligible and have indeed been appointed.

Sub-constitutional provisions integrate and even derogate to some of the constitutional provisions described above. As to the derogations, it is possible that a person's CC membership can be renewed, allowing them to stay on the institution for up to 12 years in total. That happens when the person is nominated to complete the nine-year mandate of another member, if that remaining time is less than three years.[101] The lower-level provisions thus derogate from the constitutional prescriptions in two ways: duration and renewability.[102]

As to the integration, one could mention the incompatibilities with other functions or activities, that are quite detailed. First, the Constitution provides that CC members cannot be members of government or parliament at the same time.[103] Second, sub-constitutional texts establish other incompatibilities, such as being a member of the Economic and Social Council, being the Defender of Rights, holding any elected office, being a civil servant or attorney, or carrying out any other professional or salaried activity.[104]

[101] Art 12 of the Ordonnance no 58-1067 of 7 November 1958 portant loi organique sur le conseil constitutionnel (as modified over the years. <https://www.conseil-constitutionnel.fr/en/fondements-textuels/ordinance-no-58-1067-constituting-an-institutional-act-on-the-constitutional-council> accessed 12 October 2022.

[102] Some interviewees seemed quite surprised about this observation: interviewee no 9, 21 March 2023 and interviewee no 30, 14 December 2023. The rationale of this rule was that a mandate of fewer than three years would not attract good candidates. The literature itself does not identify particular issues. See eg, the commentary by a CC's former member: François Luchaire, *Le Conseil constitutionnel* (Economica 1980) 66. But see the mention by Colombani, who states that Luchaire himself had critiqued this rule or exception: Jean-Marie Colombani, 'L'opposition, à l'exception de M Chirac, dénonce la nomination de M Badinter' *Le Monde* (Paris, 21 February 1986) 10.

In the CC's history, five people have been reappointed in this way: René Cassin who was re-nominated in 1962 after finishing the mandate of the late Maurice Délépine; Louis Joxe who was re-nominated in 1980 after finishing the mandate of the late Henry Rey; Robert Lecourt who was re-nominated in 1980 after finishing the mandate of the late Paul Coste-Floret; Maurice-René Simmonet who was re-nominated in 1986 after finishing the mandate of the late Louis Gros; and more recently, Claire Bazy Malaurie was re-nominated in 2013 after finishing the mandate of the late Jean-Louis Pezant. See on this list: <https://www.conseil-constitutionnel.fr/les-membres-depuis-1959> accessed 2 June 2023. Renewals of such 'unfinished' mandates are not automatic, as can be gleaned from the example of Paul Legatte, who was nominated in 1983 to finish the mandate of the late Achille Peretti with fewer than three years left and whose mandate was not renewed. See the list of members of the CC published in (2008) 25 Cahiers du conseil constitutionnel 80, 84 and also: Lauréline Fontaine, *La Constitution maltraitée* (Editions Amsterdam 2023) 75 fn 5.

[103] Art 57 of the French Constitution.

[104] Art 4 of the Ordonnance no 58-1067 of 7 November 1958 portant loi organique sur le conseil constitutionnel (as modified over the years) <https://www.conseil-constitutionnel.fr/en/fondements-textuels/ordinance-no-58-1067-constituting-an-institutional-act-on-the-constitutional-council> accessed 12 October 2022.

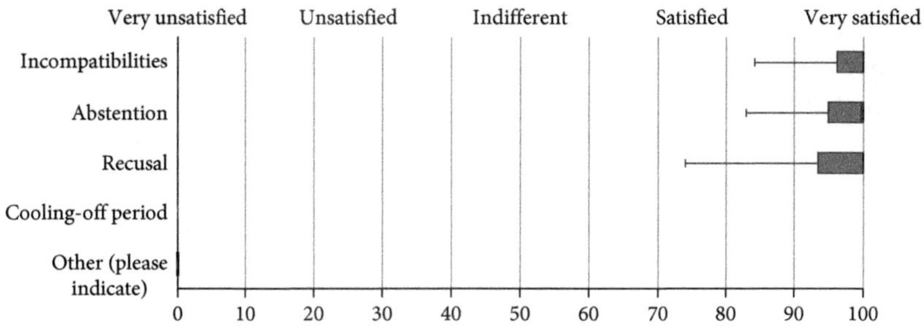

Figure 2.4 Survey answers to question 3 for France

In terms of abstentions and recusals, the Constitution generically provides that members of the CC have to exercise their functions impartially.[105] Two internal regulations by the CC have clarified the possibility of abstentions and recusals and how they should be procedurally handled.[106] As to abstentions, essentially any member who deems they should refrain from sitting on a given case informs the President of the CC.[107] As to recusals, there are some differences, depending on the type of procedure engaged before the CC. The main point is that they are possible and if the member disagrees with the arguments provided for the recusal, then the CC examines the claim without the concerned member.[108] Unlike the BVerfG, however, the CC does not adopt any public motivated decisions. One relevant aspect for this book is that, as in Germany, the previous participation in the drafting of a legislative text whose constitutionality is raised does not constitute a ground for exclusion or recusal.[109] Another parallel with the German situation is that the level of satisfaction of the CC with its own rules is very high, as Figure 2.4 shows.

The CC decides in a single bench, and the minimum quorum for valid decisions by the CC is seven members, except for a case of force majeure which is duly noted in the minutes.[110] Dissenting opinions are not allowed at the CC.

[105] Art 3 of the Ordonnance no 58-1067 du 7 novembre 1958 portant loi organique sur le conseil constitutionnel.
[106] Règlement intérieur sur la procédure suivie devant le Conseil constitutionnel pour les questions prioritaires de constitutionnalité of 4 February 2010 and Décision no 2022-152 ORGA of 11 March 2022.
[107] Art 4, para 1 of Règlement 2010 and Art 14, para 1 of Décision 2022.
[108] Art 4, paras 2 and 3 of Règlement 2010 and Art 15 of Décision 2022.
[109] Art 4, para 4 of Règlement 2010.
[110] Art 14 of the Ordonnance no 58-1067 du 7 novembre 1958 portant loi organique sur le conseil constitutionnel.

As far as its budget is concerned, the CC has the lowest of the four courts examined here, with 17.93 million euro for 2024.[111] That may be unsurprising, given that it is also the body with the fewest members. Moreover, unlike in Germany and in Italy, single judges do not have individual law clerks. Instead, they can rely on a centralized study service which is staffed essentially by five people who work under the supervision of the General Secretary.[112] Approval ratings for the CC correspond roughly to those for the VfGH, with 40% of the surveyed individuals stating that they have high or relatively high trust in the CC in February 2023; the best of the national level institutions, behind various institutions of local or regional government .[113] However, this had declined from 47% in February 2021.[114]

Under the French Constitution, only the constitutionality of statutes, and not that of other acts, can be challenged before the CC. There are two main ways of doing so. The first one is the so-called a priori procedure which takes place before legislation enters into force. Such a check is mandatory inter alia for institutional acts but also for internal regulations of parliament. In other situations, bills can be referred to the CC before their promulgation, by the President of the Republic, the Prime Minister, the President of the National Assembly, the President of the Senate, or by 60 members of the National Assembly or 60 Senators.[115] In these cases, the CC must decide within a month. The second procedure takes place once legislation has entered into force, meaning a posteriori. In that case, the recourse is incidental, in the sense that if during a court proceeding the claim arises that a legislative provision infringes the rights and freedoms guaranteed by the Constitution, then leave needs to be requested from one of France's two supreme courts, the French Supreme Administrative Court (the Conseil d'Etat—CE) or the French Supreme Court (the Cour de cassation—C Cass)[116] who then filter the cases as to their admissibility and merits.

Apart from deciding on the constitutionality of legislation, the CC performs a host of other functions that are mentioned in various provisions of the Constitution. Indeed, it declares the potential incapacity of the President

[111] Loi n° 2023-1322 du 29 décembre 2023 de finances pour 2024.

[112] <https://www.conseil-constitutionnel.fr/le-conseil-constitutionnel/les-services-du-conseil> accessed 17 January 2023.

[113] Opinionway pour SciencesPo CEVIPOF, 'Baromètre de la confiance politique/vague 14 – Février 2023', 25 <https://www.sciencespo.fr/cevipof/sites/sciencespo.fr.cevipof/files/Barometre%20de%20la%20confiance%20en%20politique%20-%20vague%2014%20-%20Fevrier%202023%20-%20vFR.pdf%20(1).pdf> accessed 8 October 2023.

[114] ibid 26.

[115] On the a priori control, see Art 61 of the French Constitution. Judgments under this procedure are identified with the docket number DC (*decision portant sur la constitutionnalité d'une loi*).

[116] On the a posteriori control, see: Art 61-1 of the French Constitution. Judgments under this procedure are identified with the docket number QPC (*question prioritaire de constitutionnalité*).

of the Republic and is more generally involved in the presidential elections at various moments;[117] it intervenes in different types of referenda[118] and when the President declares an emergency situation;[119] it checks whether international treaties conform to the French Constitution if the issue is raised by the same authorities allowed to raise an a priori constitutionality review;[120] and it intervenes in electoral litigation involving the election of members of both houses of parliament.[121]

2.1.5 Comparative overview

The overview of these basic features of the four constitutional bodies illustrates how different these constitutional courts are from each other. One (Austria) has part-time judges, whereas in the others (France, Germany, Italy) constitutional judges are full-time positions. One (France) has virtually no educational or experiential prerequisites for becoming judges, whereas in the others (Austria, Germany, Italy) there are detailed requirements and they are essentially composed of experienced lawyers. Some (Austria, France, Germany) have purely political nomination procedures, in the sense that political organs exclusively nominate the judges, whereas one (Italy) has a mix. Some (Italy, Germany) require the participation of judges, whereas others (Austria, France) do not. One (Italy) goes so far as prohibiting abstentions and recusals, whereas the others (Austria, France, Germany) have some rules. Some (Italy and France) provide no direct access for individuals, whereas others (Austria, Germany) do. Some (Austria, Italy) seem to be more critical of how some of their internal mechanisms function, whereas others (France, Germany) are quite satisfied. Some (Germany) seem to have quite high approval rates, whereas others less (Austria, France). Finally, constitutional courts' budgets and available personnel to support the judges vary, which then has an impact on the functioning of each body.

Tables 2.1 and 2.2 illustrate some of the main similarities and differences for the purposes of this book. Table 2.1 provides an overview of the institutional issues relevant for this book.

117 Arts 7 and 58 of the French Constitution.
118 Arts 11 and 60 of the French Constitution.
119 Art 16 of the French Constitution.
120 Art 54 of the French Constitution.
121 Art 59 of the French Constitution. Judgments under this procedure are identified with the docket number AN for elections to the *Assemblée Nationale* and SEN for Senate elections.

Table 2.1 Comparative overview of institutional aspects of four constitutional courts

	Austria	Italy	Germany	France
Duration in years or max age	Until 70	9	12 or until 68	9
Nomination				
Parliament[122]	x	x	x	x
President/Government[123]	x	x	x	x
Courts		x		
Number of judges	14 + 6 substitutes	15	16	9
(Min) Qualifications/ Requirements				
Age	-	-	x (min 40)	-
Civil and political rights	-	-	-	x
Legal education	x	x	x	-
Mandatory presence of judges	-	x	x	-
Minimum no of years' experience[124]	x	x	-	-
Incompatibilities with other functions	x	x	x	x
Abstention[125]	x	-	x	x
Recusal[126]	-	-	x	x
Cooling-off periods	x[127]	-	-	-
Minimum quorum for valid decisions	x	x	x	x
Dissenting opinions	-	-	x	-
Budget in million euro (annual)	18.78 (2023)	65.5 (2023)	40 (2023)	17.93 (2023)
Public trust (year)	41% (2022)	-	70% (2022/ 2023)	40% (2023)

[122] This includes where separate proposals by the two different houses (Austria, France, Germany) or a common one (Italy) are made.

[123] In Austria, the President formally nominates the judges upon proposals advanced by the government and by parliament and is bound by them, but can reject some nominations. This double reference to President/government takes into account that in France the President is the head of the government whereas in Austria, Italy, and Germany presidents have a more or less ceremonial function.

[124] Not necessarily for all judges, but for some categories.

[125] In Italy, abstention is only officially allowed for presidential impeachment procedures of which, so far, there have been none. In France, abstention is not possible for electoral litigation.

[126] In Italy, recusal is only officially allowed for presidential impeachment procedures, of which, so far, there have been none. In France, recusal is not possible for electoral litigation.

[127] In Austria, cooling-off periods are limited to the President and Vice-President of the VfGH.

Table 2.2, instead, allows for a comparative overview of the various functions these courts provide.[128]

To a certain extent, these two tables may help to understand why the presence of ex-ministers may be more or less of an issue. Indeed, while nowadays all four courts exercise some form(s) of a posteriori constitutionality control, the extent to which they are involved in other political, electoral, or impeachment litigation may expose such bodies to more or fewer critiques of not being impartial if and when too many ex-ministers sit on them. Moreover, these differences are also interesting because they indicate, from a comparative perspective, what measures could be taken to minimize any possible risk which stems from such members joining constitutional courts.

At the same time, one also needs to highlight that these institutions have not functioned in the same way from their creation. Given that I am looking at the phenomenon of ex-ministers as constitutional judges from their beginnings, some additional background information needs to be provided, both chronologically and qualitatively, to obtain a fuller picture.

Table 2.2 Comparative overview of functional aspects of four constitutional courts

Function	Procedural avenues	Austria	Italy	Germany	France
Keeping legislature in check	**Abstract constitutionality**				
	A priori	-	-	x	x
	A posteriori	x	-	x	x
	Preliminary references	x	x	x	x
Protecting fundamental rights	Constitutional complaint procedure	x	-	x	-
Resolving institutional disputes	Vertical disputes	x	x	x	-
	Horizontal disputes	x	x	x	x
Ensuring integrity of political offices and processes	Electoral disputes	x	-	x	x
	Presidential impeachment[129]	x	x	x	-
	Political parties	-	-	x	-
	Referenda	x	x	-	x

[128] This table is a simplified version of a comparative research on European constitutional courts already done by Maartje de Visser, with the addition of Austria, minus some categories that are not relevant for this book and other legal systems she considered in her work. Maartje de Visser, *Constitutional Review in Europe. A Comparative Analysis* (Hart 2014) 187.

[129] In Austria, there are two mechanisms by which to impeach a President: one in Art 60 B-VG by referendum and the other in Art 142 B-VG where the VfGH intervenes.

2.2 Evolutions of Constitutional Courts

The previous point described how these constitutional courts are regulated and function today. Nevertheless, only a diachronic comparison will allow us to better understand the structural and functional changes these institutions went through over time, and to see if they have impacted the composition in the sense of this book. Given that I will look at ex-ministers as constitutional judges in these systems from the time of creation of these courts, it is important to note that most of the constitutional courts studied here went through some more or less radical changes. I will present a selection of the most relevant ones here below in the same order as above. The brief overview of these changes will then also allow the reader to better situate the overall historical and contextual moment within which certain former government members joined a given court at a given time.

2.2.1 Austria

As to Austria, today's VfGH is very different from the earliest one. Some of the main changes took place in the early years, prior to its dissolution in 1934 and revival in 1945. Indeed, for the initial 1920 VfGH, no legal education was required to become a constitutional court judge. Hence, there were high-level politicians who were simultaneously judges in the constitutional court. Moreover, judges were nominated for life.

A series of early constitutional reforms made profound changes to this initial design.[130] A 1921 statute having constitutional rank established a first incompatibility of membership of the VfGH with government positions. This was then essentially confirmed and extended by a first constitutional reform in 1925 which added that the President, the Vice-President, and eight of the remaining members, as well as four substitute members, could not be simultaneously members of the National Council, the Federal Council, or state parliaments.[131]

An even more in-depth reform took place in 1929.[132] This reform's official goal was intended to 'de-politicize' the VfGH. It did so by introducing the requirement of legal education for constitutional judges; by eliminating the possibility for members of parliament but also for employees and other officials of political parties to simultaneously also be constitutional judges; by introducing the

[130] For the main aspects in English one can consult: Christoph Grabenwarter, 'The Austrian Constitutional Court' in Armin von Bogdandy, Peter M Huber, and Christoph Grabenwarter (eds), *The Max Planck Handbooks in European Public Law* (3rd edn, OUP 2020) esp 27–34. In German, and with a much more detailed analysis on the years from 1918–30, see: Kurt Heller, *Der Verfassungsgerichtshof* (Verlag Österreich 2010) 138–233.

[131] Art 39 of the Bundesverfassungsgesetz, 30 July 1925, BGBl 268/1925.

[132] Bundesverfassungsgesetz, 7 December 1929, BGBl 392/1929.

already mentioned cooling-off period of initially four years for the President and Vice-President of the VfGH; and by introducing an age limit of 70. The reform was critiqued because it strengthened the Executive and the President's powers, to the detriment of parliament. With regard to the VfGH, it increased the role of the government in appointing judges as well as requiring in a transitional provision[133] that all the judges who had been nominated for life, including Hans Kelsen, resign.[134] It was especially this last provision that was problematic, given that it intervened against the backdrop of a public debate over politically sensitive decisions by the VfGH on marriage regulations and was critiqued already at that time as a 're-politicization' rather than a 'de-politicization'.[135]

Looking at the 1929 reform from a calmer and more distant vantage point, it essentially led to how the VfGH is still functioning today and ironically implemented things which Kelsen had himself advocated in his writings, namely a stronger legal and less political background for constitutional court judges, with some clear and even innovative rules of incompatibility.

Other changes that took place since then concerned the nomination procedure. First, in 1994 an amendment was made whereby the President's power to choose from a list of three candidates nominated by the two chambers of parliament was abolished.[136] Unlike the candidates nominated by the government, both the National and Federal Council had to submit a list of three candidates to the President, who could freely choose one from that list. The reform eliminated this practice and since then the President has had no choice. The background to this reform is that against the practice of nominating the first name on that list of three, the then President of Austria, Thomas Klestil, had decided to nominate the first woman to the VfGH, Lisbeth Lass, who had been third on the list. The reform can thus be interpreted as a gesture of defiance to the President,[137] even though critiques against this procedure had already arisen in the 1970s.[138] Second, since 1997 the practice of non-public parliamentary hearings of the candidates for a position as judge at the VfGH was introduced.[139] Third, the qualifications needed for

[133] Art II, para 25 of the transitional rules of the 1929 Reform, 11 December 1929, BGBl 393/1929.

[134] Kelsen seemingly was one of the main targets of that reform and was offered the chance to be renominated by the mayor of Vienna, but refused. See: Kurt Heller, *Der Verfassungsgerichtshof* (Verlag Österreich 2010) 202–03.

[135] See on this expression and critique: Adolf Julius Merkl, 'Der "entpolitisierte" Verfassungsgerichtshof' (1930) 22 Der österreichische Volkswirt 509.

[136] Art I, point 28 of the Bundes-Verfassungsgesetz-Novelle 1994, BGBl 1013/1994.

[137] See in this sense: Kurt Heller, *Der Verfassungsgerichtshof* (Verlag Österreich 2010) 420.

[138] See Hans R Klecatsky, 'Über die Notwendigkeit einer grundlegenden Reform der österreichischen Verfassungsgerichtsbarkeit' in Gerhard Leibholz and others (eds), *Menschenwürde und freiheitliche Rechtsordnung. Festschrift für Willi Geiger zum 65. Geburtstag* (Mohr Siebeck 1974) 925, 933–38.

[139] Brigitte Bierlein, 'Bundesrat und Verfassungsgerichtshof. Teil I', 18 December 2020 <https://www.foederalismus.at/blog/bundesrat-und-verfassungsgerichtshof---teil-i_250.ph> accessed 18 January 2023.

becoming such a judge were also revised in 1977 and 1999, to allow certain personalities to join the institution.[140]

With regard to the VfGH's substantive tasks, one can observe that from its initial rather narrow competences there have been many changes, mostly in the sense of expanding its competences over its hundred years of existence. Just to mention some of the most important ones here, in 1925 it obtained the power to interpret legal provisions relating to the powers of the Court of Auditors (Rechnungshof);[141] in 1964, it was given the power to determine the legality of international treaties;[142] in 1975, the limited individual complaint procedure against judgments by administrative courts was introduced[143] and then broadened in 2012 to include complaints against other legislative texts (*Gesetzesbeschwerde*).[144] Moreover, access was also facilitated for other institutional actors such as members of parliament in 1975 and 1991.[145] Last but not least, the addition in 2015 of resolving litigation involving parliamentary inquiry committees[146] has contributed significantly to the work of the VfGH.[147] These developments demonstrate how, from the initial limited Kelsenian notion of what constitutional courts should or should not be doing, the VfGH today has a much wider range of competences.

2.2.2 Italy

Italy's legal system has, overall, remained comparatively stable despite some (minor) reforms.[148] Relevant changes for the purposes of this book concerned the reduction of the initial mandate from 12 years to nine, combined with the elimination of the possibility to be reappointed;[149] the limitation of impeachment

[140] Art 147, para 2 of the B-VG was amended in 1977 (BGBl 539/1977) and in 1999 (BGBl I 127/1999). The detailed reasons for this will be discussed further below in Chapter 6.1.

[141] Today Arts 126a–c and 127 B-VG (BGBl 268/1925).

[142] Today Art 140a B-VG (BGBl 59/1964).

[143] Art 144 B-VG (BGBl 302/1975).

[144] Art 140, para 1.c) B-VG (BGBl 65/2012).

[145] Art 144 B-VG (BGBl 302/1975)

[146] Art 138b B-VG. (BGBl 101/2014).

[147] See Sandra Schieder, 'Wie das Höchstgericht zum nicht mehr wegzudenkenden Streitschlichter in U-Ausschüssen wurde' *Der Standard* (Vienna, 28 December 2023) <https://www.derstandard.at/story/3000000201035/wie-das-hoechstgericht-zum-nicht-mehr-wegzudenkenden-streitschlichter-in-u-ausschuessen-wurde> accessed 28 December 2023.

[148] For a positive assessment of the relative stability, despite the other changes to the Italian Constitution, see: Paolo Passaglia, 'La disciplina della composizione come primo cardine dell'indipendenza e della legittimazione dell'organo: il caso della Corte costituzionale italiana' in Marina Calamo Specchia (ed), *Le Corti costituzionali. Composizione, Indipendenza, Legittimazione* (Giappichelli 2011) 203.

[149] Art 135 in the original version, amended and substituted by Art 1, Legge costituzionale 22 novembre 1967, no 2.

procedures only against the President and not also against members of government;[150] and wider majorities required for the election by parliament.[151] Another shift concerned the power of the C cost to verify the eligibility of the nominees. Whereas initially the C cost alone was competent to judge the validity of the titles of its members,[152] in 1967 that power was reduced to checking the subjective requirements of the nominees.[153] This change supposedly curbed the powers of the C cost to potentially also monitor the correct functioning of the nomination procedures themselves.[154]

One interesting development that took place before the C cost even started operating concerns the possibility of abstentions and recusals. The already mentioned 1953 statute specifies that, except for impeachment procedures, the rules applicable to procedures before the C cost are those established for the Cons St[155] which in turn refer to the applicable rules of the Code of Civil Procedure.[156] At least hypothetically, the ordinary rules applicable to judges were supposed to be extended to the C cost However, that same 1953 statute then authorizes the C cost to adopt supplementary rules for the procedures before it.[157] The C cost did so and introduced the prohibition for both as mentioned above. Apart from the doctrinal discussions on whether these internal regulations can derogate the legislative provisions or not and what the justifications for this exclusion could be,[158] this sentence is generally held to mean that for the C cost abstentions and recusals are not possible, except in impeachment procedures. The reasons advanced for this prohibition are various. One argument is the autonomy of the C cost[159] as well as a fear that abusive recusal requests could paralyse the institution by reducing the number of judges below the required minimum quorum.[160] Another justification is that the C cost in its early years refused to define itself as a judicial organ, with the consequence that certain rules on impartiality imposed by Article

[150] Art 135 in the original version. The reference to 'ministers' was eliminated by Art 2, Legge costituzionale 16 January 1989, no 1. An impeachment procedure for corruption against two ministers occurred only once, between 1978 and 1979 during the so-called '*Lockheed*' case which paralysed the work of the C cost and led to this constitutional amendment which transferred such competence to ordinary criminal jurisdictions. On this see: Gustavo Zagrebelsky and Valeria Marcenò, *Giustizia costituzionale, II. Oggetti, procedimenti, decisioni* (2nd edn, il Mulino 2018) 341–43.

[151] Indeed, Art 3, paras 1 and 2 of Legge 11 marzo 1953, no 87 had required a majority of three-fifths of the Parliament in a joint session and if after two rounds of secret voting such majority was not reached in subsequent rounds of voting, a majority of 'only' three-fifths of those present was required.

[152] Art 3, para 1, Legge costituzionale, 9 February 1948, no 1.

[153] Art 7, para 1, Legge costituzionale 22 November 1967, no 2.

[154] Gian Luca Conti, 'Art 135' in Raffaele Bifulco, Alfonso Celotto, and Marco Olivetti (eds), *Commentario alla Costituzione Vol III* (UTET 2006) 2621, 2626.

[155] Art 22, para 1, Legge 11 March 1953, no 87.

[156] See Art 47, Regio decreto 17 August 1907, no 642.

[157] Art 22, para 2, Legge 11 March 1953, no 87.

[158] On this discussion see eg: Gustavo Zagrebelsky and Valeria Marcenò, *Giustizia costituzionale, II. Oggetti, procedimenti, decisioni* (2nd edn, il Mulino 2018) 24–28.

[159] Gustavo Zagrebelsky, *Principî e voti* (Einaudi 2005) 64.

[160] Alessio Rauti, 'Riflessioni in tema di imparzialità dei giudici costituzionali' (2009) LIV Giurisprudenza costituzionale 4029, 4049–54, explaining that the bigger risk of operational paralysis is linked to the non-election by parliament of the new candidates.

111 of the Constitution would not extend to it.[161] Last but not least, another justification emerged from the interviews with judges and former judges of the C cost. This was most clearly expressed in the following way:

> The rules of the C. cost. do indeed not provide for either abstention or recusal. It is a choice that finds its justification in the type of judgment that the court normally makes, with respect to which the personal positions of individual judges are not at stake. Potentially, every time a statute comes before the C. cost. that in some way affects the generality of citizens, the judge may also be affected: the statute regulating the tax on real estate transfers arrives and one is concluding a contract or is planning to do so; a decision has to be made on a tax that applies to all real estate and the decision is bound to potentially affect everyone, including the judges. In other words, it is reasonable that with respect to an institution that deals with such matters, that by their nature affect everyone indiscriminately, no conflict-of-interest issues arise.[162]

I will return to some of these points in Chapter 6 of this book. For the moment, the important point of this section is that these were mostly minor changes that have not profoundly transformed the overall functioning of the C cost from how and what it was conceived for by the original constitutional drafters.

2.2.3 Germany

Like the C cost, the BVerfG remained rather stable in its attributions and functioning. Some minor, albeit important, modifications took place, especially during the early years of the BVerfG.[163] Institutionally, at the beginning the BVerfG was placed under the authority of the Federal Ministry of Justice, and only after a memorandum by the constitutional judges themselves that sparked controversy as well as legislative and constitutional amendments[164] was the BVerfG's full independence from the government established.[165]

[161] In rather critical terms of this absence and also rejecting this argument, see: Alessandro Pace, 'La Corte costituzionale nell'esperienza di un avvocato' (2006) 11 Giornale di storia costituzionale 93, 96.

[162] Interviewee no 11, 19 April 2023.

[163] On some of these changes, especially concerning the composition of the BVerfG, see: Richard Ley, 'Die Wahl der Mitglieder des Bundesverfassungsgerichtes. Eine Dokumentation anläßlich des 40jährigen Bestehens' (1991) 22 Zeitschrift für Parlamentsfragen 420, 421–23.

[164] See Art 115g as amended by the 1968 constitutional amendment (BGBl. 1968/14, 709) establishing essentially that the function of the BVerfG and its judges shall not be impaired even during a state of emergency and that during such time the GG cannot be amended unless the BVerfG itself sees it necessary to maintain its capability to function.

[165] See on this story: Donald P. Kommers and Russell A. Miller, *The Constitutional Jurisprudence of the Federal Republic of Germany* (3rd edn, Duke University Press 2012) 17-18.

In terms of composition, initially 12 judges were to sit on each Senate, something that was gradually reduced to today's eight per Senate.[166] Some shifts also took place regarding the duration of the term. Originally, four judges of each Senate were to be elected from the judicial bodies for a term as long as their office as judges in the highest courts lasted. The others were to be elected for eight years, but half of those at the first election for only four years with re-election possible.[167] Via various legislative amendments, the latest of which was made in 1970, those requirements were changed to what they are today, namely nomination for everyone for 12 years and/or until 68 years of age.[168] It is with that same 1970 reform that the possibility of having dissenting or separate opinions was introduced.

Some more recent changes also concerned the nomination procedure. Prior to a 2015 reform of the BVerfGG,[169] the election of the eight constitutional judges by the Federal Assembly, was done entirely behind closed doors by a small committee of 12 members of parliament, without any intervention or vote by the full house of parliament. This had led to many critiques for lack of transparency in the past.[170]

With regard to the competences, at the beginning the BVerfG was allowed to provide advisory opinions, but this possibility was eliminated in 1956 upon the BVerfG's own recommendation.[171] Another formal shift was that the constitutional complaint procedure was constitutionalized in 1969, having been regulated up to that point by statute only.[172] Last but not least, today's competence allocation between the two Senates was initially more clear-cut, in the sense that the First Senate was supposed to be dealing exclusively with fundamental rights issues, including constitutional complaints whereas the Second Senate was conceived as dealing exclusively with institutional conflicts. However, it quickly became clear that the First Senate was overburdened which led to a revision of the competences in the sense of what we can see today.[173] This overburdening caused by the constitutional complaints also led to other changes from the initial set-up. In fact, in

[166] These amendments mostly concerned Art 2 of the BVerfGG, as amended by statute in 1959.

[167] Art 4 of the BVerfGG, in its original version of 1951 (BGBl 1951/17, 243).

[168] Art 4 of the BVerfGG with the 1970 amendment (BGBl 1970/116, 1765).

[169] Neuntes Gesetz zur Änderung des Bundesverfassungsgerichtsgesetzes, 24 June 2015 (BGBl, 2015, I, 973).

[170] Christine Landfried, 'Die Wahl der Bundesverfassungsrichter und ihre Folgen für die Legitimität der Verfassungsgerichtsbarkeit' in Robert Chr. van Ooyen and Martin HW Möllers (eds), *Das Bundesverfassungsgericht im politischen System* (Verlag für Sozialwissenschaften 2006) 229, 233–34; Christine Landfried, 'The Selection Process of Constitutional Court Judges in Germany' in Kate Malleson and Peter H Russell (eds), *Appointing Judges in an Age of Judicial Power* (University of Toronto Press 2007) 196.

[171] See: Taylor Cole, 'The West German Federal Constitutional Court: An Evaluation After Six Years' (1958) 20 The Journal of Politics 278, 290–91.

[172] See Art 1 of the Neunzehntes Gesetz zur Änderung des Grundgesetzes of 29 January 1969 (BGBl 1969/11, 97).

[173] On the origins and evolution of the two Senate structure, see: Donald P Kommers and Russell A Miller, *The Constitutional Jurisprudence of the Federal Republic of Germany* (3rd edn, Duke University Press 2012) 18–20.

1985 the BVerfGG was amended in the sense of shifting more decisions to single chambers (*Kammern*) composed of three judges.[174] Moreover, the idea of having substitutes from the other Senate in case of successful abstentions or recusals was also introduced by this reform.[175]

It is fair to say that, by and large, the BVerfG has not changed radically from its inception, especially with regard to the topics of relevance to this book. That is certainly not the case for the next and last system analysed here.

2.2.4 France

Of the four constitutional courts, the CC possibly has undergone the most radical changes from its initial conception and function. Indeed, in the mind of the architects of the Fifth Republic, General De Gaulle and Michel Debré, the parliamentary regime of the Fourth Republic had been a failure and needed to be revised, in the sense of strengthening the Executive. In that context, the CC's function and constitutionality review of legislation was not one of ensuring that individual fundamental rights are not violated by the state but rather to make sure that the prerogatives of the Executive are not infringed upon by parliament in the newly introduced division of legislative competences between parliament and the government, as outlined in Articles 34 and 37 of the Constitution.[176] Some other mechanisms that indicate this initial design are that there exists a mandatory control of Parliament's regulations by the CC.[177] Moreover, the initial access to the CC was extremely limited in the sense that only four individuals, namely, the President of the Republic, the Prime Minister, and the Presidents of each house could refer a bill to the CC. Only a priori judicial review existed before 2008.

The original set-up and rationale of the CC as a pre-eminently political body explains the various peculiarities of this system: no legal education is required to become a member of the CC; the de jure participation of former Presidents of the Republic as members of the CC; and the regular nomination of other former politicians to this body.

A series of constitutional amendments contributed to the transformation of this body. A 1974 reform added the possibility for 60 members of the Senate or the

[174] See: Art 1 of the Gesetz zur Änderung des Gesetzes über das Bundesverfassungsgericht und zur Änderung des Deutschen Richtergesetzes of 12 December 1985 (BGBl 1985, I, 2226), adding para 15a to the BVerfGG.

[175] ibid Art 1 adding para 19(4) to the BVerfGG. The introduction of chamber decisions led to the questions about how abstentions and recusals should function in that context. On this, see: Friedrich Karl Fromme, 'Ablehnung von Richtern im Kammer-Verfahren' in Hans Joachim Faller (ed), *Verantwortlichkeit und Freiheit. Festschrift für Willi Geiger zum 80. Geburtstag* (Mohr 1989) 747.

[176] On this history in a concise manner, see Sophie Boyron, *The Constitution of France. A Contextual Analysis* (Hart 2013) 48–49.

[177] Art 61, para 1 of the French Constitution.

House of Representatives to collectively refer ordinary bills of legislation to the CC.[178] Even more importantly, in 2008 the CC's functions were increased to include not only a priori constitutionality of statutes but also a posteriori control.[179] In particular, this last change has important repercussions on the composition of the CC. Whereas in the past it made less of a difference if a former minister joined this institution, given that only new bills could be referred to the CC, today it can happen that bills that were passed with the cooperation or under the governments of those ministers end up before the CC. However, so far most of the academic and reform discussions have focused on the fact that the presence of former Presidents of the Republic is an issue and anachronism[180] but little on the regular presence of other former government members and politicians.

Another important evolution took place at the hands of the CC itself. Starting with its famous 1971 decision,[181] which has sometimes been compared to the American *Madison v Marbury* judgment,[182] the CC expanded its review powers. Indeed, over the years it held that it could review the constitutionality of statutes not only on the rather narrow technical grounds of the 1958 Constitution, but also against certain fundamental rights enshrined in various other documents, such as the Preamble of the 1946 Constitution and the 1789 Declaration, but also a whole set of other principles and objectives that the CC established for itself. This set of norms against which today the CC assesses the constitutionality of legislation has been referred to in academic literature as the 'constitutionality block' (*bloc de constitutionnalité*).[183]

Another not so anodyne change concerned the electoral litigation competence. In fact, from the 1990s onwards, that task has expanded, given that the CC now also checks on the (ir)regularity of political campaign financing.[184] This has certainly increased the potential for conflicts of interest and also dragged the CC into uneasy political situations, as will be demonstrated further below.

[178] Loi constitutionnelle no 74-904, 29 October 1974.

[179] Loi constitutionnelle no 2008-724, 23 July 2008.

[180] Art 10 of a constitutional reform bill of 2018 (*Projet de loi constitutionnelle n° 911 pour une démocratie plus représentative, responsable et efficace*) would have eliminated the ex officio participation of former Presidents of the Republic to the CC. However, the bill was withdrawn on 29 August 2019. See: <https://www.assemblee-nationale.fr/dyn/15/textes/l15b0911_projet-loi> accessed 19 January 2023.

[181] Décision no 71-44 DC, 16 July 1971.

[182] George D Haimbaugh Jr, 'Was It France's Marbury v. Madison?' (1974) 35 Ohio State LJ 910.

[183] The CC does not itself use this term in its jurisprudence. For a recent analysis of the emergence and meaning of the constitutionality block, see: Charlotte Denizeau-Lahaye, 'La génèse du bloc de constitutionnalité' (2022) 8 *Titre VII, Les catégories de normes constitutionnelles* <https://www.conseil-constitutionnel.fr/publications/titre-vii/la-genese-du-bloc-de-constitutionnalite> accessed 16 November 2022.

[184] This competence was added in 1990 when a statute introduced recourse to the CC by a national commission overviewing campaign finances in case those were either not presented at all, had been rejected, or had exceeded the statutory maximum allowed: Loi n° 90-55 du 15 janvier 1990 relative à la limitation des dépenses électorales et à la clarification du financement des activités politiques.

These major constitutional, legislative, and jurisprudential changes arguably transformed an initially political body with very narrow competences into a constitutional court. The issue is that various rules and practices, especially on composition or abstentions and recusals, have not fully reflected this shift, and are only gradually changing.

Overall, the chronological analysis reveals how these constitutional courts were not static. The most profound changes concerned the competences of these courts that have overall evolved in the sense of an expansion. Other changes affecting the nomination procedures via the introduction of parliamentary hearings or the requirements to become judges have been less dramatic. One thing that did not radically change in any of these systems is the class of institutions or persons who can nominate the judges. Yes, there were occasional modifications to the nomination procedures, but the highly political nominations, in the sense of being exclusively in the hands of political bodies, in Austria, Germany, and France, and the mixed system in Italy, were never profoundly reformed. This is particularly curious, given that at least in the constituent assemblies of Austria, Germany, and Italy this precise element had raised the most debates.[185] It seems that once the political constituent compromise on who shall be entitled to nominate constitutional judges was made, that fundamental decision would not be touched again.[186]

Having laid out the normative framework and differences on the four constitutional courts in a diachronic manner, one can move on to analyse how far the phenomenon of former government members as constitutional court judges has been reflected in the composition of these courts.

[185] Taylor Cole, 'Three Constitutional Courts: A Comparison' (1959) 53 The American Political Science Review 963, 967.

[186] That does not mean that there are no more discussions. For instance, in Austria, there has been ongoing debate on the fact that the government plays too big of a role in nominating too many constitutional judges and that they should be elected by a two-thirds majority of parliament. See in this sense: Hans R Klecatsky, 'Über die Notwendigkeit einer grundlegenden Reform der österreichischen Verfassungsgerichtsbarkeit' in Gerhard Leibholz and others (eds), *Menschenwürde und freiheitliche Rechtsordnung. Festschrift für Willi Geiger zum 65. Geburtstag* (Mohr Siebeck 1974) 925, 931 and also from the current President of the VfGH, Christoph Grabenwarter: 'VfGH Präsident Grabenwarter für Änderung des Höchstrichterbestellverfahrens' *Der Standard* (Vienna, 22 September 2022) <https://www.derstandard.at/story/2000139378549/vfgh-praesident-grabenwarter-fuer-aenderung-des-hoechstrichter-bestellverfahrens> accessed 18 January 2023.

3
Ex-Ministers in Constitutional Courts

The historical and contemporary overview of the constitutional courts under examination here provides the necessary background and context to finally describe and analyse the object of this book. In section 3.1 I will detail the names, biography, and numbers of those who had a high-level executive function prior to joining the constitutional court. I will again proceed in the order of creation of those courts. I will then, in section 3.2, provide some comparative observations.

3.1 Overview of Names and Functions

As a first observation, around the world it is not unusual for ex-ministers to join constitutional courts.[1] The extent to which this happens nevertheless varies from system to system. The tables below, organized by country, provide information on the individuals, their years spent as judges at the constitutional court,[2] the duration and governmental function they had prior to becoming constitutional judges, other functions or positions they may have occupied, and for Italy, which authority nominated them (Tables 3.1, 3.2, 3.3, and 3.4).[3]

[1] Some additional interesting examples and anecdotes on Algeria, Japan, Peru, and Brazil are mentioned in Guillaume Tusseau, *Contentieux constitutionnel comparé* (LGDJ 2021) 396–98. Other notable examples include nominations to the Belgian Constitutional Court (eg in 2001 Erick Derycke, former Federal Minister of various ministries in 1991 and 1995–99 <https://www.const-court.be/fr/court/presentation/members/erik-derycke> accessed 7 July 2023; in 2018 Joséphine Rebecca Moerman, former Federal Minister of Economy, Energy, Foreign Trade, and Science Policy (2003–04), Flemish Minister of Economy, Enterprises, Innovation, Science, and Foreign Trade as well as Deputy Minister-President of the Flemish Government 2004–07 <https://www.const-court.be/fr/court/presentation/members/josephine-rebecca-moerman> accessed 28 June 2023; and in 2020 Thierry Detienne, former Wallonian Minister of Social Affairs and Health 1999–2004 <https://www.const-court.be/fr/court/presentation/members/thierry-detienne> accessed 7 July 2023. In Spain recently the former Justice Minister, Juan Carlos Campo Moreno, was nominated to the Spanish Constitutional Court: Real Decreto 1092/2022, de 30 de diciembre, por el quel se nombra Magistrado del Tribunal Constitucional Juan Carlos Campo Moreno, Boletín Official del Estado (BOE), no 314, 3 December 2022, 193462 a 193462 <https://www.boe.es/diario_boe/txt.php?id = BOE-A-2022-24441> accessed 12 October 2023.

[2] As to the function, the names of Presidents (and for Germany, Vice-Presidents) are indicated in bold.

[3] The biographies given below have been cross-checked with information from a combination of sources that range from scientific books and articles to the webpages of each constitutional court listing the background of the current judges, as well as more unofficial Wikipedia pages. For the more official secondary sources, see: for Austria: Kurt Heller, *Der Verfassungsgerichtshof* (Verlag Österreich 2010) 602–56 and the Verfassungsgerichtshof (VfGH) website:

Ex-Ministers as Constitutional Judges. Mathias Möschel, Oxford University Press. © Mathias Möschel 2025.
DOI: 10.1093/9780198930228.003.0003

Table 3.1 Austrian ex-ministers as constitutional judges

Name and time at VfGH	Ministerial functions	Other functions
Paul Vittorelli (1919–21, Provisional VfGH and 1921–30)	Justice Minister (1918)	Judge
Michael Mayr (1921–22)	Prime Minister (1920–21)Minister of Foreign Affairs (1920–21)	University professor/ parliamentarian
Rudolf Ramek (1921–24 and 1926–30)	Prime Minister (1924–26)	Politician/ parliamentarian
Viktor Kienböck (1924–26)	Finance Minister (1922–24)	Politician/attorney
Ludwig Adamovich Snr (1930–34 and 1946–55)	Justice Minister (16 February–11 March 1938)	University professor
Wolfgang Brandstetter (2018–21)	Justice Minister (2013–17)Vice-Chancellor (2017)	University professor

<https://www.vfgh.gv.at/verfassungsgerichtshof/verfassungsrichter/mitglieder.de.html> accessed 22 November 2022; for Italy, see: Giustino D'Orazio, *La genesi della Corte costituzionale: ideologia, politica, dibattito dottrinale, un saggio di storia delle istituzioni* (Edizioni comunità 1981) 208–14; Carla Rodotà, *Storia della Corte costituzionale* (Laterza 1999) 149–58; Andrea Pertici, 'Astensione e ricusazione dei giudici costituzionali: ragioni e limiti della loro esclusione ed ipotesi di una loro introduzione' (2004) XLIX Giurisprudenza costituzionale 3105, 3127, fn 52; Patrizia Pederzoli, 'I giudici della Corte costituzionale' [2018] *disCrimen* <https://discrimen.it/i-giudici-della-corte-costituzionale/> accessed 22 November 2022; and the Corte costituzionale (C cost) websites for the President <https://www.cortecostituzionale.it/actionPresidente.do>, the other judges <https://www.cortecostituzionale.it/actionGiudiciCostituzionali.do> and past judges <https://www.cortecostituzionale.it/jsp/consulta/composizione/presidenti.do> all accessed 12 January 2023; for Germany, see: Jörg Menzel and Ralf Müller Terpitz (eds), *Verfassungsrechtsprechung* (3rd edn, Mohr Siebeck 2017) 998–1010; Marcel Kau, *United States Supreme Court und Bundesverfassungsgericht: Die Bedeutung des United States Supreme Court für die Errichtung und Fortentwicklung des Bundesverfassungsgerichts* (Springer 2007) 170–73 (including footnotes) and the official Bundesverfassungsgericht (BVerfG) website:

<https://www.bundesverfassungsgericht.de/DE/Richter/richter_node.html> accessed 22 November 2022; for France, see: Dominique Schnapper, *Une sociologue au Conseil constitutionnel* (Gallimard 2010) 147–48; the tables provided by Raphaël Franck, 'Judicial Independence Under a Divided Polity: A Study of the Rulings of the French Constitutional Court, 1959–2006' (2009) 25 Journal of Law, Economics, & Organization 262, 278–83; the tables provided by Wolfram Vogel, *Demokratie und Verfassung in der V. Republik. Frankreichs Weg zur Verfassungsstaatlichkeit* (Leske + Budrich 2001) 138–40; and the tables provided for the 50th anniversary of the Conseil constitutionnel (CC), published in [2008] Les cahiers du Conseil constitutionnel 74–87; and the website of the CC: <https://www.conseil-constitutionnel.fr/les-membres> and <https://www.conseil-constitutionnel.fr/les-membres-depuis-1959> accessed 22 November 2022.

Table 3.2 Italian ex-ministers as constitutional judges

Name and time at C cost	Ministerial functions	Other functions	Nominated by
Enrico De Nicola (1955–57)	Provisional Head of State (1946–48)	Parliamentarian/ attorney	President
Gaetano Azzariti (1955–61)	Justice Minister (1943–44)	Judge/high-level civil servant	President
Mario Bracci (1955–59)	Minister for Foreign Trade (20 February–1 July 1946)	University professor	Parliament
Paolo Rossi (1969–79)	Minister for Public Education (1955–57)	Parliamentarian	President
Oronzo Reale (1977–86)	Justice Minister (1974–76) Finance Minister (1968–69)	Parliamentarian/ attorney	Parliament
Mauro Ferri (1987–96)	Minister of Industry, Trade, and Crafts (1972–73)	Parliamentarian/ attorney	President
Giuliano Vassalli (1991–2000)	Justice Minister (1987–91)	University professor/ parliamentarian/ attorney	President
Giovanni Maria Flick (2000–09)	Justice Minister (1996–98)	University professor	President
Fernanda Contri (1996–2005)	Minister for Social Affairs (1993–94)	Attorney	President
Franco Gallo (2004–13)	Finance Minister (1993–94)	University professor	President
Sabino Cassese (2005–14)	Minister of Public Service (1993–94)	University professor	President
Luigi Mazzella (2005–14)	Minister of Public Service (2002–04)	Governmental functions/ journalist	Parliament
Sergio Mattarella (2011–15)	Minister of Relations with Parliament (1987–89) Minister of Public Education (1989–90) Defense Minister (1999–2001)	Parliamentarian/ university professor	Parliament
Giuliano Amato (2013–22)	Finance Minister (1987–89) Prime Minister (1992–93) Minister for Institutional Reforms (1998–99) Finance Minister (1999–2000) Prime Minister (2000–01) Interior Minister (2006–08)	University professor/ parliamentarian	President

(*continued*)

Table 3.2 Continued

Name and time at C cost	Ministerial functions	Other functions	Nominated by
Augusto Antonio Barbera (2015–24)	Minister of Relations with Parliament (28 April-4 May 1993)	University professor/ parliamentarian	Parliament
Filippo Patroni Griffi (2022–31)	Minister of Public Administration and of Simplification (2011–13)	Judge	Judges

Table 3.3 German ex-ministers as constitutional judges

Name and time at BVerfG	Ministerial functions	Other functions
Wilhelm Ellinghaus (1951–55)	Justice Minister of Lower Saxony (1947–51)	Parliamentarian
Hermann Höpker Aschoff (1951–54)	Finance Minister of Prussia (1925–31)Finance Minister of North Rhine-Westphalia (1946)	Parliamentarian
Rudolf Katz (1951–61)	Justice Minister of Schleswig-Holstein (1947–51)Education Minister of Schleswig-Holstein (1949–50)	Attorney/parliamentarian
Erwin Stein (1951–70)	Justice and Culture Minister of Hesse (1947–51)	Judge/attorney
Gebhard Müller (1959–71)	President of Württemberg-Hohenzollern (1948–52)Prime Minister of Baden-Württemberg (1953–58)	High-level civil servant/ parliamentarian
Ernst Benda (1969–83)	Federal Interior Minister (April 1968–October 1969)	University professor
Ernst Gottfried Mahrenholz (1981–94)	Minister of Education of Lower Saxony (1974–76)	Attorney/high-level civil servant/parliamentarian
Roman Herzog (1983–95)	Minister of Education of Baden Württemberg (1978–80)Interior Minister of Baden-Württemberg (1980–83)	University professor
Jutta Limbach (1994–2002)	Justice Minister of Berlin (1989–94)	University professor
Hans-Joachim Jentsch (1996–2005)	Justice Minister of Thuringia (1990–94)	Attorney/parliamentarian/ judge

Table 3.3 Continued

Name and time at BVerfG	Ministerial functions	Other functions
Christine Hohmann-Dennhardt (1999–2011)	Justice Minister of Hesse (1991–95)Minister of Science and Arts of Hesse (1995–99).	Judge
Wolfgang Hoffmann-Riem (1999–2008)	Justice Minister of Hamburg (1995–97)	University professor
Peter Michael Huber (2010–22)	Interior Minister of Thuringia (2009–10)	University professor
Peter Aloysius Müller (2011–23)	Prime Minister of Saarland (1999–2011)Justice Minister of Saarland (2009–11)	Judge/parliamentarian

Table 3.4 French ex-ministers as constitutional judges

Name and time at CC	Ministerial functions	Other functions
Jean Gilbert-Jules (1959–68)	Interior Minister (1956–57)	Attorney/politician
Bernard Chenot (1962–64)	Justice Minister (1961–62)	State councillor/ high civil servant
Gaston Palewski (1965–74)	State Minister (*Ministre d'Etat*)[4] for Scientific Research and Space and Atomic Questions (1962–65)	Parliamentarian/ diplomat
Pierre Chatenet (1968–77)	Interior Minister (1959–61)	State councillor/ high civil servant
Jean Sainteny (1968–77)	Minister of Former Combatants and Victims of War (1962–66)	Parliamentarian/ banker
Henry Rey (1971–77)	State Minister (May–July 1968)	Parliamentarian
Paul Coste-Floret (1971–79)	State Minister (January–May 1953)	University professor

(*continued*)

[4] This title indicates that a given minister has a special protocollary position amongst the other governmental colleagues, similarly to a Deputy Prime Minister, in the sense that a state minister can organize interministerial meetings. For a historical analysis on this, see: Bertrand Fessard de Foucault, 'Les ministres d'Etat' (1972) 22 Revue française de science politique 5.

Table 3.4 Continued

Name and time at CC	Ministerial functions	Other functions
Roger Frey (1974–83)	Communication Minister (1959–60) Interior Minister (1961–67) State Minister as Minister of Relations with Parliament (1967–71) State Minister as Minister of Administrative Reforms (1971–72)	State councillor/ parliamentarian
Louis Joxe (1977–89)	Justice Minister (1967–68) Minister of Administrative Reforms (1962–67) Minister of Algerian Affairs (1960–62) Minister of Education (January-November 1960) State Minister (1959–61)	University professor/diplomat
Robert Lecourt (1979–89)	Justice Minister (26 July–11 September 1947; 13 February–28 October 1949; 6 November 1957–1 June 1958; State Minister in various functions (1959–61)	Attorney
Robert Badinter (1986–95)	Justice Minister (1981–86)	University professor/attorney
Maurice Faure (1989–98)	Interior Minister (14–17 May 1958) Minister of European Institutions (17–28 May 1958) Justice Minister (22 May–21 June 1981) State Minister as Minister of Equipment and Housing (1988–89)	University professor/ parliamentarian
Roland Dumas (1995–2000)	Delegated Minister[5] of European Affairs (1983–84) Minister of Foreign Affairs (1984–86) State Minister as Minister of Foreign Affairs (1988–93)	Attorney/ parliamentarian
Yves Guéna (1997–2004)	Minister of Information (31 May–10 July 1968) Minister of Mail and Telecommunications (1968–69) Minister of Transports (1973–74) Minister of Industry, Trade, and Crafts (1 March–27 May 1974)	State councillor/ parliamentarian

[5] Delegated ministers are ministers who exercise certain specific functions either under the Prime Minister or under another minister. See <https://www.vie-publique.fr/fiches/19466-quest-ce-quun-ministre-detat-ministre-delegue-secretaire-detat> accessed 16 January 2023.

Table 3.4 Continued

Name and time at CC	Ministerial functions	Other functions
Monique Pelletier (2000–04)	Delegated Minister for the Female Question (1978–81)	Attorney/judge
Simone Veil (1998–2007)	Health Minister (1974–79) Minister of Social Affairs, Health, and the City (1993–95)	Judge/(European) parliamentarian
Pierre Joxe (2001–10)	Defence Minister (1991–93) Interior Minister (1989–91) Industry Minister (22 May–22 June 1981)	Judge/ parliamentarian
Jean-Louis Debré (2007–16)	Interior Minister (1995–97)	Parliamentarian
Jacques Barrot (2020–14)	Minister of Trade and Crafts (1978–79) Minister of Health and Social Security (1979–81) Minister of Employment and Social Affairs (1995–97)	Parliamentarian/ high-level civil servant
Michel Charasse (2010–19)	Delegated Budget Minister (1988–92) Budget Minister (2 April–2 October 1992)	Parliamentarian
Lionel Jospin (2015–19)	Prime Minister (1997–2002) Education Minister (1988–92)	Diplomat/ parliamentarian
Laurent Fabius (2016–25)	Delegated Budget Minister (1981–83) Minister of Industry and Research (1983–84) Prime Minister (1984–86) Minister of the Economy, Finances, and Industry (2000–02) Foreign and International Development Minister (2012–16)	Parliamentarian
Jacques Mézard (2019–28)	Minister of Territorial Cohesion (2017–18) Minister of Agriculture and Food (17 May–21 June 2017)	Attorney/ parliamentarian
Alain Juppé (2019–28)	Delegated Budget Minister (1986–88) Prime Minister (1995–97) State Minister as Minister of the Environment, of Development, and Sustainable Development (May–June 2007) State Minister as Minister of Defence and Veterans (2010–11) State Minister as Foreign and European Affairs Minister (2011–12)	Parliamentarian
Jacqueline Gourault (2022–31)	Minister at the State Ministry of the Interior Minister (2017–18)Minister of Territorial Cohesion and Relations with Local Collectivities (2018–22)	Parliamentarian

3.2 Comparative Analysis

From the names listed above by country, one immediately notices certain differences in the phenomenon. I will look at these differences from a quantitative-descriptive perspective (sub-section 3.2.1), from a qualitative angle (sub-section 3.2.2), and integrated with views from inside the four constitutional courts (sub-section 3.2.3).

3.2.1 Quantitative and descriptive observations

In terms of quantitative, statistical, and descriptive observations, France certainly stands out. Here the participation of high-level politicians remains the rule rather than the exception.[6] Indeed, of the 88 members of the CC to date (August 2024), a staggering 26 (or 29.5%) had at some point served in a governmental position in the sense used in this book; this is without counting the former Presidents who are (still) constitutionally entitled legally to be members for life of the CC.

Somewhat surprisingly, the phenomenon is not confined to France, but also occurs in Italy and Germany, where quite a few ex-ministers have joined the respective constitutional courts over the years. Unlike the political origins of the CC, in the other three jurisdictions the jurisdictional nature of their respective constitutional courts, as well as the fact that judges are required to have a legal education and some years of professional experience, might to some extent exclude the availability, or desirability of, more or less openly political candidates. In any case, especially in Germany and Italy, the politicization of the judiciary is not an entirely marginal phenomenon. In Italy, of a total of 121 judges (August 2024), 16 (13.2%) had a political background in the sense used in this book. None of these 16 had been part of regional governments. In Germany, the numbers are similar. Of a total of 118 judges to date (August 2024), 14 (11.8%) had a political/executive background in the sense used in this book. In terms of division per Senate, there does not seem to be a particular preference for one Senate or the other. Eight of these individuals sat in the First Senate, dealing mostly with fundamental rights issues, and six sat in the Second Senate, dealing with the more institutional issues. Another observation is that they practically all held executive positions at the state rather than federal level. Of the constitutional courts analysed here, only in Austria is the phenomenon limited and, with one exception, associated exclusively with the early years of the VfGH's existence.

[6] One might even speak of a longer tradition of political constitutional control, given that the predecessor of the CC, the Constitutional Committee of the Fourth Republic, also was exclusively constituted of politicians. Going further back in French constitutional history, at some point the Senate was in charge of controlling the constitutionality of statutes. See on these two points, Alec Stone, *The Birth of Judicial Politics. The Constitutional Council in Comparative Perspective* (OUP 1992) 29 and 30.

A separate question is whether there is a trend that former high-level members of government might be nominated more often to the position of President of the constitutional court? It is difficult to provide a clear answer, in part due to the different roles constitutional court presidents play in the various courts considered here. I would attempt to say that there is a certain propensity for them to end up in such a position. In Austria, of the six, Vittorelli and Adamovich Snr held that position. However, the introduction in 1929 of a 'cooling-off period' for the President and Vice-President made the repetition of such an occurrence less probable. In Germany, six of the 13 identified became President of the BVerfG. In France, from 1986 to 2004 and then again from 2007 until today a former minister has presided the CC. For Italy, the numerical analysis is a little less clear due to the practice of having (very) short presidencies, meaning that many constitutional judges have occupied this position.

Another question that can be answered by looking at the tables comparatively is whether having been Justice Minister heightens the probabilities of becoming a constitutional court judge? In Austria, Germany, and, to a lesser extent, in Italy, that seems to be the case. For France, it rather appears that any ministerial position, including that of Justice Minister, can potentially lead to membership of the CC.[7] This observation could confirm the rather political nature or perception of the CC, and the rather judicial nature of the other constitutional courts. If a minister needs to be nominated in those other systems, then at least it should be a Justice Minister, so as to not make the political aspect too overt and highlight the expertise and thematic proximity.

Another specific observation regarding Italy is that the politically neutral President of the Republic is the person most likely to nominate former politicians to the C cost.[8] One might have expected these to come from the ranks of parliamentary nominees, but that is clearly not the case.

Finally, on the quantitative, statistical, and descriptive observations, except for Fernanda Contri, Jacqueline Gourault, Christine Hohmann-Dennhardt, Jutta Limbach, Monique Pelletier, and Simone Veil, all of these 'political' judges were men. In other words, of the 61 judges identified in the manner explained in this book, only six were female, ie 10%. The low number of women is in line with the fact that women are overall underrepresented both in politics and in these institutions.[9]

[7] What also seems to be happening is that former constitutional court judges become Justice Ministers, as the above-mentioned examples of Hans Klecatsky (Austria), Marta Cartabia (Italy), and Nicole Belloubet (France) demonstrate.

[8] One exception and novelty is the 2022 judicial nomination of Filippo Patroni Griffi who had been Minister of Public Administration and of Simplification between 2011 and 2013.

[9] For analyses of women on high courts worldwide, see: Maria C Escobar Lemmon and others, *Reimagining the Judiciary: Women's Representation on High Courts Worldwide* (OUP 2021) and Melody E Valdini and Christopher Shortell, 'Women's Representation in the Highest Court: A Comparative

3.2.2 Qualitative analysis

Looking at numbers alone does not provide a full picture. As such, an assessment in qualitative terms is necessary. I will start by using the classification proposed by Dominique Schnapper in her landmark work on the CC, in which she broadly distinguished her former colleagues into two ideal-types: the 'politicians' and the 'lawyers'.[10] In her view, for the former, the position at the CC was a downgrading in terms of status and also material conditions, and at times required quite some adaptation in terms both of expectations and of learning to make themselves forgotten by being quiet.[11] For the lawyers, however, nomination was often the coronation of a career.[12] A related observation with one major difference was made by another interviewee for the German system, where instead a certain respect and trust in the justice system overall, and possibly in the BVerfG more specifically, leads to the fact that for both lawyers and politicians, joining that institution is seen as an 'upgrade' rather than the opposite:

> In Germany, it also has to do with the fact that we Germans have a special respect for the office of judges, more so than for politicians. This means that for many people, politicians' reputation does not fall when they come to the BVerfG from an operational political area, but rather rises.[13]

The underlying perception of constitutional courts and justice in a given political system and trust in them more broadly may thus also have an impact on what kinds of personalities they attract or scare away.

It may not come as a surprise that Schnapper's classification emerged from the French context, which stands out from the four systems not only in quantity but also in quality. In fact, France is exceptional not only in terms of numbers but also in terms of 'quality' of ex-ministers who have joined the CC. Indeed, in many cases, we are speaking about former Prime Ministers, Interior Ministers, Justice Ministers: high-level and high-visibility ministerial positions that then transfer

Analysis of the Appointment of Female Justices' (2016) 69 Political Research Quarterly 865. For a testimony of the first female member of the CC, see: Noëlle Lenoir, '1992–2001: Souvenirs d'une femme au Conseil constitutionnel' (2008) 25 Les cahiers du Conseil constitutionnel 15 <https://www.conseil-constitutionnel.fr/nouveaux-cahiers-du-conseil-constitutionnel/1992-2001-souvenirs-d-une-femme-au-conseil-constitutionnel#:~:text=La %20d%C3%A9cision%20du%20Conseil%20a,soit%20statu%C3%A9%20sur%20sa%20demande%20%C2%BB> accessed 22 December 2022.

[10] Dominique Schnapper, *Une sociologue au Conseil constitutionnel* (Gallimard 2010) 155. One of the interviewees thought that a better categorization would be 'technician' and 'politician', because otherwise the presumption is that politicians are not lawyers, which instead they are, from time to time. Interviewee no 32, 14 December 2023.

[11] ibid 157–72.

[12] ibid 172–75.

[13] Interviewee no 33, 2 February 2024.

this visibility and weight over to the CC. In many cases, nominees have also been members of parliament, state councillors or high-level civil servants in ministries or in parliament, meaning that sociologically, the political element went beyond their ministerial functions. In addition, the presence of academics or judges is rare and, at the time of writing, there is no university professor at the CC.

At the same time, Schnapper's classification does not fully overlap with my own in this book. On the one hand, hers is broader, because she also includes former members of parliament and high-level civil servants, such as state secretaries, in the category of politicians. On the other hand, it is narrower, because she does not count Robert Badinter, the former Justice Minister, amongst the political members. She probably considers him more of an academic and lawyer on the substance, who later became a politician. Regardless of the differences, it is interesting to keep in mind the observations made by Schnapper in the French context when looking at the other countries here under examination, even when they differ.

As a related observation to the quality of the ex-ministers and their political nature, the mere fact of having been a minister does not automatically mean that the political element is stronger than, for instance, that of having been a member of parliament or for having been at a ministry as a high-level civil servant for many years and then being nominated to the constitutional court. In that sense, there is a certain arbitrariness or formality in 'only' looking at ex-ministers. Their political role, experience, and influence can be inferior to those of other political actors, such as former members of parliament or long-term high-level civil servants who made it into the constitutional court.

In Italy and Germany, in only a few cases can one truly speak about 'true politicians', in the sense of high-level and high-visibility ministers. For Italy, Giuliano Amato stands out, but one can also mention Oronzo Reale, Sergio Mattarella, and Giuliano Vassalli amongst those who had important or long-lasting ministerial combined with parliamentary functions. In contrast, some of the Italian constitutional judges, like Gaetano Azzariti, Mario Bracci, or Augusto Antonio Barbera, were ministers for only a (very) short time, in line with the frequently rather short duration of Italian governments. One could surmise that it was probably less their political pedigree or past than their other functions that led to them being nominated to the C cost.

Similarly, in Germany, many of the former government members identified as such for the purposes of this book are not pure-blooded politicians like in France. Moreover it has already been mentioned how, given the federal nature of the country, most had been ministers at the state rather than federal level, meaning that they might not have had the same national visibility as a French minister. Nevertheless, two judges also stand out as probably falling into the political rather than legal category of Schnapper: Ernst Benda and Roman Herzog. For the others, the nomination was probably a combination of legal and university expertise, coupled with a certain political visibility.

Besides the question of whether someone is or is not sociologically a politician, Schnapper's analysis and categorization might also not be fully pertinent for those legal systems where judges are constitutionally required to sit on the constitutional court. As we have seen, that is the case for Germany and Italy, where one might need to make the picture nuanced by introducing separate socio-professional (sub-)categories of analysis for the broader 'lawyer' group. For the C cost there has been a classification into 'judges', 'academics', and 'practitioners'.[14] Interestingly, former politicians as a separate category are not mentioned here, given that 'practitioners' are considered practising attorneys with more than 20 years of experience.

For the BVerfG instead, two interviewees spoke of 'professor-judges', 'judges-judges', and the smaller group 'politician-judges',[15] meaning that here the (former) politicians can be considered as a separate category. But even here, we have already seen that the category of 'politician-judges' might not be as clear-cut as that. One interviewee mentioned how he considered himself 90% a professor and 10% a politician.[16]

As for the Austrian VfGH, one could most probably eliminate the category of politicians and add that of 'high-level civil servants' as a separate socio-professional category,[17] with a note that thanks to the part-time nature of constitutional judges, the practitioners are well represented therein. On the contrary, at the time of writing, the judges are completely absent from that institution, something that was deplored and explained by an interviewee in the following way:

> One disadvantage of the entire system is that judges from the administrative courts and, above all, from the ordinary courts are not sufficiently represented in the VfGH. This has to do with a certain 'judicial remoteness' of the judiciary. Therefore, when the National Council, the Federal Council or the federal government make a proposal, the judges are not 'visible' enough.[18]

Again, these are ideal-types and not always easily identifiable because in some cases there is overlap: Giuliano Amato, Robert Badinter, Wolfgang Brandstetter, Sabino Cassese, or Jutta Limbach were both ministers *and* academics. Their nominations to the respective constitutional courts was arguably due to their combined academic and political records, rather than merely their political past. Rarer is the combination of judge and politician, like Filippo Patroni Griffi in Italy, Peter

[14] See in this sense the categorization of the former Italian constitutional court judge Giuseppe Branca, 'Collegialità nei giudizi della Corte costituzionale' in Corte costituzionale (ed), *1956–2006: Cinquant'anni di Corte Costituzionale* (Corte Costituzionale 2006) 494, 496.

[15] Interviewees no 21, 8 September 2023 and no 33, 2 February 2024.

[16] Interviewee no 21, 8 September 2023.

[17] Interviewee no 22, 12 September 2023.

[18] Interviewee no 23, 12 September 2023.

Müller in Germany, or Jean-Louis Debré in France. While the categorizations might not be fully pertinent even within one given system, and have their limitations, the Schnapperian grouping into 'politicians' and 'lawyers' might, nevertheless, provide helpful indications for thinking about constitutional courts outside France as well.

Indeed, a short ministerial time in a less important ministry or at the state level in Germany might not have the same qualitative impact and visibility as having been a Prime Minister. Yet, even for what are sometimes called technical, caretaker governments or ministers in Italy (ie individuals who become ministers not so much for their political opinions or affiliations but for their technical competence), such positions allow for gaining government experience and for creating contacts and links which later may have repercussions on the constitutional court, in terms of their perception. For example, Sabino Cassese and Franco Gallo had both been ministers for little over a year under the government of then Prime Minister, Carlo Azeglio Ciampi in the mid-1990s. When Ciampi later became President of Italy he nominated both to the C cost. Fernanda Contri had been part of that same Ciampi government and was the first woman to be nominated to the C cost by another President of the Republic, Oscar Luigi Scalfaro.

Last but not least, another element to take into account is the role of trained lawyers in a given political culture of a country. In many countries lawyers do play an important role as a political elite—this certainly is the case for Germany, Austria, and Italy. In France, their role is reduced due to the different institutional set-up in which the fact of having spent some time at the former *Ecole Nationale de l'Administration* (ENA) constituted a better predictor of whether or not someone might later on have a high-level political career.

The collegial nature of these courts, the existence of the already referenced 'Becket effect', the role of lawyers in a given political culture or elite, and the acknowledgement, if not admission, that a full-time parliamentary member or high level civil servant is possibly more political than a short-lived, less visible minister, are things that certainly influence the observations and comparative analyses in this book. As was already mentioned above, the purpose here is not to inquire whether a person's previous political past has a bearing on the judicial output of a given constitutional court. That this is often not the case has also been recently ascertained in relation to the Second Senate of the BVerfG.[19] In that study, the authors also observe that, besides politics, biographical elements, such as social and professional background, position within the courts as well as length of service play a certain role.

[19] Benjamin G Engst and others, 'Zum Einfluss der Parteinähe auf das Abstimmungsverhalten der Bundesverfassungsrichter – eine quantitative Untersuchung' (2017) 72 Juristen Zeitung 816.

It is precisely to some of these biographical elements that I turn next. The comparative study of the biographies and personal histories of those judges and how they intertwine with that of the constitutional courts they joined at a given time also provides important elements in understanding what benefits or risks their presence brings. Some of these elements and stories will be considered in more detail in Chapter 4.

I limit myself to some observations on how these biographies also highlight some important differences in how constitutional courts have been located and understood as a break from a difficult past, in theory and in practice. While such a break is more evident in the case of Germany, where many of the initial BVerfG judges had either been expelled from Nazi Germany and/or participated in the constitution drafting process,[20] the personal continuities at the highest level are much more visible and troubling in Italy. For instance, the already mentioned Gaetano Azzariti, who briefly became Justice Minister in 1943–44, spent a large part of his professional life at the Justice Ministry under various regimes (monarchy, Fascism, transitional governments, and the new Italian Republic). More problematically, he presided over an infamous Commission dubbed the 'Race Tribunal' (*Tribunale della razza*), whose role it was to determine whether or not someone belonged to the Aryan race. Despite this past, he survived the lustrations at the end of World War II and was nominated by the President of the Republic to the C cost, of which he served as the second President for four years from 1957–61. He was not the only member of this Race Tribunal to make it to the C cost; indeed, he shared this dubious honour with Giuseppe Lampis and Antonio Manca, who both became constitutional judges respectively between 1955–56 and 1956–68 as 'judicial' nominees.[21]

The story is somewhat different in France, even though the capacity of the CC's first President, Léon Noël, to survive relatively unscathed and at high(est) levels

[20] This is not to say that some judges with questionable Nazi pasts did not make it onto the BVerfG, as demonstrated by Willi Geiger. On Geiger's past and the difficulties this created within the BVerfG, see eg: Helmut Kramer, *Willi Geiger. Vom Antisemiten und Staatsanwalt am NS Sondergericht zum Richter am Bundesverfassungsgericht* (Kugelberg Verlag 2017) and Rolf Lamprecht, *Ich gehe bis nach Karlsruhe. Eine Geschichte des Bundesverfassungsgerichts* (Spiegel Buchverlag 2011) 98–100. On the importance of Geiger's internal role during the early years of the BVerfG, see the short autobiographical account by Theodor Ritterspach, 'Erinnerungen an die Anfänge des Bundesverfassungsgerichts' in Eckart Klein (ed), *Grundrechte, soziale Ordnung und Verfassungsgerichtsbarkeit. Festschrift für Ernst Benda zum 70. Geburtstag* (CF Müller 1995) 202–03.

[21] See on these personalities most recently: Massimiliano Boni, *In questi tempi di fervore e di gloria* (Bollati Boringhieri 2022) and Saverio Gentile, '"Le mani nella pasta, gli occhi al cielo" e la coscienza sporca: la magistratura e la legislazione antiebraica tra fascismo e Repubblica' in Antonella Meniconi and Guido Neppi Modona (eds), *L'epurazione mancata. La magistratura italiana tra fascismo e Repubblica* (il Mulino 2022) 115, 117–20. In 2012, a request to remove the bust of Azzariti at the C cost was denied. See: <http://www.libertaegiustizia.it/2015/03/29/respinta-la-richiesta-di-rimuovere-lopera-che-ricorda-gaetano-azzariti/> accessed 22 November 2022. Nevertheless, the bust somehow disappeared, allegedly to be restored, together with others. On this latest information see: Massimiliano Boni, *In questi tempi di fervore e di gloria* (Bollati Boringhieri 2022) 209.

throughout various régime changes from the Third Republic, to the Vichy Régime, and on to the two post-war Republics, resembles uncannily the life and career of Azzariti.[22] The difference, however, was that part of the function and birth of the CC and the Fifth Republic was to distance itself not from dictatorship but from the previously existing parliamentary regimes of the Third and especially the Fourth Republics and their perceived shortcomings and dysfunctions. It is no secret that until 1980, many staunch De Gaulle followers were nominated to that body,[23] amongst which were many of his former ministers. Even after 1980, with Yves Guéna, a young follower of De Gaulle in London during World War II, and Jean-Louis Debré, the son of De Gaulle's right-hand man, Michel Debré, the General's presence at the CC could be felt all the way into the 2000s. In one way, there was a break from the previous parliamentary 'regime' but in another way that break was strongly linked to a specific persona which had repercussions also on the interpretations by the CC.

In Austria, the biography of the second President of the VfGH after World War II, Ludwig Adamovich Snr, also reveals some interesting—though less spectacular—transformations, compared to his Italian or French counterparts. He became judge at the VfGH in 1930, as a substitute for Hans Kelsen, after the 1929 Reform. In 1938, for a very short time, he also became Justice Minister under the Austro-Fascist Schuschnigg regime. While he could not retain his professorship during the annexation of Austria by Nazi Germany in 1938, his conservative, authoritarian roots and pedigree as well as capacity to maintain political positions, while remaining apolitical and legal in appearance, allowed him to be reinstated and to become President of the VfGH in 1946.[24]

The point about these stories is not to draw any conclusions on whether these individuals managed to influence the jurisprudence of these courts in a given way.[25] Nevertheless, the biographical approach to looking at these courts makes things emerge that at least in traditional legal scholarship are not (as) visible. Coincidentally, a few of these judges were also ex-ministers who had been nominated to these constitutional courts. Some of these biographical elements will re-emerge further below when discussing the advantages and risks of having such personalities on the bench of a constitutional court.

[22] On this story, see: Yves Beauvois, *Léon Noël de Laval à de Gaulle via Pétain (1888–1987)* (Presses Universitaires du Septentrion 2001).

[23] Wolfram Vogel, *Demokratie und Verfassung in der V. Republik. Frankreichs Weg zur Verfassungsstaatlichkeit* (Leske + Budrich 2001) 141–42.

[24] On this story, in critical sense, see: Thomas König and Tamara Ehs, 'Ludwig Adamovich. Jurist, Minister, Rektor und Verfassungsrichter' in Mitchell G Ash and Josef Ehmer (eds), *Universität—Politik—Gesellschaft* (Vienna University Press 2015) 305. Less critical, his son: Ludwig Adamovich, 'Mein Vater Ludwig Adamovich (1890–1955)' in Peter Häberle, Michael Kilian, and Heinrich A Wolff (eds), *Staatsrechtslehrer des 20. Jahrhunderts* (De Gruyter 2015) 371.

[25] Even though this is what is argued at least with regard to Willi Geiger at the BVerfG: Helmut Kramer, *Willi Geiger. Vom Antisemiten und Staatsanwalt am NS Sondergericht zum Richter am Bundesverfassungsgericht* (Kugelberg Verlag 2017).

3.2.3 Views from inside constitutional courts

An important aspect of this book is the interviews conducted with those actors directly involved and concerned with the phenomenon of ex-ministers as constitutional judges. How is this perceived from within constitutional courts? Is it seen as a problem or as an advantage? Can one make some comparative observations or even models?

One thing that certainly emerges is a certain path-dependency of an existing practice. Moreover, I could not detect any differences between various categories of interviewees. Whether they were former constitutional judges, current constitutional judges, high-level personnel, former politicians, professors, judges, men or women, the answers resembled each other and differed rather per legal system than per internal categorizations. In this sense, if one wanted to make a model, France is certainly where ex-ministers are assessed most positively and least critically. It is almost as if such roles are a sign of a particular understanding of the state's institutions and of the state's or the public's general interest that is needed at the CC. One of the interviewees put it as follows:

> I think it is a very good thing that a certain number of members of the CC have experience of the State. I insist on that. Let us look at some examples. We often have to take decisions here on the reconciliation of public freedoms and individual freedoms, as well as on defending the public order or individual freedoms, health, etc. It is obvious that when we have to decide what is legally possible to intervene in demonstrations, the fact of having headed the State or of having been a minister at a certain time allows us to make fairly informed decisions. It is the same in a number of areas: it is useful to see how a society and the state work.[26]

Others stated this less directly but still highlighted the positive aspects that are, for example, evoked by the French administrative culture to which both politicians and administrative officials are exposed:

> Yes, there are some former politicians here, but many of them, especially those I have known, were still steeped in the French administrative culture of impartiality. ... The convictions that appear in the deliberations of the CC, whether on the part of former politicians or former administrative officials, are convictions that have to do with their idea of public affairs, of the balance between the general interest and individual freedom. ... [S]ometimes there is a debate about the nature of the general interest, or when there are several ones, which one is overriding? And only then do we have the most delicate question, which is whether the

[26] Interviewee no 4, 8 February 2023.

> infringement is justified by the general interest, is it proportionate, is it relevant? And it is here that we come up against the idea that each person may have based on his or her own culture, in particular the very French culture of public service in the general interest, which exists in many other legal systems, but which we have pushed with certain logics in our traditional French culture.[27]

Another one rather framed the issue in terms of diversity and the diverse experiences such personalities bring with them:

> Having headed a government, having been a minister, having seen what the life of a group or a company was like, or of being an academic and of being very familiar with a line of reasoning or a doctrine of comparative law ... these are all factors that will enable us to reach a decision that is not only founded in law, but also a decision that will be fair because it is felt to be fair, in the sense that the parties involved will have weighed up the effects in these different fields.[28]

A fourth one saw the issue in terms rather of political power(s) of the institution:

> I am not against having a political element, because at this level, we cannot be in a position of legal absolutism. I consider that in certain ways today the President of the CC has almost more power than the President of the Republic. The latter may have some problems in getting a certain statute passed but if the CC wants to strike down a statute, it can do so in two seconds.[29]

In Italy and Germany the views are somewhat more nuanced. One argument that emerged in favour of having ex-ministers on their respective constitutional courts was a qualitative one, in the sense that they combined legal and political qualities at the highest levels:

> I think of recent examples like Giuliano Amato, Augusto Barbera and Sergio Mattarella, or older ones like Leopoldo Elia or Giuliano Vassalli. They were all politicians but what politicians! And what lawyers! ... I do not recall exactly who and how many they were out of the more than one hundred constitutional judges overall. ... But the ones I remember personally were great judges. I think having specific technical requirements and qualifications is not irrelevant.[30]

[27] Interviewee no 9, 22 March 2023.
[28] Interviewee no 3, 8 February 2023.
[29] Interviewee no 5, 16 February 2023.
[30] Interviewee no 11, 19 April 2023.

In Germany, the qualitative argument is raised, too. I will analyse the benefits which those personalities bring to constitutional courts below, but clearly the fact of being excellent lawyers is a (pre-)requisite. One interviewee stated that '[u]ntil now, we were always lucky that we had good or very good lawyers here. The important thing is the level.'[31]

Quantitative arguments constituted a second set and were framed in more cautionary terms along the lines that former politicians would be welcome but there should not be too many. In this sense, one of the interviewees mentioned that a 50–50 composition would be seen as problematic, while an 80–20 one could be fine.[32] In the German reality, quite a few judges or former judges used the same formulaic expression of Paracelsus, according to which 'the dose makes the poison'.[33] Put differently, in small doses, such personalities are good but in larger ones they would be a poison. Others were even more precise and indicated numerical limits:

> The presence of one or two politicians is fine but I would also say that there should not be too many.[34]

> I think the way it has been so far, with a maximum of one politician per Senate and sometimes a slight increase, is fine.[35]

Another argument that was raised explicitly for the German context is that the rules, especially on abstention and recusal, were drafted in such a way as to make it possible for former politicians to join the BVerfG:

> As far as the question of bias is concerned and the rule that the mere participation in a legislative procedure of a piece of legislation whose constitutionality is being checked, does not constitute grounds for recusal, the background to this is, of course, that the intention was to enable someone from politics to become a member of the court.[36]

> On the grounds of exclusion, if you want to have politicians here, but that they would be excluded from judging in the case of any previous involvement, then no

[31] Interviewee no 27, 15 November 2023.

[32] Interviewee no 10, 19 April 2023.

[33] In this exact wording: interviewee no 26, 15 November 2023; interviewee no 28, 16 November 2023; and also the former President of the BVerfG, Andreas Voßkuhle, in a 2021 interview: Heinrich Welfing, 'Die Parteiloyalitäten zählen nicht mehr' *Die Zeit* (Hamburg, 15 September 2021) 10<https://www.zeit.de/2021/38/andreas-vosskuhle-bundesverfassungsgericht-ehemaliger-praesident-interview> accessed 18 December 2023.

[34] Interviewee no 20, 30 August 2023.

[35] Interviewee no 27, 15 November 2023.

[36] Interviewee no 20, 30 August 2023.

> federal politician could come, because they were involved in all legislation. Then you might just as well write that federal politicians are not allowed to come, even if they were not in office and only dealt with the matter in some distant way.[37]

If one wanted to make a model or categorization on this issue, both Germany and Italy situate themselves somewhere in an intermediate category, where in terms of practice and experience, ex-ministers were perceived as bringing positive elements to the table, with the idea that they should not become too many and that their legal expertise should be very high-level.

The most adverse system to such personalities is the Austrian one. Here from the conversations had with various members of the VfGH, the tone was very doubtful as to what ex-ministers could bring to a constitutional court. One interviewee mentioned that '[a]s far as the involvement or appointment of former politicians is concerned, I am very sceptical'.[38] Another was even more doubtful, when referring to a recent experience:

> [A] politician makes little sense in a constitutional court ... From my point of view, he was not a lawyer who wanted to deal with legal issues in detail. He was in the right place in politics, where things are about management functions, about activities that are very different from those in the legal profession. In my opinion, it is an example of how a politician is no good at all [in a constitutional court], not even when I imagine the ideal figure of an intellectual, legally highly educated politician.... I fail to see what added value they can bring because they held a political position.[39]

This clear opinion was also echoed in another interview:

> The former Minister of Justice was certainly the complete exception to the long standing rule. It has also been shown that a quick change from a high-ranking government office to the constitutional court is not a good idea for our system.[40]

This scepticism arguably also extends to substitute judges, as can be gleaned from another mention indicating how the (former) Austrian Christian Democratic Party had nominated the lawyer representing this party in court proceedings as a substitute judge, with the result that—to the best knowledge of the interviewee—he has not been called to sit on a case, yet.[41] Of course, a lawyer is not an ex-minister

[37] Interviewee no 27, 15 November 2023.
[38] Interviewee no 23, 12 September 2023.
[39] Interviewee no 24, 19 September 2023.
[40] Interviewee no 14, 17 May 2023.
[41] Interviewee no 23, 12 September 2023. The decision on who to call as substitute judge is completely up to the President of the VfGH.

but the example was brought up when enquiring more specifically about the issue, indicating how far the scepticism goes.

Overall, one can say that each system seems to assess the presence of ex-ministers according to their rules, practices, and experiences. So, there is a certain path-dependency. If former politicians are usually nominated, or nominated in limited numbers, or not nominated at all, that is the practice which is then viewed as acceptable. Austria in this sense is an interesting comparator because here we have seen that essentially since the 1929 Reform on the de-politicization of the VfGH, the practice became not to have former politicians on this body. This long-standing practice was then disrupted with the nomination of Wolfgang Brandstetter in 2018, which has been perceived as an overall negative experience that will be discussed further below under Chapter 4.2. Such a negative experience then influences how the issue is thought of in broader terms, just as the perceived positive experiences influence how the French, German, or Italian interviewees see, understand, and analyse the issue.

France is interesting in the opposite sense. Here the CC's functions changed quite radically since its creation, but the path-dependency remained. Of course, this institution was designed to be a political one from its inception, which explains the difference in terms of numbers and quality of ex-ministers being nominated to it. However, the surprise is how the constitutional changes, which arguably transformed this body from a political to a judicial one, have not affected the overall nomination practices.

Apart from the models and practices, and how they are assessed and viewed from inside the constitutional courts, one can provide a first answer to the hypothetical question raised in the Introduction to this book. In the legal systems under observation, the phenomenon of former government members in constitutional courts exists, but it is neither clearly increasing nor decreasing. The Austrian VfGH is an exception for the reasons of legal and constitutional change in the early years just explained. Otherwise, one rather sees continuities or path-dependency than trends or evolutions. If any politicization of the judiciary occurs, it does not take the form of politics increasingly naming former high-level politicians to constitutional courts.[42]

If some change can be observed, it is that possibly the nomination of (ex-)ministers seems to have become more contested, or more visible. In Austria, that happened earlier in the political context of the 1920s. In France, Germany, and Italy the issue seems to be more recent and more contested when the passage is directly from active politics into the constitutional court. The detailed reasons for these critiques will be analysed below in the next chapter.

[42] This seems to be somewhat in contrast to what has been observed for the United States, Canada, and Australia and their supreme courts, where instead there is a clear trend and shift towards fewer former politicians on those bodies. Douglas MacDonald, 'Worlds Apart. The Appointment of Former Politicians as Judges' (2016) 41 Alternative LJ 17.

4
Assessing the Participation of Ex-Ministers as Constitutional Judges

The previous chapter demonstrated that former members of government join constitutional courts as judges more often than is widely known. What do they bring to the table at such institutions? Put differently, what benefits and risks does their political past bring to constitutional courts? I will first survey the positive aspects of such participation (section 4.1) before turning my attention to the attendant risks (section 4.2).

4.1 The Benefits

The political or judicial nature of constitutional courts has been a point of contention and discussion since their invention. As laid out at the beginning of this book, the debate between Kelsen and Schmitt brought to light the fact that constitutional courts judges with neither political experience nor democratic legitimacy could nonetheless strike down legislation in a manner standing in stark contrast with the notion of parliamentary sovereignty. Kelsen tried to address and justify this issue in two ways. First, on a conceptual level, he theorized that when constitutional courts review the constitutionality of legislation, they act as a 'negative legislator'.[1] Second, he tried to design explicit links between constitutional courts and politics via the nomination procedure. By involving parliament in the nomination of constitutional court judges, some representative legitimacy would be achieved, at least indirectly. While serving politicians do not sit as judges on such courts due to ineligibility rules, political representation is indirectly exercised by the parliaments or governments that nominate the judges.

The presence of former ministers in constitutional courts takes this logic one step further. Unlike 'simple' or 'pure' university professors, judges, civil servants, or other law practitioners who mostly never held a political mandate, former members of government (or parliamentarians) most probably—except for the case of appointed caretaker 'technical' governments, especially in Italy, where they are

[1] *Negativer Gesetzgeber* in the original German version. See, at various points in Kelsen's work as republished in Robert Chr. van Ooyen (ed) and Hans Kelsen, *Wer soll der Hüter der Verfassung sein?* (2nd edn, Mohr Siebeck 2019) 26, 78–79.

Ex-Ministers as Constitutional Judges. Mathias Möschel, Oxford University Press. © Mathias Möschel 2025.
DOI: 10.1093/9780198930228.003.0004

known as *governi tecnici*—have won some sort of elective mandate in the past. This could be understood to mitigate the counter-majoritarian critique that constitutional judges have no popular or democratic legitimacy to strike down parliamentary legislation. One might surmise that the presence of former politicians provides constitutional courts with a degree of political legitimacy in the eyes of the people and the political class. They have stood for elections and thus at least once represented the people via a democratic process. This argument has interestingly not come up even indirectly during the interviews, the reason why I do not engage with it further here.

Connected to the political and democratic representativity of constitutional courts is another argument, namely that the presence of former politicians injects a degree of professional diversity into these institutions. In other words, constitutional courts composed exclusively of career judges, law professors, legal practitioners, or civil servants would lack diversity in their viewpoints, personalities, and experiences.

For example, one interviewee stated that 'the worst thing would be to have a CC made up entirely of law professors. I have a lot of admiration for law professors, but 80% of the time they are out of the loop'.[2]

A second one also highlighted how 'it would certainly not be good if there were only professors on a constitutional court, just as I do not think it would be good if there were only civil servants or judges on the court. I think professional diversity is certainly a value'.[3]

This diversity is then also reflected in how differently cases may be approached by the various professional categories in a given court, thus adding to the diversity in decision-making. Without wanting to over-essentialize the sociological categorization of politicians versus lawyers or the other categorizations provided in the previous chapters, the interpretive positions of the former may be seen as less rigid, doctrinal, and/or conservative than those of judges or law professors.

In his memoirs referred to earlier, Debré mentions how the 'lawyers' at the CC have a thinly veiled disregard for the 'politicians' and how they know all without admitting other points of view.[4] A certain rigidity of law professors in their approaches to constitutional decision-making or judging more generally has also been observed in Italy, where it has been written that judges stress and defend the value of precedents as well as the negative consequences of a declaration of unconstitutionality, while law professors seem to be less concerned with such issues but may be beholden to dogmatic formulas.[5]

[2] Interviewee no 32, 20 December 2023.
[3] Interviewee no 25, 20 September 2023.
[4] Jean-Louis Debré, *Ce que je ne pouvais pas dire* (Robert Laffont 2016) 33.
[5] Giuseppe Branca, 'Collegialità nei giudizi della Corte costituzionale' in Corte costituzionale, *1956–2006: Cinquant'anni di Corte Costituzionale* (Corte Costituzionale 2006) 494, 496.

For the BVerfG, the classification into professor-judges, judge-judges, and politician-judges allows one to identify different socio-professional approaches to judging. With regard to the first two categories, those belonging to the former group have been identified as being more creative and systematizing, whereas those belonging to the latter have been socialized in a community of judges and are more willing to compromise in chambers. However, '[p]rofessors are sometimes a little harder to get to compromise, because the professor also embodies a claim to truth and not just a claim to finding the law'.[6]

As to the Austrian VfGH, the importance of diversity in composition emerged in a somewhat different manner and not related to former politicians because they barely existed on this institution. One interviewee mentioned how:

> a mixed composition is extremely important. The professors often want something new and the civil servants are looking for safe ground. When they find previous case law, preferably 10–20 cases, they are happy. And where the professors consider whether we should rethink it, [civil servants] do not even think about it, unless [that line of cases] has always bothered a lot. But if a certain line of cases bothers a civil servant . . . it is a fact that has to be worked with.[7]

Similarly, another interviewee mentioned that the different socio-professional backgrounds have an influence on:

> the way one argues and which aspects one brings in and how they are weighted. And that is probably also a value of this composition that an attorney is more likely to recall: How does this affect the practical consequences of the case? Someone who comes from the civil service perhaps has more of an eye on what something means for enforcement or how is this handled? And the professors are more inclined to break something down into its individual parts or to pay very close attention to the dogmatic categorisation of the status quo, so to speak. I would thus rather say that [the diversity] is reflected in the way the cases are prepared and which aspects are perhaps used more in the discussion, but not in the understanding of roles [of constitutional judges] as such.[8]

The direct or indirect implications from these observations are that politician judges may enrich a constitutional court sociologically by adding professional and viewpoint diversity thanks to more flexible approaches to law than professor-judges. The latter might be seen as being more creative and curious in testing out new solutions but may, at the same time, be too dogmatic, rigid, and less inclined

[6] On these points, see interviewee no 33, 2 February 2024.
[7] Interviewee no 22, 12 September 2023.
[8] Interviewee no 25, 20 September 2023.

to compromise in certain situations, especially in their areas of speciality. Judge-judges and civil-servant judges instead might be seen as more willing to compromise in chambers but at the same time be too timid and less creative because seeing themselves as (too) bound by precedent. Again, some of these observations may be too essentializing and even contradictory as such, but clearly the diversity which ex-ministers may bring to constitutional courts could benefit these institutions as compared to a homogenous constitutional court dominated by other socio-professional categories.

Apart from some elements of democratic representativity and (viewpoint) diversity, another benefit ex-ministers or politicians bring to constitutional courts is specific expertise and knowledge. This knowledge or expertise can be understood in two ways.

A first understanding is that former politicians contribute their specific insider knowledge of how legislative and governmental processes work; something that is otherwise difficult to access for university professors or judges who lack such experience. This point is particularly relevant to—and appreciated by—constitutional judges themselves, as demonstrated by interviews made by others in the context of their research as well as my own ones for this book.

In his work on the BVerfG, Uwe Kranenpohl cites a judge who indicated that 'former politicians bring a knowledge of the political processes with them, that are quite helpful in many cases'.[9] Another judge indicated that especially during Germany's reunification process, politicians had a vast background knowledge on political processes that allowed them to understand the meaning of certain legislative formulations which would have been lost on judges from non-political backgrounds.[10] Another interview highlights the technical element, ie that judges who were formerly politicians consider and add perspectives which go beyond the purely juridical but which draw on knowledge of the legislative process, of difficulties in the implementation thereof, or with a focus on the practical consequences of one's judicial approach.[11] The overall impression that emerges from Kranenpohl's interviews is that from the perspective of BVerfG insiders, there are too few—rather than too many—'political' judges with the experience or expertise to properly consider political-administrative perspectives when deciding on the constitutionality of a given act.[12] Of course, this knowledge could arguably be obtained in different ways, for example via external experts. But, as one interviewee put it, there is a certain advantage of having such information at hand and in a given court without having to go to call in an external expert which may cost time and money.

[9] Uwe Kranenpohl, *Hinter dem Schleier des Beratungsgeheimnisses. Der Willensbildungs- und Entscheidungsprozess beim BVerfG* (Verlag für Sozialwissenschaften 2010) 208, citing interviewee no 19.

[10] ibid 209, citing interviewee no 1.

[11] ibid, citing interviewee no 15.

[12] ibid.

> A constitutional court must also understand the political processes, not in order to be overly considerate, but to ensure that a transitional period or a requirement as to how the legislator should decide is not dysfunctional. It is not a question of making any political concessions, but of not misunderstanding the reality. And at times it is very helpful if someone tells that something can no longer be decided in this legislative period because there is still a certain deadline. Of course, there are other ways of finding out such things, but a practitioner from the political field simply knows them from their experience.[13]

Of course, the specific nature and composition of the BVerfG, which is known for being a rather professorial court, contrasts with that of the French CC where, on the contrary the knowledge and experience of professors or judges has been lacking or underrepresented. But even in that institution, its former President who was, in principle, against the continued participation of former French Presidents sitting ex officio on the CC, observed that Sarkozy's 'interventions in a case that we are examining were pertinent and the reflection of a real experience'.[14] Hence, even in a heavily politicized body, such experience can be welcome.

Despite certain differences existing between the four constitutional courts and their judges analysed in this book, the perspectives in interviews conducted by Kranenpohl in Germany or of the occasional information gleaned from the memoirs of former judges on the CC resonate with the viewpoints solicited during my own interviews with judges, former judges, or high-level personnel of constitutional courts in the four jurisdictions analysed here. These excerpts are also relevant for the diversity element described above. One interviewee explained that:

> it is a very good thing that a certain number of the CC members have government experience. I insist on that. Let us look at some examples. We often must make decisions about reconciling public freedoms and individual freedoms, as well as the defence of public order with individual freedoms and health. It is obvious that when we must decide what is legally possible to intervene in demonstrations, the fact of having headed the State or of having been a minister at a certain time allows us to make informed decisions. It is the same in several areas: it is useful to see how society and the state work. That does not mean that you cannot appoint university professors. But having only university professors on the CC, if I can put it that way, is another matter.[15]

Another interviewee explained for the Italian C cost how such personalities can bring certain knowledge:

[13] Interviewee no 33, 2 February 2024.
[14] Jean-Louis Debré, *Ce que je ne pouvais pas dire* (Robert Laffont 2016) 182–83.
[15] Interviewee no 4, 8 February 2023.

> of politics and certain times also of parliamentary dynamics that escape those who have been judges or professors. So they certainly bring useful experience, but what is particularly important is that they divest themselves of their political hat and play the full role of judges.[16]

Remaining with Italy, yet another interviewee confirmed that:

> generally speaking, the presence of ministers or of people who have had institutional experience of another kind, is very important to prevent the C cost from having ideal, very pure or very lofty positions that are not rooted in a knowledge of the dynamics of institutions.[17]

The same interviewee highlighted how, with the benefit of hindsight, ministerial experience gained *after* having been a constitutional court judge might have changed how to approach certain cases as a judge.

The second understanding of this expertise and knowledge is that former politicians are perceived as experts in a particular field or subject matter due to their involvement in relevant political and technical debates around specific pieces of legislation.

For France, one could mention Simone Veil and her involvement as a minister in the decriminalization of abortion in the 1970s. In France, her name and face became inextricably associated with this piece of legislation, partly due to the intensity of the parliamentary debate surrounding it. When a revision of this legislation was brought before the CC in 2001, she did not abstain from judging in that case, probably because she was seen as the expert in this domain. Similarly, Pierre Joxe's previous knowledge and involvement as a minister in relation to Corsica made him particularly competent to judge on revisions of its legal status later on.[18]

In Germany, Höpker Aschoff's knowledge as former Prussian Finance Minister seemed to give him an important, if not decisive, influence on the outcome of a BVerfG judgment on a specific financial matter.[19] In Italy, nominations are sometimes made to address a lack of expertise in a given area on the C cost.[20] As examples of former ministers who were probably nominated for that reason, one could mention Franco Gallo, former Finance Minister, who was nominated by the President for his expertise in tax law, and Giuliano Vassalli, the Justice Minister, who had just ensured the adoption of an important reform of the Criminal Procedure Act a few

[16] Interviewee no 16, 7 June 2023.
[17] Interviewee no 7, 3 March 2023.
[18] Fabrice Hourquebie, 'Les nominations au Conseil constitutionnel' [2001] Les Petites Affiches 79.
[19] Uwe Kranenpohl, *Hinter dem Schleier des Beratungsgeheimnisses. Der Willensbildungs- und Entscheidungsprozess beim BVerfG* (Verlag für Sozialwissenschaften 2010) 209–10, citing Konrad Zweigert.
[20] See in this sense: interviewee no 2, 1 February 2023 and interviewee no 11, 19 April 2023.

years before joining the C cost, for his expertise in criminal law and procedure.[21] Reasoning *a contrario*, the appointment of a former minister who lacks such legal expertise could be considered problematic and rather political than technical. Put differently, one's prior political knowledge and/or involvement in an area of legislation whose constitutionality is being challenged can be seen as a sign of expertise and thus comes with a series of advantages.[22] I will come back to this issue later when discussing the downsides and risks connected with this view.

Another not wholly unrelated point, of more biographical and psychological nature, may be that former politicians are perceived as having stronger public personalities and thicker skin due to their experience dealing with situations that have little to do with legal interpretation and more to do with political positioning, strategy, and (institutional) conflicts. High-level politicians might bring a certain prestige, respect, visibility, and leadership qualities to an institution that others lack.

This could be particularly relevant for young institutions and leading positions within such courts and may help bolster and guarantee their independence. For instance, the former constitutional judge, Theodor Ritterspach, mentions his great respect and admiration for the first President of the BVerfG, Hermann Höpker Aschoff, 'who had been Prussian Finance Minister when the younger ones of us were still in high school'.[23] Of course, a previous ministerial position does not automatically entail higher prestige, respect, or visibility. Other factors—such as age or personality—also play a certain role. Indeed, the same Ritterspach mentions how another former state minister, Rudolf Katz, would not have been a great presidential figure because he did not have the same representative dignity of Höpker Aschoff.[24]

Nevertheless, someone who already has experience of political conflicts and who has personal knowledge of political games and personalities from their past, might be less fazed by the publicity brought by a position on the constitutional court than someone who is completely inexperienced in such affairs and who has predominantly worked within less publicly visible university or judicial contexts. Moreover, the presence of former ministers may mean that politicians, nominating authorities and/or personnel in ministries might feel more inclined to refer cases under certain procedures to constitutional courts because someone

[21] See: Gian Luca Conti, 'Art. 135' in Raffaele Bifulco, Alfonso Celotto, and Marco Olivetti (eds), *Commentario alla Costituzione Vol. III* (UTET 2006) 2621, 2625.

[22] This positive assessment of former politicians joining constitutional courts does not extend to the participation of former Presidents in France and the limited benefits they have brought to the institution overall. In this sense: Antoine Chopplet, 'Les membres de droit à vie du Conseil constitutionnel: inutile réforme ou abrogation nécessaire?' in Elina Lemaire and Thomas Perroud (eds), *Le Conseil constitutionnel à l'épreuve de la déontologie et de la transparence* (IFJD 2022) 123, 136.

[23] Theodor Ritterspach, 'Erinnerungen an die Anfänge des Bundesverfassungsgerichts' in Eckart Klein (ed), *Grundrechte, soziale Ordnung und Verfassungsgerichtsbarkeit. Festschrift für Ernst Benda zum 70. Geburtstag* (CF Müller 1995) 203.

[24] ibid.

they know, trust, and/or esteem is sitting in that institution. Especially during the initial process of establishing a constitutional court, it may be a consideration to compose it of battle-hardened former politicians who bring a certain respect and respectability, as well as personal connections to the political realm, to such new institutions.

As examples, one could mention the difficulties and controversies in Germany and Italy in the period immediately following World War II. In Italy, these related to the position of the C cost and its judges in the official protocols for public events.[25] In Germany, the issue was the BVerfG's independence, due to its controversial formal subordination to the Justice Ministry, something which had been raised by the BVerfG itself in a famous memorandum.[26] In such cases, the strong and respected personalities as well as the political clout of former politicians such as Höpker Aschoff in Germany or De Nicola in Italy had advantages both internally and externally.[27]

But even when constitutional courts are established, former Italian constitutional judge, Gustavo Zagrebelsky, indicates that strong personalities are needed. He stated that:

> Against the risk of politicisation, should unknown, faded and second-rate lawyers be chosen for the constitutional court? Are these the antidotes to the politicisation of the Court? Certainly not. On the contrary, what is important, is that those named to become constitutional judges are strong personalities, with a dignified personal history that deserves to be claimed and defended. The half-figures, the lukewarm, the Nicodemi who have the courage of their ideas only under the cover of darkness and not in the light of the sun: these are precisely the kind of people who are always ready, as they say, to 'follow the wind'.[28]

In Zagrebelsky's words, the question is not whether politicians or non-politicians compose constitutional courts—of course, one can well imagine the nomination of a weak, puppet politician who executes whatever the government wants—but rather whether strong or weak personalities compose such courts.[29]

[25] See for Italy: Carla Rodotà, *Storia della Corte costituzionale* (Laterza 1999) 27–28.

[26] On this story, see more in detail: Donald P Kommers and Russell A Miller, *The Constitutional Jurisprudence of the Federal Republic of Germany* (3rd edn, Duke University Press 2012) 17–18.

[27] The search for a first President for the BVerfG was not an easy one and other former state-level ministers, like Josef Beyerle, Gebhard Müller (later President of the BVerfG) and Adolf Süsterhenn, had been considered. On this long search and how eventually Höpker Aschoff became the BVerfG's first President against his will, see: Thomas Aders, *Die Utopie vom Staat über den Parteien. Biographische Annäherungen an Hermann Höpker Aschoff (1883–1954)* (Peter Lang 1999) 300–08.

[28] Gustavo Zagrebelsky, *Principî e voti. La Corte costituzionale e la politica* (Einaudi 2005) 62.

[29] Similar ideas are confirmed and highlighted by another judge at the Italian Constitutional Court: interviewee no 11, 19 April 2023.

This brings us back to the Becket effect and the story of an evidently strong personality, Thomas Becket, defending the independence of his institution despite his friendship with and political indebtedness to King Henry II. Without necessarily endorsing a binary understanding of strong politicians versus weak, technical lawyers which could result from a combined reading of Dominique Schnapper's categorization with the citation of Zagrebelsky, the political members of such courts, especially when they have been in governmental positions, could be nevertheless perceived as sign of strength that helps establishing or keeping the respect of a constitutional court both in an external and in an internal dimension.

Seasoned political personalities may also bring with them another element that strengthens constitutional courts: age. We have already seen that in Austria and Germany this aspect is limited by the fact that their judges need to retire at 70 and 68 respectively. However, particularly in France, the relatively old age of CC members is widely seen as an advantage, not only from the perspectives of political credibility, diversity of viewpoints, or experience, but also those of independence and impartiality. This is referred to directly in a few interviews, by quoting Robert Badinter, former Justice Minister and President of the CC, who said that the meaning of independence is to 'have nothing to expect and nothing to fear'.[30] However, it is not only in the French context that the issue of age comes up as a benefit. In fact, another interviewee from Italy stated that:

> Since the mandate as constitutional judge is not for life it would be good if only people who are old enough not to aspire for any public position or function afterwards are nominated or elected.... It is very dangerous when public mandates are infected by such aspirations.[31]

Of course, age and experience are not automatically associated with a political career and could extend to anyone, from judges to law professors. But at least in the way things have played out and functioned in France, nominating politicians at the end of their career has been interpreted as a sign of their independence. Younger politicians would be a different reality.

Summarizing the benefits, ex-ministers can bring democratic representativity, socio-professional and interpretational diversity, professional knowledge and experience, as well as a certain political stamina that may serve constitutional courts well.

[30] In French: *Rien à espérér et rien à redouter*, quoted by interviewees nos 3, 8 February 2023; 4, 8 February 2023; and 9, 22 March 2023 in relation to the issue of age and independence/impartiality.

[31] Interviewee no 18, 3 July 2023.

4.2 The Risks

The benefits outlined above come with a certain number of risks. In outlining them, one ought to bear in mind the nuance that the degree of risk depends on whether the political-personality-turned-judge occupied a high ministerial position (eg Prime Minister, Justice Minister or Interior Minister), whether they were a politician for a long time, and also whether that personality became the President or Vice-President of a constitutional court or an 'ordinary' constitutional judge. One can safely presume *ceteris paribus* that a former minister in charge of a minor and less visible/important ministry who held office for a short time prior to being nominated to the constitutional court and had otherwise few, if any, political activities presents comparatively few risks.

Several of the risks I will outline below will be exemplified by what I call 'scandals' that involved constitutional judges.[32] I do not distinguish between fully blown public scandals or more limited 'gossip' noted within a given national legal public. The point of these anecdotes is neither to name and shame the individuals mentioned nor to insult some of them personally, nor to discredit the institutions they have been working in. Rather, the idea is to exemplify the potential risks associated with former ministers as constitutional judges, as they have emerged from bigger or smaller controversies in the four systems analysed here.

Bearing these points in mind, many of the risks discussed below often represent the flipside of the benefits discussed above. In this sense, a given benefit or advantage could just as well be a risk or disadvantage. I will analyse the risks, starting with the more theoretical ones and moving to more operational ones. A certain degree of overlap amongst the various categories identified is to be taken into account.

4.2.1 Politicization and separation of powers

The most important risk is linked to separation of powers and the idea that the legislative, executive, and judicial powers are meant to hold each other in check. As already mentioned in the Introduction, counting constitutional courts as part of the judicial branch may be slightly more controversial than in the case of supreme courts. The latter function both as courts of final instance for statutory interpretation as well as for constitutionality review of legislation and thus are formally at the top of the judicial pyramid. Constitutional courts often operate alongside ordinary, administrative or other supreme courts who are each on top of their own judicial pyramid. Moreover, due to the many other functions they often perform,

[32] For an overview and application of scandal theory to European judges, see: Mitchell de SO-L'E Lasser, *Judicial Dis-Appointments: Judicial Appointments Reform and the Rise of European Judicial Independence* (OUP 2020) 273–341.

they are arguably of a dual judicial and political nature.[33] Since Kelsen and World War II, the addition of the fundamental rights review of legislation to the list of constitutional courts' competences has reinforced their judicial nature. Moreover, supranational judicial dialogue between national constitutional courts and inter alia the ECtHR and/or CJEU has further highlighted the judicial nature of these national institutions.

If (too many) former politicians or members of government are nominated to constitutional courts and their increasingly judicial nature (ie an over-politicization), that may shift their centre of gravity away from the judicial towards the political. This is a frequent criticism made against the French CC, whose origins were political but whose judicial nature has been reinforced by a series of reforms and internal innovations over the years. However, this has had little (if any) effect on the political nature of nominations and the CC's composition.[34]

A separate yet related issue is that of mono-politicization, ie when all judges, regardless of their professional origin and background, have been nominated or are known to come from the same political spectrum and thus there is a lack of political diversity in a constitutional court. This point will be addressed more in detail below when looking at the supranational level. Ex-ministers do not have a monopoly over mono-politicization, which could also occur with no former politicians being in a given constitutional court.

Even if one refrains from considering the judicializing evolution of constitutional courts and goes back to Hans Kelsen, one would find that he also stressed the legal/judicial nature of constitutional courts. As mentioned in the Introduction, Kelsen objected to the practice of allowing serving politicians to sit on constitutional courts as a mingling of legislative, executive, and judicial power. Incompatibility rules have been introduced to reduce some of these risks. However, little is said about the temporal aspect or sequence of these functions, but when these aspects are neglected, this causes not only theoretical but also concrete problems.

Another observation to be made with regard to separation of powers is that constitutional courts are very special institutions of judicial power. Unlike ordinary courts, whose daily bread and butter is the adjudication of individual cases, one of the main functions of constitutional courts is to rule on the constitutionality of statutes or to adjudicate competence conflicts between various state and federal powers. In addition, as described in Chapter 2, they often fulfil and intervene in a series of other situations which very much have an explicitly political dimension.

[33] On this ambiguity and mix of natures at constitutional courts, see eg: Enzo Cheli, *Il giudice delle leggi* (il Mulino 1996) 45.

[34] See most recently and explicitly on such critiques: Lauréline Fontaine, *La Constitution maltraitée* (Editions Amsterdam 2023).

Hence, they are not a typical part of the judicial power, given their position between a political and a judicial body. Nevertheless, nowadays one increasingly reads the argument that—due to their increasing role as fundamental rights protectors and judicial dialogue with the ECtHR and the CJEU—European constitutional courts in particular have been transformed from playing the role of mere political arbiters to that of a full-blown court and actor of the judiciary intended in a broad sense.[35] This is true even for France, where such a development is probably the most spectacular, as detailed in Chapter 2.2.4. From that perspective, a clearer separation of functions from a temporal point of view may also be necessary. Having worked as a parliamentarian or as a high-level politician prior to joining a constitutional court may put at risk the separation of powers more than having been a university professor or a judge would do.

Where such mingling of functions first becomes visible is at the nomination stage to a position as constitutional judge if and when potential names circulate and are exposed to critiques. Of course, some of these controversies need to be analysed carefully, given that these problematizations may themselves be instrumentalized towards various political ends. Nevertheless, a common thread is that from the perspective of appearances, they seem to politicize constitutional courts far beyond the realm of necessity.

As examples of contested nominations, one could mention that of Wolfgang Brandstetter to the Austrian VfGH in 2018, which has been described as 'craziness from an optics perspective';[36] for Italy, those of Giuliano Vassalli in 1991[37] and Giuliano Amato in 2009;[38] and for Germany, that of Peter Michael Huber in 2010[39] and Peter Aloysius Müller in 2011.[40] Even

[35] Anja Seibert-Fohr, 'Richterbestellung im Verfassungswandel: Der Einfluss des Individualrechtsschutzes auf Funktion und Auswahl oberster Richter in Europa' (2010) 49 Der Staat 130; and for Italy: Elisabetta Lamarque, *Corte costituzionale e giudici nell'Italia repubblicana* (Laterza 2017) 25–29.

[36] Renate Graber and Günther Oswald, 'Brandstetter als Verfassungsrichter: "Von der Optik her ein Wahnsinn"' *Der Standard* (Vienna, 6 February 2018) <https://www.derstandard.at/story/2000073694277/brandstetter-als-verfassungsrichter-von-der-optik-her-ein-wahnsinn> accessed 20 December 2022.

[37] Veronica Magrini, 'L'astensione e la ricusazione quali strumenti per la realizzazione dell'imparzialità del giudice costituzionale' (DPhil thesis, University of Pisa, 2016) 91 at fn 62 <https://core.ac.uk/download/pdf/79621805.pdf> accessed 15 February 2023.

[38] Rquotidiano, 'Corte costituzionale, Amato giudice. M5S: "All'insaputa della Costituzione"' *Il fatto quotidiano* (Rome, 12 September 2013) <https://www.ilfattoquotidiano.it/2013/09/12/corte-costituzionale-amato-giudice-m5s-ad-insaputa-della-costituzione/709484/> accessed 18 July 2024.

[39] The controversial nature was also noted by foreign commentators: Francesco Palermo, 'La giurisprudenza costituzionale tedesca nel biennio 2009–2010' (2011) LVI Giurisprudenza costituzionale 3921, 3922.

[40] 'Peter Müller. Ex-Ministerpräsident wird Verfassungsrichter' *Der Spiegel* (Hamburg, 25 November 2011) <https://www.spiegel.de/politik/deutschland/peter-mueller-ex-ministerpraesident-wird-verfassungsrichter-a-799880.html> accessed 20 December 2022.

in France, where former politicians on the bench of the CC are the norm, the nominations of Robert Badinter in 1986[41] or of Jacqueline Gourault in 2022[42] were anything but uncontroversial.[43]

Sometimes these early contestations may result in the nominating authorities ultimately not nominating (former) members of government because they are perceived as being too political or unacceptable due to their clear positions on certain controversial topics. This seems to be particularly the case in Germany where the fact of needing to reach a political compromise for the nomination procedure may exclude former members of government who were potential candidates for the BVerfG.[44]

The French system has a particularly interesting story concerning a former minister who was ultimately not admitted to the CC. Here the opposition did not arise from the broader public but from the CC itself, which expressed the view that the former minister and politician, Michel Mercier—whose nomination by the President of the Senate had already been confirmed by the Senate—would not be welcomed to the CC due to a suspicion that the employment of his two daughters by the French parliament had been fraudulent.[45]

Allowing myself to stray a little from this book's narrower focus on former members of government, the nomination of Stephan Harbarth, the current President

[41] See: Alec Stone, *The Birth of Judicial Politics in France. The Constitutional Council in Comparative Perspective* (OUP 1992) 52 and 86. For comments relating to this nomination at the time in the French newspapers, see eg: Jean-Marie Colombani, 'L'opposition, à l'exception de M Chirac, dénonce la nomination de M Badinter' *Le Monde* (Paris, 21 February 1986) 1 and 10; Bertrand Le Gendre, 'Un homme de droit' *Le Monde* (Paris, 21 February 1986) 8; Maurice Duverger, 'Une fraude à la Constitution? *Le Monde* (Paris, 22 February 1986) 7; and François Luchaire, 'La nomination de Robert Badinter au Conseil constitutionnel. Réponse à Maurice Duverger' *Le Monde* (Paris, 26 February 1986) 9.

[42] Tristan Quinault-Maupoil, 'Conseil constitutionnel: les nominations de la macronie font polémique' *Le Figaro* (Paris, 15 February 2022) <https://www.lefigaro.fr/politique/emmanuel-macron-propose-de-nommer-jacqueline-gourault-au-conseil-constitutionnel-20220215> accessed 21 December 2022.

[43] On this last nomination and that of Jacques Mézard, even internally some doubts not as to the quality but the opportunity of nominating former politicians to the CC have been very cautiously alluded to as not being conducive to transforming the CC from a political body to a more judicial one: interviewee no 8, 21 March 2023.

[44] This was the case for Hertha Däubler Gmelin, a former socialist Justice Minister in Germany whose nomination was blocked in 1993 by the Christian Democrats. On this botched nomination and its background, see: Michaela Hailbronner, *Tradition and Transformations. The Rise of German Constitutionalism* (OUP 2015) 110; Thomas Dieterich, *Ein Richterleben im Arbeits- und Verfassungsrecht* (Berliner Wissenschaftsverlag 2016) 219; and Rolf Lamprecht, *Ich gehe bis nach Karlsruhe. Eine Geschichte des Bundesverfassungsgerichts* (Spiegel Buchverlag 2011) 230–31. The last author also mentions the failed nomination of former Justice Minister, Jürgen Schmude, for that same post. Ibid 230.

[45] Interviewee no 4, 8 February 2023. On this event also in the literature, see: Patrick Wachsmann, 'Les membres du Conseil au risque de la déontologie' in Elina Lemaire and Thomas Perroud (eds), *Le Conseil constitutionnel à l'épreuve de la déontologie et de la transparence* (IFJD 2022) 33, 38–39. The suspicions were eventually confirmed by a conviction in 2023: <https://www.lemonde.fr/politique/article/2023/01/26/michel-mercier-ancien-garde-des-sceaux-condamne-a-trois-ans-de-prison-avec-sursis-pour-des-emplois-fictifs_6159441_823448.html> accessed 23 April 2023.

of the BVerfG, was not met with unanimously positive assessments. He had been a parliamentarian and a former deputy chairman of the Christian Democrats—ie a relatively high-level politician—prior to being nominated to the BVerfG.[46]

Straying even further away, this time geographically, Spain's recent nomination of Juan Carlos Campo in 2022 was heavily criticized, with some referring to the event as a 'constitutional crisis'.[47] The first nomination of a former minister as constitutional court judge came against the backdrop of a four-year wait for judicial nominees to the Spanish Constitutional Tribunal (the *Tribunal Constitucional*—TC) as well as the rise of populism in that country.

In many, if not all of these cases, it is the swift passage from the role of an active and partial politician to that of an impartial, constitutional judge that is seen as a threat to democracy and the rule of law.[48] Nevertheless, the assessment of such individuals is rarely completely negative.[49] Indeed, often it has little to do with the actual competences of these single judges. The issue is more that when former politicians join constitutional courts, doubts linger over the politicization of such bodies due to the possibility that they retain their political friendships or relationships from the past, and that this may leave the public with the perception that specific cases and matters are being discussed or decided behind closed doors.[50]

One way to reduce such doubts of politicization is to request is that constitutional judges, in general, but especially if they are former politicians, should give up any formal party affiliation. In some systems such affiliation is prohibited explicitly, while in others it is a widely adhered to as best practice. Theodor Ritterspach, one of the first judges of the BVerfG, mentions that during the early days of this institution, the question of judges simultaneously retaining membership of political parties or otherwise remaining closely associated with a given political party (pre-)occupied the institution, and he felt that it was better not to maintain such affiliations.[51] In France, one of the interviewees similarly observed that, whilst it is possible to retain membership of a political party as a constitutional judge, he was

[46] See in this sense: Volker Boehme Nessler, 'Politiker als Richter?' *Die Zeit* (Hamburg, 25 December 2018) <https://www.zeit.de/politik/2018-12/rechtsstaat-parteipolitik-wechsel-politiker-verfassungsrichter-bundesverfassungsgericht> accessed 14 April 2023.

[47] See: Elisa de la Nuez, 'Crisis constitucional' *El Mundo* (Madrid, 20 December 2022) <https://www.elmundo.es/opinion/2022/12/20/63a1b503e4d4d8cf4f8b4589.html> accessed 12 April 2023.

[48] In this sense explicitly for all: Volker Boehme Nessler, 'Politiker als Richter?' *Die Zeit* (Hamburg, 25 December 2018) <https://www.zeit.de/politik/2018-12/rechtsstaat-parteipolitik-wechsel-politiker-verfassungsrichter-bundesverfassungsgericht> accessed 14 April 2023.

[49] Indeed, Peter Müller's nomination was also assessed positively in the literature: Markus Höreth, 'Sollen Politiker Verfassungsrichter werden?' (2011) 60 Gesellschaft, Wirtschaft, Politik 5.

[50] See in this sense again: Renate Graber and Günther Oswald, 'Brandstetter als Verfassungsrichter: "Von der Optik her ein Wahnsinn"' *Der Standard* (Vienna, 6 February 2018) <https://www.derstandard.at/story/2000073694277/brandstetter-als-verfassungsrichter-von-der-optik-her-ein-wahnsinn> accessed 20 December 2022.

[51] Theodor Ritterspach, 'Erinnerungen an die Anfänge des Bundesverfassungsgerichts' in Eckart Klein (ed), *Grundrechte, soziale Ordnung und Verfassungsgerichtsbarkeit. Festschrift für Ernst Benda zum 70. Geburtstag* (CF Müller 1995) 206.

unaware of any judge doing so. If some did, he asserted that this practice must be very rare.[52]

One last point to be mentioned under this heading relates to the observations made with regard to the benefits stemming from former politicians as constitutional judges in terms of socio-professional diversity and viewpoints. As for some of the other analyses made here under the risks section, they often constitute the flip side of the benefits.

The (over-)politicization may have yet other unexpected or unintended sociological negative consequences, put forward by another interviewee, and that relate more to the internal culture and functioning of constitutional courts.

> Everyone has their own reference group. If I come from a university background, then I am also interested in the opinions and votes of the other professors who are constitutional judges. If they all critique me, it has a greater psychological effect than if a politician scolds me because that is not my reference group. … In my experience, I would not advise to send too many [former] politicians to [constitutional courts]. They are socialised in [these courts] because they meet independent judges. And if there is one, or at most two, from the political sphere there, then they will be socialised by the climate of impartiality and judicial independence. But if you had six from the political sphere on a panel of eight judges, there would be a danger that things would develop differently.[53]

Put differently, apart from the external appearance that will be referred to also in the next point with regard to objective impartiality, internally too many former politicians in a constitutional court might create their own reference group to which they pay more attention to than to other colleagues. If they are only one or two, then they will be socialized by the internal culture of judicial independence that is certainly different to a 'normal' political culture.

4.2.2 Independence and impartiality

The participation of former politicians on constitutional courts also raises issues from the related theoretical perspective of independence and impartiality. Before detailing how the participation of former members of government on constitutional courts may affect these two areas, I will briefly outline how these intimately linked concepts are defined.

[52] Interviewee no 9, 21 March 2023.
[53] Interviewee no 33, 2 February 2024.

As regards judicial independence, a classic distinction in political science literature which understands such independence in relational terms refers to two separate dimensions: the judiciary as a whole or the individuals sitting in courts.[54] With regard to that first structural dimension, its main meaning is that courts, including constitutional courts, are independent from outside influences hailing either from the other state powers (legislative or executive) or from the litigating parties taking part in the underlying controversies. Lord Bingham famously stated that:

> Any mention of judicial independence must eventually prompt the question: independent of what? The most obvious answer is, of course, independent of government. I find it impossible to think of any way in which judges, in their decision-making role, should not be independent of government. But they should also be independent of the legislature .... Judges should not defer to expressions of parliamentary opinion, or decide cases with a view either to earn parliamentary approbation or avoiding parliamentary censure.[55]

It is important to note that Lord Bingham first identifies independence from government and adds to that independence from parliament. This reinforces the choice in this book to focus on former ministers who join constitutional courts, rather than also explicitly including parliamentarians. In any case, this notion of independence is also referred to as objective or formal independence.[56] Mechanisms to ensure such independence are often inscribed directly into constitutions and can include providing for lengthy non-renewable judicial terms, guaranteeing financial independence and/or regulatory autonomy for constitutional courts, and similar mechanisms.

With regard to the second and more individualized and personal aspect of judicial independence, this is sometimes referred to as subjective independence.[57] It can further be subdivided into two subtypes that are of external and internal nature. Such a distinction also emerges from interviews with the constitutional judges. As to the external level of subjective independence, reference is made to the functioning of these courts and their decision-making processes. For instance, with regard to the French CC, one risk to its independence is that some

[54] See eg Peter H Russell, 'Toward a General Theory of Judicial Independence', in Peter H Russell and David M O'Brien (eds), *Judicial Independence in the Age of Democracy: Critical Perspectives From Around the World* (UVA Press 2001) 1, 11–13.

[55] Tom Bingham, *The Business of Judging: Selected Essays and Speeches* (OUP 2000) 61.

[56] See eg: Frans Van Dijk and Geoffrey Vos, 'A Method for Assessment of the Independence and Accountability of the Judiciary' (2018) 9 International Journal for Court Administration 1. In German this is also called *sachliche Unabhängigkeit*. See: Gerd Pfeiffer, 'Die innere Unabhängigkeit des Richters' in Walther Fürst, Roman Herzog, and Dieter C Umbach (eds), *Festschrift für Wolfgang Zeidler* (Walter de Gruyter 1987) 67.

[57] ibid. In German called *persönliche Unabhängigkeit*.

non-lawyer members might be too dependent on internal legal services and the pre-report drafted by those services, and ultimately to the President of the CC.[58] In Italy, one could point to the internal election of the President. On the one hand, this can be interpreted as a sign of the C cost's autonomy and independence. On the other hand, it is viewed critically as disturbing the serenity of its work and thus its internal independence.[59] Put differently by yet another judge, 'one is not elected without making a campaign',[60] and such campaigns can lead to bargaining and raise the question of independence of the candidate from one's colleagues within the institution.

The internal personal level of independence has been referred to as 'independence from oneself'[61] or 'inner independence'[62] from one's own convictions, one's own doctrinal interpretations, one's own background etc. Undoubtedly these forms of personal independence apply to anyone joining these constitutional courts, regardless of their previous experience. The non-lawyers at the CC might be perceived as more impressionable, while law professors may find it more difficult to free themselves from their doctrinal opinions and intellectual hobby horses when judging cases.[63]

It is not always easy to distinguish these different categories. If one considers the subject matter of this book, one could think that both the issue of objective independence but also the external side of subjective independence could be at play. For instance, how—if at all—do the former associations and political friendships in government, which ex-ministers certainly have, influence their decisions? An archetypal example of risks to independence is that of external contacts or pressures, for instance a phone call from a serving member of government or parliament to a specific judge in order to influence the outcome of a concrete case. Most interviewees deny that any such calls, threats or tests to their independence have occurred.[64] I will leave it up to the reader to determine whether such a call falls into one or the other category of judicial independence. The factual and systemic context may lead to slightly different outcomes.

Regardless of the categorization, despite the denials of the interviewees, a closer look, especially at the French reality, shows a slightly different picture. The memoirs by Jean-Louis Debré, the former President of the CC, provide some interesting insights into the rather frequent contacts between members of the CC and

[58] In this sense, interviewee no 1, 23 January 2023.
[59] Interviewee no 7, 3 March 2023.
[60] Interviewee no 4, 8 February 2023.
[61] ibid.
[62] Gerd Pfeiffer, 'Die innere Unabhängigkeit des Richters' in Walther Fürst, Roman Herzog, and Dieter C Umbach (eds), *Festschrift für Wolfgang Zeidler* (Walter de Gruyter 1987) 67.
[63] An example of the contrary was given by one of the interviewees, who stated that when judging on a case where he had held a doctrinally different opinion, he nevertheless abandoned the opinion in the broader interests of stability of jurisprudence and foreseeability. Interviewee no 2, 1 February 2023.
[64] Most clearly in this sense: interviewee no 2, 1 February 2023 and interviewee no 9, 21 March 2023.

politicians. At best, such contacts can be seen as attempts to obtain insights into future decisions; at worst they are attempts to influence the outcome of decisions. One particularly detailed example came in conjunction with a case involving the constitutionality of legislation intending to modernize the exercise of local executive powers. Specifically, this legislation would have eliminated the accumulation of certain elective mandates, which would have affected Gérard Collomb, Mayor of Lyon since 2001, and who would not have been allowed to keep his parliamentary mandate while also being Mayor of Lyon. In the wake of the decision, Jean-Louis Debré received a call by the then Prime Minister, Jean-Marc Ayrault, letting him know that he was being harassed by Collomb, who wanted the CC not to annul that part of the legislation which concerned him.[65] One other member of the CC had seemingly also received a note from Collomb and another one had been contacted informally by the President of the Senate.[66] Those 'interventions' arguably created some changes of opinions on the matter, Debré commenting that 'the phones must have been running hot in certain offices, as one says'.[67] Despite—or maybe due to—the reasonable interferences that can be drawn from these phone calls, Collomb was allowed to keep his mandate for the remaining six years as a transitional measure.[68]

If one reads these memoirs in detail, one gets a sense that phone calls, and also lunches or dinners with various politicians, at least with regard to Jean-Louis Debré, were anything but exceptional. Nothing written here intends to say that all of these events were pressurizing the then President of the CC to decide in one way or another. As to phones running hot, or other conversations, apart from the one just mentioned, Debré also mentions a call by then President, François Hollande, on his wish to submit the ratification of the 2012 Treaty on the European Union for a constitutionality check by the CC;[69] various calls at various moments on various matters received by then Prime Minister, Jean-Marc Ayrault;[70] another call from Christian Jacob, the president of an opposition group and his friend, informing him that he would deposit the recourse against a hotly contested gay marriage bill.[71]

As far as lunches or dinners are concerned, there are many examples mentioned in that book, of which I will only select a few here: one with the then President of the Republic, Nicolas Sarkozy, on 23 January 2008;[72] one with the Justice Minister,

[65] Jean-Louis Debré, *Ce que je ne pouvais pas dire* (Robert Laffont 2016) 305.
[66] ibid.
[67] ibid 306–07.
[68] CC, Decision no 2013-678 DC of 23 January 2014.
[69] Jean-Louis Debré, *Ce que je ne pouvais pas dire* (Robert Laffont 2016) 151–52.
[70] ibid 156 and 169.
[71] ibid 211.
[72] ibid 38.

Rachida Dati, on 6 February 2008;[73] one with ten unnamed friends and members of parliament from the ruling party on 28 April 2008;[74] one with the Minister of State Reforms, Decentralization and Civil Service, Marylise Lebranchu, on 20 March 2013;[75] and another one with the Prime Minister, Jean-Marc Ayrault, on 26 November 2013.[76] Whereas many of these lunches or dinners took place at the CC, rather than in the ministries or at the French Presidency, or with all the members of the CC,[77] nevertheless, the constant formal and informal contacts with members of the Legislative and the Executive described throughout the book raise more than one question.

Another example demonstrating what problems the participation of former politicians at the CC can bring in theory and in practice arose in 2012. The case concerned Gérard Ducray, a former politician, who had been convicted for sexual harassment. He successfully challenged the constitutionality of the statute defining sexual harassment on the grounds that it was insufficiently clear.[78] The issue from the perspective of this book was that Ducray knew two members of the CC and had also worked in the governments of two former Presidents who were ex officio members of the CC but who did not take part in the judgment, as one can read from the names indicated at the end of the decision.[79]

While each of these single events might be considered normal interactions amongst state authorities, the overall picture one obtains—at least for the French CC at that time—is rather disconcerting. It seems to be confirmed at least by one interviewee who mentioned that she was contacted in the context of an electoral dispute raised by two politicians whom she knew well, for the purposes of influencing her vote. But she was quick to assert that this attempt to influence her upset her so much that even if she had intended to vote as asked, she would have ended up voting the opposite.[80]

The picture of where to fit such events into classifications of judicial independence becomes even more blurred when taking into account judicial impartiality. Indeed, some of these anecdotes are possibly even more relevant for this second important concept, that cannot be read without reference to the issue of independence of constitutional court judges.

With regard to impartiality, one can distinguish between two different notions: subjective impartiality and objective impartiality. This distinction is made explicit in the case law of the ECtHR on the right to fair trial, which will

[73] ibid 41.
[74] ibid 47.
[75] ibid 206.
[76] ibid 281.
[77] ibid 170, 206, and 281.
[78] CC, Decision no 2012-240 QPC of 4 May 2012.
[79] In more detail on this matter, see: Lauréline Fontaine, *La Constitution maltraitée* (Editions Amsterdam 2023) 56–59.
[80] Interviewee no 5, 16 February 2023.

be analysed in more detail in Chapter 5. Suffice to say here, for the moment, that subjective impartiality relates to the judge in his or her personal and human interactions, whereas objective impartiality is linked to his or her institutional or functional interactions. In the first case, the question is whether the judge, in reaching a decision, was subjectively motivated by feelings in favour of or against one party. In the second case, the question is whether, irrespective of the judge's personal feelings, the mere fact that he or she had previously held a particular position was likely to influence his or her convictions.[81] Sometimes the objective impartiality is also identified with the doctrine of appearances and the aphorism that 'justice must not only be done, but must also be seen to be done' that has been used in many cases,[82] including that of the ECtHR, that will be referred to below.

We have already seen under the previous point how the nomination of former politicians as constitutional judges can lead to debate at the nomination stage and politicize constitutional courts in unwanted ways.[83] But even once those debates have calmed down and settled, former members of government can continue to raise doubts from the perspective of objective impartiality and the principle or doctrine of appearances once they judge certain cases.

Of course, the notion of objective impartiality may call into question any judge, even those who have never been politicians. Indeed, for law professors—but not only for them—the principle of objective impartiality gives rise to serious and justified discussions of a different nature and, in particular, regarding whether they ought to refrain from adjudicating matters that they have expressed opinions on, either orally or in writing. Interviewees have referred to such matters in various ways in highlighting how academics who become constitutional judges are also not immune from partiality. This was best expressed by the following example, where the distinction of problems to impartiality arising between former politicians and former professors or judges was not seen as stark as presented in this book. The example highlights the fact that university professors also come with their own political baggage and that they do intervene as experts publicly in legislative processes and that these positions are not necessarily as neutral or anodyne as may seem at first sight. Hence, their objective impartiality is just as problematic as that of former politicians. Even law review articles have been referred to as problematic or political in this context:

[81] See in this sense, Pierre Bon, 'Recuser un membre du Conseil constitutionnel' (2010) 186 Recueil Dalloz 2007, 2008 citing E Glaser's conclusions to a case before the French Conseil d'Etat.

[82] For an early use in the British context, see Lord Hewart, then Lord Chief Justice of England, who stated that 'a long line of cases shows that it is not merely of some importance but of fundamental importance that *justice must not only be done, but should manifestly and undoubtedly be seen to be done*'. *R v Sussex Justices* [1924] 1 KB 256, 259 (emphasis added).

[83] As the example of the United States demonstrates, passionate debate also arises around non-politician nominees to the USSC. But probably this system is not representative of overall trends, and arguably not of European constitutional courts, at least from this angle.

> [F]or law professors who took position in a certain law review in favour of this or that law, nothing is said. When they would tell me: 'When you were a Member of Parliament, you voted in favour', I would respond: 'But Professor, you wrote a whole article in the *Revue du Droit Public* on gay marriage, did you not? You took position?!' Let us be careful. It is not a one-way street. All the law professors and even the Vice-President of the CdE [Conseil d'Etat] have written articles on case law. And I used to show them what they had written in the *Revue du Droit Public* or in the *Jurisclasseur* when they had expressed themselves on important issues.[84]

It is obvious that scientific publications or interventions can have a relevance in assessing the objective impartiality of a constitutional judge. However, doubts about the objective impartiality of former politicians and ministers sitting as judges on constitutional courts are probably more acute and qualitatively different. Their objective impartiality is viewed as compromised due to their previous links to government and/or the legislature. It is one thing to be seen as partial because of one's academic, religious, or personal opinions as expressed earlier in one's professional life. In that case, the doubt stems from a perception that a judge's personal beliefs are so influential on their judicial work, that their objective impartiality as a neutral arbiter of the law is impossible. It is another thing to be seen as partial because of one's previous political experience and associations, of previously being part of a different state power than the judiciary, which may both call into questions one's objective impartiality, but possibly even one's independence from politics and political influence over the decision-making of the constitutional court such personalities sit on. This was expressed most clearly by one of the interviewees:

> The only group that is suspected of constituting a risk to independence is that which comes from the political arena, because they have their friends and references in the political arena. If on top of that I was also a party politician, then it cannot be entirely irrelevant whether a decision is made in favour of or against a party, perhaps in a dispute between constitutional organs. That is why the public is sensitive when it comes to constitutional judges. You do not normally hear anything like that for 'professor-judges' and 'judge-judges'.[85]

One way to informally address and reduce such a risk would be to shun former political friends and colleagues, so as to avoid any appearances of partiality arising.[86] The legal ways to address some of these issues will be explored in the next chapter.

[84] Interviewee no 32, 20 December 2023.
[85] Interviewee no 33, 2 February 2024.
[86] This is seemingly what one of them opted to do, despite having been a politician and being friends with several former high-level politicians. Interviewee no 4, 11 April 2023.

The degree to which the participation of former politicians on constitutional courts is seen as problematic depends on the specific competences of the relevant constitutional court. Indeed, as we have seen in Chapter 2, in most cases, the competences of constitutional courts are not merely limited to the constitutionality review of legislation, but often include intervention in and adjudication of other procedures, such as impeachment procedures, competence conflicts amongst various state powers and organs, disputes amongst constitutional validating referenda, or electoral litigation. In such procedures, the presence of former politicians can prove 'uncomfortable' from the perspectives of separation of powers, independence, and impartiality. For example, when the C cost had to intervene in an impeachment procedure of two ministers in the famous *Lockheed* case mentioned previously,[87] it is obvious that sitting judges deciding on the legal fate of their former political colleagues and adversaries has the potential to cause problems.

Again, with regard to Italy, it is not hard to imagine how competence conflicts between state powers adjudicated by the C cost drag former ministers into delicate situations. This depends on the sensitivity of individual judges to perceptions of judicial impropriety and the degree of judicial impropriety required for them to recuse themselves from the adjudication of a given case. As examples one could mention Giovanni Maria Flick, who abstained from judging in a case concerning a conflict between the Senate and the Italian Judicial Council over the initiation of a disciplinary procedure for opinions expressed by a judge who had become a Senator and against whom Flick had initiated a disciplinary procedure at the time when he was still a Justice Minister.[88] Similarly, one of the interviewees mentioned how he abstained from judging in a case involving a conflict between the Executive and the Judiciary concerning the declaration of a state secret in a specific case by the government which he had himself been part of at the time.[89]

The French CC's role in electoral litigation also demonstrates the dangers of political partiality and the potential for conflicts of interest. As we have already seen, the French Constitution allows the CC to intervene in and monitor both presidential[90] and parliamentary elections.[91] While for the latter, they primarily check for irregularities during the election, for the former during the 1990s, the CC was also entrusted with the delicate task of checking that election campaign

[87] See n 150 of Chapter 2.

[88] C cost, Judgment no 270/2002 of 17 June 2002; mentioned by Alessandro Pace, 'La Corte costituzionale nell'esperienza di un avvocato' (2006) 11 Giornale di storia costituzionale 93, 96. Pace did not attribute the same sensitivity to other constitutional judges who had not abstained even though they had previously defended one of the parties involved in the underlying case before them.

[89] Interviewee no 18, 3 July 2023. Also mentioning this abstention, see: <https://www.ilfattoquotidiano.it/2014/01/14/abu-omar-consulta-sul-segreto-di-stato-da-ragione-al-governo/843831/> accessed 12 July 2023.

[90] Art 58 of the French Constitution.

[91] Art 59 of the French Constitution.

expenditure remained below the upper financial limits imposed by law.[92] On the one hand, this led to one of France's biggest 'judicial' scandals, when the CC validated the French presidential election campaign finances of Jacques Chirac and Edouard Balladur, even though both clearly exceeded the limits prescribed by law, especially Balladur's. The suspicion that the CC's President, Roland Dumas, had acted under political influence was exacerbated by the fact that he asserted that invalidating Balladur's finances would have entailed the annulment of the presidential elections, when simply returning the surplus expenditure could also have satisfied legal requirements. Additionally, public statements he made on the matter certainly did not do anything to restore the CC's image of independence and impartiality.[93]

On the other hand, when the CC invalidated the electoral campaign accounts of Nicolas Sarkozy years later,[94] a different and possibly even more delicate problem arose. In fact, this examination of the campaign accounts took place after Nicolas Sarkozy's term as President of the Republic, when Sarkozy was therefore an ex officio member of the CC. Even though Nicolas Sarkozy did not sit on this case, and thereafter never again took part in the CC's activities, the whole case raised questions concerning the potential for future ex-Presidents to influence their colleagues at the CC, even if they choose to abstain from cases involving blatant conflicts of interest such as this one.[95] Similar arguments could be made for ex-ministers.

Lauréline Fontaine explains it when she lists the names of former ministers and parliamentarians (Michel Charasse, Huberta Haenel, Jean-Louis-Debré, Jacques Barrot, Lionel Jospin or Alain Juppé), none of whom abstained from judging electoral conflicts concerning former colleagues, even those they had worked with almost immediately prior to their appointments to the CC.[96] When looking at these examples and potential conflicts of interest, the ongoing exclusion of electoral litigation from any rules of abstention and recusal in France looks even more problematic, a point which will be mentioned again in Chapter 6.

A related issue and risk which former politician-ministers may cause for objective impartiality is that they may be tempted to continue with political-representative

[92] For a short overview on this, see: Sophie Boyron, *The Constitution of France. A Contextual Analysis* (Hart 2013) 156–58.

[93] See on this lately: Lauréline Fontaine, *La Constitution maltraitée* (Editions Amsterdam 2023) 105 and 139–40. See also the description from the inside of the difficulties the electoral campaign financing litigation poses to the CC, in relation also to this case: Jacques Robert, *La garde de la République* (Plon 2000) 154–78. This event is still on the CC's mind, given that it was mentioned in two interviews with former and current members of this institution: interviewees nos 4, 8 February 2023 and 5, 16 February 2023.

[94] CC, Decision no 2013-156 PDR of 4 July 2013.

[95] Details on how this played out behind the scenes and the kinds of embarrassment and difficulties it created for the institution can be found in the memoirs of the former President of the CC at the time: Jean-Louis Debré, *Ce que je ne pouvais pas dire* (Robert Laffont 2016) 185–87, 190–93, 196–97, 210 and 225–38.

[96] Lauréline Fontaine, *La Constitution maltraitée* (Editions Amsterdam 2023) 46.

activities. France, yet again, provides some good examples of such occurrences. Actually, legal texts even allow for such a continuation. In fact, a 1959 decree allows members of the CC to take leave to run a campaign seeking an elective office.[97] Apart from the fact that this possibility exists and what it says about the continued political nature of the CC, this leave has been (mis-)used for other situations that had little to do with the CC member wanting to run a campaign for their election. Thus, the then-President of the CC, Roland Dumas, used it in the above-mentioned political-financial scandal before eventually stepping down. Even more famously, Simone Veil went on leave when campaigning in favour of a referendum on the European Constitution between April and June 2005.[98]

Moving closer to contemporary examples, and unrelatedly to this possibility of taking leave, Laurent Fabius, the current President of the CC, intended to remain President of the United Nations Climate Change Conference in Paris (COP 21) upon his nomination to the CC in 2016, also maintaining an office at the French Foreign Ministry for that purpose. However, the public reaction nudged him to step down from that function. Nevertheless, in 2017, he was nominated UN Environment Patron on Environmental Governance, an honorific function but which potentially would lead to participation in political and policy decisions in the global environmental domain.[99]

Admittedly, many of the examples cited here above concern the French CC and the political origins and nature of this institution make it stand out. But it is precisely these examples that give a sense of what can happen when ex-ministers join constitutional courts. Probably the unofficial practices and expectations would place higher levels of constraint in the other constitutional courts examined here. Nevertheless, such practices and expectations can change, shift, or simply be disregarded.

4.2.3 *Nemo iudex causa sua*

The previous paragraphs demonstrate the risks of another complication taking place that former politicians joining constitutional courts may pose from yet another angle. Indeed, in the case of Nicolas Sarkozy, he could have taken part in the decision on his own campaign finances. This stands in contrast with the natural law principle encapsulated in the Latin axiom *nemo iudex causa sua*: no one should be judge in their own cause.

[97] Art 4, Decree no 59-1292, 13 November 1959.

[98] On these two examples, see: Alexia David, 'L'impartialité du Conseil constitutionnel' (DPhil thesis, Normandie Université 2021) 167–69 <https://normandie-univ.hal.science/tel-03331880v2/file/sygal_fusion_27488-david-alexia.pdf> accessed 12 October 2023.

[99] ibid 172–74.

Apart from this possibly extreme and obvious case, what about former politicians or ministers who participated in drafting legislation whose constitutionality is under review by a court they now sit on? The level of participation a given politician has in legislative drafting varies from simply voting in favour of a given piece of legislation but without making any public comments on it in one way or the other, all the way through to being part of the government which initiated the legislation or to even being the initiator behind the legislation. It is difficult to identify the contours of this axiom in this context, because where exactly the line should be drawn before someone is judging their own cause is a matter on which reasonable people could disagree.

One way to limit this danger is to have rules on abstention and recusal in place. They will be critically analysed more in detail in Chapters 5 and 6. But we have already seen that at the Austrian VfGH, recusals by third parties are not allowed, while at the Italian C cost neither abstentions nor recusals are allowed. Interestingly, in Italy already during the constituent assembly debates, it was deemed problematic that former members of parliament could sit as constitutional judges, because it might have meant that those who elaborated a piece of legislation could then judge its constitutionality, thus directly speaking to the issue at stake.[100] That in the end such an incompatibility, which would arguably extend also to former members of government, was not introduced, can partly be explained by the fact that assembly member Bulloni did not insist and declared himself satisfied as long as it went on record that in future in such cases, judges should mandatorily abstain,[101] a possibility which as we have seen has since been eliminated.

In France and Germany, existing rules indicate that mere participation in the passage of a given piece of legislation does not in itself constitute a cause for recusal for a judge. Applicants may still challenge the participation of a judge who was involved in the elaboration of legislation but probably such participation must go beyond what is normal and would probably require particular statements in favour of or against a given piece of legislation whose constitutionality is being challenged. Otherwise, one must essentially rely on the judges' goodwill, personal understanding, sensitivity, and ethical integrity for them to step down.

There are some examples of constitutional judges not having necessarily demonstrated such qualities and sensitivity. Possibly one of the most known cases comes from Italy. Giuliano Vassalli, the former Justice Minister, had initiated an overhaul of the Criminal Procedure Code which reformed the previously inquisitorial Italian criminal procedure into a new accusatorial system. The new

[100] See in this sense the constituent assembly members Bozzi and Bulloni: Assemblea Costituente, Commissione per la Costituzione, Seconda Sottocommissione (Seconda Sezione), 23 January 1947, respectively 168 and 169.

[101] ibid 169.

code was also dubbed as the 'Pisapia-Vassalli Code'.[102] Many—if not most—of the constitutionality challenges to this statute reached that institution while Vassalli sat as a judge at the C cost. Vassalli not only participated as a judge, but he was also the judge rapporteur in 155 cases, placing him in charge of drafting decisions ranging from the rejection of applications on formal grounds to declarations of unconstitutionality.[103] Interestingly, none of this is mentioned in his, admittedly, brief memoirs on his time at the C cost written a few years later.[104]

During my interviews, it was either denied that he took part in any of these matters, in the sense that he allegedly always abstained from participating in any judgments on 'his' code by not participating in the deliberations,[105] or it was indicated that he used this occasion to review the text made during the reform and that, in any case, the situation had been exceptional.[106]

The French CC again provides several examples where the principle of *nemo iudex causa sua* could be seen as having been violated, or at least touched upon.[107] I have already mentioned Simone Veil and her participation in adjudicating the constitutionality of the reform of the abortion law, which she had pushed through parliament in the 1970s. More recently, the CC's President, Laurent Fabius, declined to abstain from judging the constitutionality of an important and controversial labour law reform initiated by a previous government in which he had been Foreign Minister.[108] Even more recently, questions arose over whether Jaqueline Gourault and Jacques Mézard should have refrained from participating in a judgment on the constitutionality of legislation which limited judicial recourse on permissions to build that they had contributed to as ministers and for which Gourault had issued implementing decrees.[109] This matter has some international repercussions that will also be discussed in the next chapter.

Of course, some of the issues surrounding whether and how far one is really judging in one's own cause when the constitutionality of abstract and general legislation is at stake is always a question of degree. Each concrete case needs to be looked at in detail, and hasty generalizations of principle are not necessarily

[102] The code took the form of a presidential decree: Decreto del Presidente della Repubblica, 22 September 1988 no 447.

[103] See on this more in detail: Veronica Magrini, 'L'astensione e la ricusazione quali strumenti per la realizzazione dell'imparzialità del giudice costituzionale' (DPhil thesis, University of Pisa 2016) 91, esp fn 62 <https://core.ac.uk/download/pdf/79621805.pdf> accessed 15 February 2023.

[104] Giuliano Vassalli, 'Testimonianza' (2006) 11 Giornale di storia costituzionale 55, 61–64.

[105] Interviewee no 6, 3 March 2023.

[106] Interviewee no 7, 3 March 2023.

[107] The examples here are mentioned in: Lauréline Fontaine, *La Constitution maltraitée* (Editions Amsterdam 2023) 43–46. I only selected those relating to former ministers even though other conflicts arose also with regard to parliamentarians.

[108] CC, Decision no 2016-736 DC of 4 August 2016.

[109] CC, Decision no 2022-986 QPC of 1 April 2022.

helpful. But this is yet another theoretical risk which must be factored into the assessment of the practice of having former ministers participating as judges on constitutional courts, especially when to an uninformed public the appearance of partiality can arise.

4.2.4 Public trust, competence, transparency, and ethics

Each of the previous points raises issues that in and of themself might not be intrinsically and automatically problematic. Indeed, the presence of a former politician on a constitutional court neither automatically leads to its politicization, problems with the separation of powers, or objective impartiality, nor is this inexorably the case just because someone who had been a minister or politician finds themselves judging legislation that they initiated. Such problems are only a possibility, albeit a heightened one.

Nevertheless, what almost always arises because of these practices are derivative issues concerning public support of and trust in constitutional courts that are intimately linked with questions of transparency and ethics. Constitutional courts are fragile institutions. One way in which they ensure their public prestige is by projecting an image of neutrality and competence. Close attention has been paid to these factors in studies which attempt to explain the success and *modus operandi* of the BVerfG. On the one hand, it has been argued that the BVerfG's value formalism and judicial style have contributed to its success and have functioned so as to somewhat insulate it from accusations of (over-)politicization.[110] Comparative political science literature has highlighted that public support and transparency can influence how constitutional courts operate. For instance, the BVerfG lost some of its popularity in the mid-1990s and thereafter adopted a low profile, which led to a rebound in public support for the institution.[111]

One risk of having former politicians on board is that constitutional courts lose that aura of being technical and independent arbiters of controversial legal-political issues and are instead perceived to be political and politicized actors, due to the nomination of former politicians as judges. As a result, their public approval ratings and trust could plummet. Put differently, high-level politicians might politicize constitutional courts, with detrimental consequences on the public perception of their purported neutrality.

I will mention further below the ongoing issue of dinners and hunting parties attended by apex court judges and sitting members of government in various countries. In order not to bore the reader with repetitive anecdotes, I will describe

[110] Michaela Hailbronner, *Tradition and Transformations. The Rise of German Constitutionalism* (OUP 2015).

[111] George Vanberg, *Constitutional Politics in Germany* (CUP 2005).

but a couple here. The French CC again provides a wealth of examples thanks to the publication of biographies and memoirs by its former members. The fact that many of the Presidents of the CC maintained friendships or political alliances with the President of the Republic is no secret.[112] For instance, Léon Noël, the CC's first President, met regularly with Charles de Gaulle, as is amply demonstrated in his memoirs on the beginnings of the Fifth Republic.[113] Quite tellingly, Gaston Palewski, the second President of the CC, also explained how constrained he and the CC were in interpreting the French Constitution while De Gaulle was still around.[114] As we have already seen in the discussion on the memoirs of the former President of the CC, Jean-Louis Debré, the practice of regular contacts with members of the executive seems to continue today, as much as he also repeatedly stresses the importance of the independence and impartiality of the CC.[115] Again, the French CC may be an outlier in the four jurisdictions analysed here. However, the point is that these former members of government for various personal and professional reasons made contacts during their political careers that did not simply disappear once they joined their respective constitutional courts. These practices potentially damage public trust and support for these institutions.

Public support and perceptions of constitutional courts are (also) reinforced by transparency and rigorous ethics rules. It has long been argued that ethics and trust in public institutions are playing an increasing role, in the sense that the appearance of exercising public functions in an unethical—and for courts, partial—manner generates distrust in institutions.[116] One interviewee stated that: '[t]he most important asset that constitutional courts have is trust, and one can only establish that if one discloses things'.[117] Possibly for this reason, rules of ethics and transparency are increasingly extended to constitutional courts as such public institutions, where they have so far, for different reasons, been exempted from their application.[118] Transparency and ethics for constitutional courts can be guaranteed inter alia in the context of nominations,[119] but also by providing clear and

[112] See Lauréline Fontaine, *La Constitution maltraitée* (Editions Amsterdam 2023) 69–70.

[113] Léon Noël, *De Gaulle et les débuts de la Ve République* (Plon 1976).

[114] Gaston Palewski, *Mémoires d'action. 1924–1974* (Plon 1988) 292.

[115] Jean-Louis Debré, *Ce que je ne pouvais pas dire* (Robert Laffont 2016).

[116] Dennis F Thompson; 'Paradoxes of Government Ethics' (1992) 52 Public Administration Review 254.

[117] Interviewee no 26, 15 November 2023.

[118] More broadly on this notion of public ethics and their application to public institutions, see: Guillaume Tusseau, *La déontologie publique: trajectoire et présence d'une notion ambiguë* (IFJD 2019); more specifically and recently on how ethics and transparency apply to constitutional or supreme courts, see: Elina Lemaire and Thomas Perroud (eds), *Le Conseil constitutionnel à l'épreuve de la déontologie et de la transparence* (IFJD 2022); and Mariana Almeida Kato, *La transparence de la justice constitutionnelle. Une étude de droit comparé (France, Brésil, États-Unis)* (Dalloz 2023).

[119] This was the already mentioned critique for Germany, see: Christine Landfried, 'Die Wahl der Bundesverfassungsrichter und ihre Folgen für die Legitimität der Verfassungsgerichtsbarkeit' in Robert Chr. van Ooyen and Martin HW Möllers, *Das Bundesverfassungsgericht im politischen System* (Verlag für Sozialwissenschaften 2006) 229, 233–34.

transparent rules on abstentions and recusals[120] that will be discussed further below. Moreover, any kind of appearance of wrongdoing—even when nothing has actually and factually been done wrong—must be avoided. This is what has been referred to as the paradox of appearances, whereby '[a]ppearing to do wrong while doing right is really doing wrong', because appearances are often the only way in which citizens can assess official conduct by a public actor.[121] Applying this principle to constitutional courts, whose judges are public officials and actors, gives us reason to think that a failure to take this paradox into account may reduce trust in such institutions.

Of course, *all* constitutional court judges must or should live by the highest ethical standards, not just the former politician judges. The examples provided above seem to indicate that the participation of former politicians as judges on constitutional courts raises specific ethical issues both in quality and in quantity that are not necessarily present for judges from other backgrounds. Therefore, the more former politicians become constitutional judges, the higher the risk that constitutional courts will be perceived by the broader public as more of a political than an impartial judicial body. Moreover, there remain doubts that former politicians can shed their partial political role for an impartial judicial one overnight, and these doubts and questions are increased with every appointment of a former politician as a constitutional court judge.[122]

4.2.5 Practical socio-organizational risks

The participation of former ministers or high-level politicians also poses certain organizational risks, especially if the rules on abstention and recusal are well drafted to take the issue of impartiality into account and/or when single judges take their ethical obligations very seriously. The problem at that point from an organizational perspective is that if a judge abstains or has to abstain regularly from cases because of a potential involvement in a given case or the perception that there is a conflict of interest, this creates a whole set of issues.

First, judges might be excluded from deciding a whole set of cases, with several consequences.[123] The Austrian case illustrates the practical organizational

[120] In this sense, see also: Mariana Almeida Kato, *La transparence de la justice constitutionnelle. Une étude de droit comparé (France, Brésil, États-Unis)* (Dalloz 2023) 333–57.

[121] Dennis F Thompson; 'Paradoxes of Government Ethics' (1992) 52 Public Administration Review 254, 257.

[122] This argument has been raised in conjunction with the nomination of Stephan Harbarth in Germany: Volker Boehme Nessler, 'Politiker als Richter?' *Die Zeit* (Hamburg, 25 December 2018) <https://www.zeit.de/politik/2018-12/rechtsstaat-parteipolitik-wechsel-politiker-verfassungsrichter-bundesverfassungsgericht> accessed 14 April 2023.

[123] This was one argument raised in conjunction with the nomination of Wolfgang Brandstetter in Austria: Renate Graber and Günther Oswald, 'Brandstetter als Verfassungsrichter: "Von der Optik her

difficulties this caused. In fact, due to the rules and practices developed, the former justice minister, Wolfgang Brandstetter, was essentially not hearing any cases, or very few, during the first years of his mandate, let alone being a judge rapporteur. This means that other colleagues need to take up some extra work. In the Austrian case, it also meant that the allocation and planning of cases became more difficult, especially because substitute members had to be called in. This was how the issue was described from the inside:

> As a result, he had to abstain in many cases. It was said that he cannot examine laws where a government bill was passed with his involvement. That is simply not possible. And that affected many cases. So there was a practical problem. A substitute member had to step in very often. At the same time, of course, this prevented him [Brandstetter] from participating in a decision as being specifically biased. But I think it was practically quite complicated to have to call in a substitute member so often.[124]

A slightly different element and practical argument arose from another conversation, namely that the strict abstention and recusal rules that were applied to Brandstetter could also lead to different judicial outcomes:

> This means that the composition of the regular judicial chamber changed more often. This is not such a huge problem, but there is a tendency to keep the composition of the regular judicial chamber stable for important cases, to avoid different outcomes in similar cases.[125]

Apart from these practical aspects, another consequence of abstentions and recusals that apply to former politicians could lead to the scenario that the minimum quorum for taking a valid decision is not reached. As we have already seen above in Chapter 2.2.2, this risk is being cited, amongst others, in Italy to justify the prohibition of rules on abstentions and recusals for the C cost. The truth is that the greater risk of not reaching the minimum quorum stems from the fact that in Italy, parliamentary nominations notoriously are often considerably delayed, thus reducing the numbers of judges.

A similar observation can be made in France. Here arguably the failure to reach the minimum quorum is not taken very seriously in the first place,[126] and secondly

ein Wahnsinn"' *Der Standard* (Vienna, 6 February 2018) <https://www.derstandard.at/story/2000073694277/brandstetter-als-verfassungsrichter-von-der-optik-her-ein-wahnsinn> accessed 7 April 2023.

[124] Interviewee no 29, 5 December 2023.

[125] Interviewee no 22, 12 September 2023.

[126] See most recently on this issue: Jérémy Martinez, 'L'absence de quorum dans la QPC François Fillon: les tourments de la "juridictionnalisation" du Conseil constitutionnel' (*JP Blog*, 8 November

the problems in the CC's functioning due to the absence of certain CC members are rather caused by resignations or deaths of members and a failure to promptly nominate new ones, rather than by the rules on abstentions and recusals.[127]

The argument that well-functioning rules on abstentions and recusals could paralyse a constitutional court is not convincing, and rather speaks to technical solutions that need to be adapted to foresee any lack of quorum, in general. As we have seen, the structure of the BVerfG allows it to select judges from the other Senate to sit as substitutes. The Austrian system established substitute members from the beginning, something that could be thought of also for France and Italy. As a last resort, one could think of ad hoc solutions, as was the case in the United States, when the USSC could not reach a minimum quorum due to the abstentions of several judges and Congress passed a special statute assigning the case to the US Court of Appeals of the Second Circuit.[128] While such ad hoc solutions bear their own risks of manipulation, the point is rather that the argument that courts could be blocked via abstention and recusal rules is rather a practical obstacle than a theoretically unsurmountable hurdle and thus does not fully justify why such rules should not be introduced in the first place.

Another practical risk comes from a somewhat different angle. Former high-level politicians might see the constitutional court as just a stepping stone or placeholder in their political career. A consequence of this could be a negative effect on the image and stability of the institution. Some of the information here is necessarily anecdotal. Nevertheless, Dominique Schnapper's sociological analysis indicated that often the CC's 'politicians' perceived their presence at the Conseil as a 'downgrading' from their status,[129] indicating a potential willingness to leave the institution sooner rather than later to move to more politically, more visible, prestigious, or powerful positions.

Here it is interesting to note cases where constitutional court judges left the institution *prior* to the expiration of their judicial mandate to pick up political positions. Examples of this can be found in France and Italy. As to France, Georges Pompidou left the CC after only three years to take up the office of Prime Minister in 1962, and later still became President of France. In 1967, Edmond Michelet left the CC because he was elected as parliamentarian. Many years later, Nicole Belloubet left the CC prior to the expiration of her mandate to become Justice

2023) <https://blog.juspoliticum.com/2023/11/08/labsence-de-quorum-dans-la-qpc-francois-fillon-les-tourments-de-la-juridictionnalisation-du-conseil-constitutionnel-par-jeremy-martinez/> accessed 11 November 2023.

[127] See on this in detail: Alexia David, 'L'impartialité du Conseil constitutionnel' (DPhil, Normandie Université, 2021) 400–01 <https://normandie-univ.hal.science/tel-03331880v2/file/sygal_fusion_27488-david-alexia.pdf> accessed 12 October 2023.

[128] *United States v Alcoa*, 148 F 2d 416 (2d Cir 1945).

[129] Dominique Schnapper, *Une sociologue au Conseil constitutionnel* (Gallimard 2010) 157–72.

Minister. In Italy, one could mention Sergio Mattarella who had previously been a minister and later left the C cost to become President. In Germany, this seems unthinkable, as indicated by one of the interviewees:

> It would be completely inconceivable to simply stop your mandate [as constitutional judge], in order to make a [professional] change. That never happened. Sometimes someone leaves earlier due to illness, but in principle it goes without saying that the mandate will be finished.[130]

Outside of the jurisdictions analysed in detail here, one could mention the example of Portugal, where Antonio Vitorino was appointed to the Portuguese constitutional court in 1989 at 32 years of age, only to resign five years later in 1994 for a political mandate and after that becoming a minister.[131]

Of course, resignations can happen for many different reasons, but if a constitutional court is perceived as a simple step on a political career ladder, rather than the final rung, this causes additional practical problems. This is particularly true if nomination procedures are not always swift, as is notoriously the case in Italy for judges named by parliament, or in Spain for judges named from the judicial level. Hence, there is a risk that such personalities dropping out before the end of their mandate will cause issues as regards the minimum quorum for judicial decisions but also for the allocation of the workload among judges and other such issues.

As already mentioned above, the advantage of having seasoned and experienced politicians is that they have nothing to fear, and nothing to hope for. Their generally advanced age seems to act as a partial safeguard against politicians using a position on the constitutional court as a mid-career stepping stone. However, age and experience criteria also have a dark side. One former judge in Italy mentioned that those judges coming from a long political career needed time to return to a professional working mode and to leave their networking mentality—typical of the political milieu—behind.[132] As to France, the reformed—almost revolutionized—competences of the French CC have changed the job description quite a bit and the work load for its members has increased accordingly. However, the average age of the French constitutional judges has not changed accordingly, leading to very carefully framed doubts as to whether all judges can actually shoulder the increased responsibilities and work load.[133]

[130] Interviewee no 34, 22 February 2024.

[131] See on these biographical details: <https://institutdelors.eu/en/tous-les-contributeurs/vitorino-antonio/> accessed 11 November 2023.

[132] Ugo de Siervo, 'Riflessioni su un'esperienza di lavoro alla Corte costituzionale' (2006) 11 Giornale di storia costituzionale 81, 84. That is not to say that the constitutional judges with backgrounds as professors or judges do not have their own drawbacks.

[133] Interviewee no 8, 21 March 2023.

Another element that is the flip side of the coin of a benefit is that the greater public visibility and status that former politicians bring to constitutional courts also increases the chances of negative 'publicity'. Are former politicians more involved in judicial and political scandals than non-politicians? The answer to this question is not unambiguous. But it is probable that due to their previous public roles, when scandals or controversies do occur, they will be all the more visible. The comparative glance at the four systems seems to demonstrate that what may look anecdotal at the national level becomes less so when seen alongside anecdotes from the other jurisdictions. I am not claiming to provide an overall and exhaustive empirical study of scandals or controversies. I will leave it to the critical reader to reach their own conclusions. One thing, however, is sure: these events are 'potential reputation and "trust depleters"'.[134]

Certainly, one can distinguish between controversies at the nomination stage and those following appointments to the relevant constitutional court. Given that I have already presented some of the controversies arising at the nomination stage above, I will focus on controversies or scandals that have arisen while such personalities were sitting constitutional judges.

In fact, quite a few of the 'political' judges have found themselves at the heart of political scandals during their mandate, thereby confirming some of the misgivings that had arisen during the nomination stage. The most prominent example is Wolfgang Brandstetter in Austria, who was involved in a series of scandals that confirmed some of the misgivings that had arisen in the course of his nomination. In fact, due to a number of separate criminal inquiries, his electronic communications with various individuals were made public. In the first inquiry, his possible role in tipping off a businessman friend about a planned search of his house as part of a corruption investigation did not induce him to resign from the VfGH.[135] A second exchange of messages that went public was with a high-level official in the Justice Ministry, Christian Pilnacek, who hailed from the same political party. Those messages revolved around a news item about a plan to deliver Austrian refuse trucks to Cuba. Pilnacek commented that one might just as well transfer the whole VfGH to Cuba, which would be happy to receive the Vice-President of the VfGH.[136] He also wrote to Brandstetter that another female member of the VfGH would make a great refuse lady (*Müllfrau*). The fact that Brandstetter did not react

[134] John B Thompson, *Political Scandal: Power and Visibility in the Media Age* (Polity Press 2000) 252.

[135] Theodor Anders and Fabian Schmidt, 'MS vor Hausdurchsuchung. Ex-Minister Brandstetter an Investor Tojner: "Wenn die heute kommen: ganz ruhig bleiben"' *Der Standard* (Vienna, 27 February 2021) <https://www.derstandard.at/story/2000124524659/ex-minister-brandstetter-an-investor-tojner-wenn-die-heute-kommen> accessed 21 December 2022.

[136] The not very veiled reference was to Verena Madner, the Vice-President of the VfGH who also happens to be a woman of colour. <https://www.vfgh.gv.at/verfassungsgerichtshof/verfassungsrichter/Verena_Madner.en.html> accessed 21 December 2022.

in a critical way to these disparaging messages about his colleagues was the straw that broke the camel's back, eventually leading to his (voluntary) resignation.[137]

In Italy, the first example of a constitutional judge resigning voluntarily was Enrico De Nicola, first President of the C cost and provisional head of state, allegedly due to some internal conflict at the C cost.[138] Much more problematic Italian anecdotes include a dinner organized by the constitutional court judge Luigi Mazzella at his home in June 2009, where then Prime Minister Silvio Berlusconi and Justice Minister Angelino Alfano were guests. The incident caused quite a few public and academic ripples. Mazzella had been minister under Berlusconi, and the dinner took place at the same time as the constitutionality of a particular piece of legislation was being discussed at the C cost. This legislation had been proposed by Alfano (it was even called 'Lodo Alfano') and it would have insulated Prime Minister Berlusconi from ongoing criminal prosecution,[139] though the legislation was eventually struck down as unconstitutional.[140]

France's CC members hailing from the political branches have been at the heart of some of the CC's biggest scandals and controversies during their mandate. First and foremost, one must mention the resignation of Roland Dumas, at the time President of the CC, who had dragged 'his' institution into a difficult situation.[141] As we have already seen, there have been other resignations from the CC that took place mostly due to members taking on other (political) roles. In the case of Dumas, instead, it was a criminal inquiry into whether he had contributed to concealing the misuse of corporate assets that led to his resignation. He was suspected to have (ab)used his position as Foreign Minister to secure the employment of his former lover, Christine Deviers-Joncour, at the large French oil company, Elf-Aquitaine, as well as to have personally benefited from a portion of the (large) salaries and

[137] On this story, see: Renate Graber and Fabian Schmidt, 'Posten, Fouls und Verfassungsrichterinnen als Müllfrauen in Pilnaceks Chats' *Der Standard* (Vienna, 2 June 2021) <https://www.derstandard.at/story/2000127094571/posten-fouls-und-verfassungsrichterinnen-als-muellfrauen-in-pilnaceks-chats> accessed 21 December 2022; and 'Wolfgang Brandstetter zieht sich als Verfassungsrichter zurück' *Der Standard* (Vienna, 3 June 2021) <https://www.derstandard.at/story/2000127133522/wolfgang-brandstetter-tritt-als-verfassungsrichter-zurueck> accessed 21 December 2022.

[138] See on this: Gustavo Zagrebelsky, *Principî e voti* (Einaudi 2005) 65. An interesting debate arose with regard to De Nicola, who as a former President of Italy was also de jure senator for life. Was this compatible with his role as a constitutional judge, or could/would he need to resign or suspend his role as senator? See, on this debate which ultimately became moot: Amedeo Giannini, 'Ineleggibilità ed incompatibilità dei giudici costituzionali' (1956) 5–6 Il Consiglio di Stato 5, 7.

[139] On the details of this affair, see: Alessio Rauti, 'Riflessioni in tema di imparzialità dei giudici costituzionali' (2009) LIV Giurisprudenza costituzionale 4029, 4040–41 and Alessandro Morelli, 'La Corte imparziale e i suoi nemici. L'inapplicabilità nei giudizi costituzionali delle norme sull'astensione e la ricusazione dei giudici' (2009) Forum dei quaderni costituzionali 1–2 <https://www.forumcostituzionale.it/wordpress/images/stories/pdf/documenti_forum/temi_attualita/corte_costituzionale/0004_morelli.pdf> accessed 12 January 2023.

[140] C cost, sentenza no 262/2009 of 7 October 2009.

[141] How the long shadow of this scandal still hovers over the institution became clear also from the interviews during which two interviewees (interviewees nos 4 and 5) referred to it in some depth during the conversation.

commissions paid by Elf to her.[142] After initially voluntarily suspending his functions as President of the CC, he eventually resigned, for ethical rather than strictly legal reasons—he was ultimately declared innocent—and the initiation of the CC's internal exclusion procedure was thereby avoided. Had it not been resolved by his resignation, this scandal could have had even greater repercussions on the CC.[143]

The perception of independence and impartiality was also linked to another example of voluntary suspension of one's functions (*congé*)—a practice without any foundation in law—in a less egregious controversy involving Simone Veil. The former minister had been the first President of the European Parliament (EP), and she suspended her membership at the CC while she took part in the pro-Europe campaign for France's ratification of the European Constitutional Treaty in 2005. This led to difficult questions being asked about the independence and impartiality of the CC and its members.[144]

Nothing in the preceding paragraphs is meant to imply that non-political judges are not also involved in controversies or scandals of their own. Again, some of the admittedly anecdotal evidence shows that over the years, there have been various issues involving them, too. In Germany, Gerhard Leibholz, judge at the BVerfG from 1951 to 1971, was allegedly almost forced to resign for copying a passage from his earlier work into a BVerfG judgment on electoral matters.[145] Another former BVerfG judge, Helmut Simon, mentions two situations involving his daughter's alleged political actions and friendships that had become public and almost led to his resignation as constitutional judge, and could have prevented his re-election.[146]

More recently, a dinner of some judges of the BVerfG with members of the German government raised public eyebrows,[147] unsuccessful recusal requests, and also led to academic analyses on the practice of informality, including such dinners at the BVerfG.[148]

Moving to Italy, the above-mentioned dinner at Judge Mazzella's home was also attended by a non-political judge, Paolo Maria Napolitano. Open doubts over

[142] 'Roland Dumas doit-il démissioner?' *Nouvel Observateur* (Paris, 22 February 2000) <https://www.nouvelobs.com/societe/20000221.OBS2216/roland-dumas-doit-il-demissionner.html> accessed 22 December 2022.

[143] On the details of this story as well as the 'internal' difficulties the CC had to face in that situation, see: Jacques Robert, *La garde de la République. Le Conseil constitutionnel raconté par l'un de ses membres* (Plon 2000) 145–53 and Patrick Wachsmann, 'Sur la composition du Conseil constitutionnel' (2010) Jus Politicum 30–31 <http://juspoliticum.com/article/Sur-la-composition-du-Conseil-constitutionnel-294.html> accessed 22 December 2022.

[144] ibid Wachsmann 31.

[145] See on this: Gustavo Zagrebelsky, *Principî e voti* (Einaudi 2005) 101.

[146] Helmut Simon, *Leben zwischen den Zeiten* (Nomos 2020) 115–16.

[147] See on this: Marlene Grunert, 'Ein Abendessen mit Nebenwirkungen' *Frankfurter Allgemeine Zeitung* (Frankfurt a M, 18 October 2021) <https://www.faz.net/aktuell/politik/inland/corona-notbremse-vor-bundesverfassungsgericht-antrag-abgelehnt-17590738.html> accessed 21 December 2022.

[148] Silvia Steininger, 'Talks, Dinners, and Envelopes at Nightfall: The Politicization of Informality at the Bundesverfassungsgericht' (2023) 24 German Law Journal 1300.

the impartiality also hovered over two other 'non-political' Italian constitutional judges, Carlo Mezzanotte and Romano Vaccarella, who had both represented Prime Minister Silvio Berlusconi's companies as their lawyers and had been declared 'close' to him.[149] Like Giuseppe Ferrari in 1987, Vaccarella resigned from his mandate in 2007; both allegedly due to political pressure.[150]

Last but not least, also in Austria, the public statements made by Johannes Schnizer concerning a ruling by the VfGH which led to the cancellation of the run-off election for the federal presidency had attracted public criticism to him and the VfGH.[151]

Arguably, the discussions around the impartiality and/or secrecy of deliberations concerning non-political constitutional court judges are less visible and revolve around somewhat different topics. For (former) university professors, it is interviews, public declarations, or publications on subject matters they had dealt with before becoming constitutional judge or also after they ceased to be one. For (former) judges, it is that they may have been involved in the same or a related matter prior to coming to the constitutional court. So, the issues giving rise to abstentions or recusal requests are less blatantly related to politics or separation of powers, and possibly more related to issues of etiquette. Examples include the regular public interventions by former President of the C cost, Antonio Baldassarre,[152] or an interview published in a major German newspaper which led to the recusal decision of BVerfG judge, Astrid Wallrabenstein.[153] But in many situations, especially in Austria, France, and Italy, such situations are handled discreetly with constitutional judges simply abstaining and not being involved in a given judgment. Some examples that emerged during the interviews will be mentioned below under Chapter 6.3 when describing the practices of abstentions, especially in Austria, Italy, and France. At times, even in the three systems mentioned, these abstentions become public. Just to provide one example, in the early 2000s a famous judicial saga around the issue of whether parents of a severely disabled child could claim wrongful life damages for medical error from doctors shook France. Without entering into the details of the whole complex litigation history, the case had ended before the French C Cass which had ruled in favour

[149] See: Antonio Ruggeri and Antonino Spadaro, *Lineamenti di giustizia costituzionale* (Giappichelli 2014) 59.

[150] In the case of Giuseppe Ferrari, those pressures allegedly took place around the elections he lost to become President of the C cost. See on this: Carla Rodotà, *Storia della Corte costituzionale* (Laterza 1999) 105–07. In the case of Romano Vaccarella, a former lawyer of Silvio Berlusconi, the presumed pressures occurred around the vote on a referendum. See: Alessio Rauti, 'Riflessioni in tema di imparzialità dei giudici costituzionali' (2009) LIV Giurisprudenza costituzionale 4029, 4040.

[151] On this matter, see: Alexander Somek, 'Das Hohe und das Menschliche: eine Anmerkung zur Affäre Schnizer' (*VerfBlog*, 3 October 2016) https://verfassungsblog.de/das-hohe-und-das-menschliche-eine-anmerkung-zur-affaere-schnizer accessed 26 August 2024.

[152] Carla Rodotà, *Storia della Corte costituzionale* (Laterza 1999) 121–23.

[153] BVerfG, 2 BvR 2006/15, 12 January 2021, ECLI:DE:BVerfG:2021:rs20210112.2bvr200615.

of the plaintiffs and of which Guy Canivet had been judge at the time.[154] When years later legislation that had partly 'overruled' the C Cass's decision ended up before the CC, Canivet abstained, given his previous involvement as a supreme court judge in the underlying issue.[155]

Put differently, scandals or controversies are not the monopoly of former high-level politicians in constitutional courts. However, the 'political' judges tend to be more visible, possibly have more high-level political acquaintances and consequently probably draw (more) public attention to their past and present actions.[156] Moreover, without providing definitive answers on whether these 'political' judges are numerically or proportionally more involved in such controversies or scandals than non-political ones, there seems to be a difference in the 'quality' and seriousness of the respective issues present amongst these two groups. All of this may have repercussions on constitutional courts and how the public perceives them.

Overall, readers will assess for themselves whether, in their view, the benefits or risks of having ex-ministers on constitutional courts prevail. My intent here is not to cast *ad hominem* or *ad feminam* aspersions, nor to prescribe an ideal about how constitutional courts ought to operate. The question is simply whether and how the practice of having former ministers as guardians of the Constitution positively or negatively affects constitutional courts. Do these anecdotes and stories coupled with the theoretical principles of separation of powers, independence, impartiality, and public trust justify the practice?

Such an assessment would not be complete without looking at the international level. I will next turn to an analysis of the supranational level for an additional assessment of the issue.

[154] C Cass (Plenary), no 99-13.701, 17 November 2001. The case and the whole issue became known by the family name *Perruche*. For an overview in English, see: Cécile Manaouil, Maxime Gignon, and Olivier Jardé, '10 Years of Controversy, Twists and Turns in the Perruche Wrongful Life Claim: Compensation for Children Born with a Disability in France' (2012) 31 Medicine and Law 661.

[155] Dominique Rousseau, 'Le procès constitutionnel' (2011) 137 Pouvoirs 47, 53.

[156] This observation also includes legal-political scandals preceding the time that some individuals joined their respective constitutional courts, raising the additional question of what such baggage brings to these courts in terms of ethical, moral and social requirements. See the example of former Prime Minister, Alain Juppé, now a member of the CC, who had been found guilty of illegal campaign financing of the Gaullist party in 2004. On this, see: Antoine Vauchez, 'Judicialization: A sociohistorical perspective (lessons and questions from the French Fifth Republic)' in Mikael Rask Madsen and Chris Thornhill (eds), *Law and the Formation of Modern Europe. Perspectives from the Historical Sociology of Law* (CUP 2014) 96.

5

Supranational Requirements and Standards

In addition to the weighing of the pros and cons of appointing former members of government as constitutional judges, supranational standards must also be taken into consideration when analysing certain issues that were discussed in the previous chapter, especially with regard to European constitutional courts.

Indeed, over recent years, the CJEU, ECtHR, and other supranational bodies have issued binding judgments and non-binding standards that have implications for the practice of ex-ministers becoming constitutional judges, especially in light of the previously discussed risks attendant thereto. For a large part, these supranational institutions have yet to directly address this question.

The first set of issues dealt with in this chapter relate to the risk of (over-or mono-)politicization of (constitutional) courts (section 5.1). The second set of issues concerns whether the rules and practices on abstentions and recusals discussed above are in line with the case law on the right to a fair trial, as elaborated by the ECtHR in particular (section 5.2).

5.1 Politicization

We have already seen how the presence of former politicians can politicize constitutional courts and, if there are too many, may even over-politicize them. In that sense, the potential danger is that such courts may come to be perceived not as impartial or independent institutions, but instead as 'just another' political body. This risk is particularly high if constitutional judges all hail from a single party, or from a narrow range on the political spectrum, and constitutional courts thereby end up lacking political diversity and representativeness because they are mono-politicized.[1]

So far, the phenomenon of the judicialization of politics as understood in this book has led to neither open debates or accusations of (over-)politicization nor of (mono-)politicization. That does not mean that the four constitutional courts considered here have not gone through periods where their judges were cut from the same political cloth, so to speak. Again, the French CC stands out amongst the

[1] See recently on this: Gertrude Lübbe-Wolff, 'One-sidedly Staffed Courts: A Problem of Impartiality – not only in Poland' (*VerfBlog*, 8 January 2024) <https://verfassungsblog.de/one-sidedly-staffed-courts/> accessed 9 January 2024.

Ex-Ministers as Constitutional Judges. Mathias Möschel, Oxford University Press. © Mathias Möschel 2025.
DOI: 10.1093/9780198930228.003.0005

systems under scrutiny. From its creation in 1958 through to 1983, and again in the years 1995–97 and 2002–12, the French CC was composed exclusively of members from the right of the political spectrum.[2]

The recent rise of illiberal regimes and (constitutional) court capture raises questions about how long the situation will remain as it is, both in countries where politically one-sided constitutional courts have not yet existed, but also in France, where the possibility of another period of exclusively right-wing CC membership cannot be excluded. Even if such a situation never actually arises, it is nonetheless important to consider the potential limitations that supranational law may place on the (over- or mono-)politicization of constitutional courts when their membership is composed—be it partially or completely—of former high-level politicians.

I will first look at the standards elaborated under EU law (subsection 5.1.1) before moving on to those decided or elaborated by bodies of the Council of Europe (subsection 5.1.2).

5.1.1 European Union law

All four countries analysed in this book are part of the EU and their constitutional systems are thus subject to the limitations to sovereignty that EU membership entails. Discussions about the not always harmonious relations between national constitutional courts and the CJEU go well beyond the scope of this book.[3] Recently, a new dimension has been added to those relations with regard to the issue of deliberately instituted rule-of-law backsliding, put into effect via various legislative and constitutional reforms in countries such as Hungary, Poland, and Romania. This issue has opened a new field in the development of EU and comparative constitutional (law) studies which aims to ascertain the extent to which the EU can and will go to address their concerns about constitutional backsliding and illiberalism in certain Member States.[4]

The European Commission (EC) and the CJEU in particular have been at the forefront of interventions in this field and have strengthened political and judicial scrutiny from mere formal checks to far more substantive analysis. However,

[2] Guillaume Tusseau, *Contentieux constitutionnel comparé* (LGDJ 2021) 485–86.

[3] See on this: Monica Claes, 'Luxembourg, Here We Come? Constitutional Courts and the Preliminary Reference Procedure' (2015) 16 German Law Journal 1331.

[4] Today, the literature on this subject in law and political sciences is immense. For some examples of books, see: András Jakab and Dimitry Kochenov (eds), *The Enforcement of EU Law and Values* (OUP 2017); Wojciech Sadurski, *Poland's Constitutional Breakdown* (OUP 2019); Astrid Lorenz and Lisa H Anders (eds), *Illiberal Trends and Anti-EU Politics in East Central Europe* (Palgrave Macmillan 2021); Tímea Drinóczi and Agnieszka Bień-Kacała, *Illiberal Constitutionalism in Poland and Hungary: The Deterioration of Democracy, Misuse of Human Rights and Abuse of the Rule of Law* (Routledge 2022); Martin Krygier, Adam Czarnota, and Wojciech Sadurski (eds), *Anti-Constitutional Populism* (CUP 2022); and Petra Bárd, *Rule of Law: Sustainability and Mutual Trust in a Transforming Europe* (Eleven 2023).

these initiatives have not yet involved any cases dealing directly with the question of former ministers becoming constitutional judges in connection with the aforementioned problem of rule of law backsliding. Many such judgments have instead dealt with broader judicial reforms that do not always directly involve national constitutional courts. I posit that the case law that is being developed could in future become applicable if too many former politicians join a particular constitutional court. Whenever the (over- or mono-)politicization of constitutional courts takes place as part of a broader rule of law backsliding process, it may be deemed problematic from an EU law perspective in light of the actions and case law that will be described below. Their description is merely intended to be an outline of an ongoing trend toward a more sustained control of national judicial rules and is not supposed to be an in-depth case-by-case analysis because the relevance of such cases to the object of this book's study is, at this point, largely hypothetical.

In terms of primary EU law, the relevant provisions are Article 2 of the Treaty on the European Union (TEU), which stipulates that the EU 'is founded on the values of respect for human dignity, freedom, democracy, equality, the *rule of law* and respect for human rights, including the rights of persons belonging to minorities'.[5] Article 7 TEU establishes procedures whereby the Council of the EU may determine, as a first step, that there is a clear risk of a serious breach of the values enshrined in Article 2 TEU by a Member State, and they may issue recommendations on that basis.[6] As a second step, the Council of the EU may determine the existence of a serious breach of the values enshrined in Article 2 TEU, and on this basis they may ask the Member State concerned for observations and thereafter, they suspend certain rights of that state.[7] Moreover, Article 19 TEU provides that 'Member States shall provide remedies sufficient to ensure effective legal protection in the fields covered by Union law'.[8]

Article 47 of the Charter of Fundamental Rights of the European Union (EUCFR) establishes the right to an effective remedy and to a fair trial, stipulating that '[e]veryone is entitled to a fair and public hearing within a reasonable time by an *independent and impartial tribunal* previously established by law'.[9]

Secondary EU law has begun to provide detailed integrations to some of these rather generic provisions. In particular, the new rules on the EU budget being 'conditional' (ie contingent) on Member States' respect of rule of law deserve mention.[10]

[5] Art 2 TEU (emphasis added).
[6] Art 7 TEU, para 1.
[7] Art 7 TEU, paras 2 and 3.
[8] Art 19 TEU, para 1, second subpara.
[9] Art 47 TFEU, para 2 (emphasis added).
[10] Regulation (EU, Euratom) 2020/2092 of the European Parliament and of the Council of 16 December 2020 on a general regime of conditionality for the protection of the Union budget [2020] OJ L 433I/1–10. This instrument's validity was challenged by both Hungary and Poland, with the CJEU rejecting both cases: CJEU (Full Court), Case C-156/21 *Hungary v European Parliament and the Council of European Union* ECLI:EU:C:2022:97 (16 February 2022) and Case C-157/21 (Full Court), *Poland v European Parliament and the Council of European Union* ECLI:EU:C:2022:98 (16 February 2022).

Rule of law is defined as 'the principles of legality implying a transparent, accountable, democratic and pluralistic law-making process; legal certainty; prohibition of arbitrariness of the executive powers; *effective judicial protection, including access to justice, by independent and impartial courts, also as regards fundamental rights; separation of powers*; and non-discrimination and equality before the law'.[11] A breach of the rule of law can be identified through various criteria, which include 'endangering the independence of the judiciary'.[12]

These primary and secondary EU law provisions have been 'operationalized' by both the EC and the CJEU. There are some serious and well-founded doubts about the efficacy of these mechanisms and of the reach of the CJEU's case law.[13] Despite all these shortcomings, it is worth delving into these cases for the purposes of this book.

Early attempts to challenge rule of law backsliding failed to address questionable judicial reforms head-on, and instead approached the problem in a rather oblique way. The best example of this is a 2012 judgment concerning a judicial reform in Hungary which forced many prosecutors and judges into early retirement, presumably because they were perceived to be hostile to the constitutional and statutory reforms which Viktor Orbán's then new 2010 government intended to carry out.[14] While the CJEU was able to find a violation of EU law, it did not find a breach of the primary or secondary rule of law provisions mentioned above, but instead a violation of the age discrimination rules contained within Directive 2000/78/EC.[15] The CJEU only started directly addressing questions of rule of law and judicial independence as a matter of EU law since the *Portuguese Judges* case,[16] where the crucial link between Article 19(1) and Article 2 TEU first entered judicial cognizance.

It was only in response to Poland's judicial reforms, which took place in the context of rule of law backsliding, that EU institutional control of Member State judiciaries became more substantial and thus potentially more relevant to the object of this book's study. Without rehashing the details of this so-called 'constitutional breakdown',[17] the gist is that a number of judicial reforms initiated by the

[11] Art 2, para (a) of Regulation 2020/2092 (emphasis added).

[12] Art 3, para (a) of Regulation 2020/2092.

[13] Considering the now rather vast literature on the topic, I will limit myself to citing Petra Bárd, 'In Courts We Trust, or Should We? Judicial Independence as the Precondition for the Effectiveness of EU Law' (2021) 27 European LJ 185.

[14] CJEU, Case C-286/12 *European Commission v Hungary* ECLI:EU:C:2012:687 (6 November 2012).

[15] Council Directive 2000/78/EC of 27 November 2000 establishing a general framework for equal treatment in employment and occupation [2000] OJ L 303/16–22.

[16] CJEU (GC), Case C-64/16 *Associaçao Sindical dos Juízes Portugueses* ECLI:EU:C:208:117 (28 February 2018). For commentary on this issue, see: Matteo Bonelli and Monica Claes, 'Judicial Serendipity: How Portuguese Judges Came to the Rescue of the Polish Judiciary' (2018) 14 EU Cons L Rev 622; and Laurent Pech and Sébastien Platon, 'Judicial Independence Under Threat: The Court of Justice to the Rescue in the ASJP Case' [2018] CMLR 1827.

[17] For elucidation on the meaning of this impression and a detailed critique of the Polish rule of law crisis, see: Wojciech Sadurski, *Poland's Constitutional Breakdown* (OUP 2019).

incumbent populist Law and Justice Party (*Prawo i Sprawiedliwość*, also known as *PiS)* targeted the Polish Constitutional Court (the *Trybunał Konstytucyjny*—TK), in order to capture it and/or obstruct it from effectively functioning as the guardian of the constitution. Various aspects of these reforms were then challenged internally but also supranationally.

Apart from the initiation of a series of infringement procedures before the CJEU that are discussed below, the EC also triggered the Article 7(1) TEU procedure against Poland.[18] However, little progress has been made on this front, and even less is expected of the more forceful procedure established under Article 7(2) and (3) TEU that allows the suspension of certain Member State rights. Part of the reason for this is a lack of political will and also the very high majorities—and even unanimity—that some steps in the procedure require.[19] In terms of results, the infringement procedures brought before the CJEU by various actors have been comparatively successful.

The first case directly addressing the question of whether Polish judicial institutions in general remained independent and impartial was initiated by an Irish preliminary reference. The question was whether a European arrest warrant for an individual in Ireland issued by the Polish courts could or should be rejected on the basis of Polish courts' lack of independence and impartiality. The CJEU essentially held that a refusal to comply with a European arrest warrant is possible only if there 'is a real risk of [a] breach of the fundamental right to a fair trial guaranteed by the second paragraph of Article 47 EUCFR, on account of systemic or generalised deficiencies so far as concerns the independence of the issuing Member State's judiciary'.[20] What is relevant in this judgment is that the CJEU explicitly linked the fundamental rights aspect under Article 47 EUCFR to the question of rule of law enshrined in Article 7 TEU, even though it ultimately allowed the Irish courts to make the final determination in the case at hand.[21]

A second case dealt with reforms to the National Judicial Council and the impossibility of lodging appeals against decisions to propose or not propose specific candidates for appointments to positions as judges at the Polish Supreme Court. Whereas the CJEU mainly relied on Article 19 TEU to find a violation of EU law, in this case, it also used the principle of sincere cooperation enshrined in Article 4(3) TEU to do so.[22]

[18] See on this: <https://ec.europa.eu/commission/presscorner/detail/en/ip_21_7070> accessed 28 September 2023. A separate attempt to trigger Art 7(1) was started by the European Parliament (EP) in 2018, with little success. See on some details of this action that was challenged before the CJEU by Hungary: CJEU (GC) Case C-650/18 *Hungary v European Parliament* ECLI:EU:C:2021:426 (3 June 2021).

[19] For a recent in-depth analysis on the political obstacles to these actions against Poland and Hungary, see: Gráinne de Búrca, 'Poland and Hungary's EU Membership: On Not Confronting Authoritarian Governments' (2022) 20 ICON 13.

[20] CJEU (GC), Case C-216/18 PPU *LM* ECLI:EU:C:2018:586 (25 July 2018), main holding.

[21] This linkage had not been made in AG Tanchev's opinion: ibid ECLI:EU:C:2018:517 (28 June 2018). See on this: Wojciech Sadurski, *Poland's Constitutional Breakdown* (OUP 2019) 202–08.

[22] CJEU (GC), Case C-824/18 *AB and Others* ECLI:EU:C:2021:153 (2 March 2021).

A third case addressed legislation that gave the Polish Justice Minister the power to assign a judge to a higher criminal court without any publicly available criteria and without any possibility of the secondment being challenged. Moreover, these secondments could be terminated by the same minister without any predefined criteria or justification. The CJEU held that this violated inter alia Article 19 TEU read in light of Article 2 TEU.[23]

More recently in yet another Grand Chamber decision by the CJEU,[24] the action initiated by the European Commission (EC) concerned a 2019 statute which conferred disciplinary competence over the judiciary to the Disciplinary Chamber of the Polish Supreme Court, a chamber whose independence and impartiality were not guaranteed. Moreover, the same statute made it a disciplinary offence for ordinary judges to examine the compliance of Polish laws with EU requirements for independent and impartial tribunals, and instead mandated that all such matters be transferred to another special chamber of the Polish Supreme Court for consideration. The CJEU found all this to be in violation of Article 19, para 1 TEU and of Article 47 EUCFR.[25]

A few Romanian cases are also relevant to this chapter's discussion, especially because they involved the Romanian Constitutional Court (*Curtea Constituțională a României*—CCR). The background to those cases is fairly similar to the Polish cases. In view of its accession to the EU, Romania had adopted legislation in 2004 to reform its judicial system with the goal of improving the independence and effectiveness thereof. Between 2017 and 2019, various amendments were made to those statutes whose compatibility with EU law was being questioned by lower court judges via the preliminary reference procedure.

In the first judgment that arose from these preliminary references, the CJEU essentially had to ascertain how far some of these reforms conformed with Decision 2006/928,[26] a monitoring mechanism established for the Romanian judicial reforms and the fight against corruption that had been established prior to Romania's accession to the EU.[27] This last instrument is worth mentioning because

[23] CJEU (GC), Joined Cases C-748/19 to C-754/19 *WB and Others* ECLI:EU:C:2021:931 (16 November 2021).

[24] CJEU (GC), Case C-204/21 *European Commission v Republic of Poland* ECLI:EU:C:2023:442 (5 June 2023).

[25] Not all judgments involving Poland and its justice system were found to be violating EU law. See eg: CJEU (GC), Case C-132/20 *BN and Others v Getin Noble Bank SA* ECLI:EU:C:2022:235 (29 March 2022).

[26] Commission Decision of 13 December 2006 establishing a mechanism for cooperation and verification of progress in Romania to address specific benchmarks in the areas of judicial reform and the fight against corruption [2006] OJ L354/56.

[27] CJEU (GC), Joined Cases C-83/19, C-127/19, C-195/19, C-291/19, C-355/19, and C-397/19 *Asociația Forumul Judecătorilor din România* ECLI:EU:C:2021:393 (18 May 2021). For a first comment on this judgment, see: Madalina Moraru and Raluca Bercea, 'The First Episode in the Romanian Rule of Law Saga: Joined Cases C-83/19, C-127/19, C-195/19, C-291/19, C-355/19 and C-397/19, Asociația 'Forumul Judecătorilor din România, and Their Follow-up at the National Level' (2022) 18 European Constitutional L Rev 82.

it stipulated that the pre-accession monitoring of Romania's judicial independence would continue even after Romania's accession. In essence, the CJEU held that various judicial reforms, including the disciplinary regime applicable to judges, the financial liability of the state, and the personal liability of judges as a result of judicial error, were precluded by Decision 2006/928 and the principle of the primacy of EU law.

A second set of cases more directly involved the CCR.[28] Charges of corruption and the misuse of EU funds levelled against several Romanian politicians had been dropped thanks to a series of judgments by the CCR, and judges who disregarded the CCR's judgments faced potential disciplinary sanctions. Most importantly for the purposes of this book, by drawing upon existing case law, the CJEU stated that 'although the organisation of justice in the Member States, including the establishment, composition and functioning of a constitutional court, falls within the competence of those Member States, they are nonetheless required, when exercising that competence, to comply with their obligations deriving from EU law'.[29] The CJEU agreed that nothing in EU law prevents Member State constitutional court decisions being binding on ordinary courts, as long as the constitutional court is independent of that country's legislature and executive. However, the CJEU did find that the possibility that judges might face disciplinary sanctions for the disapplication of internal law they deem contrary to EU law to be a violation of EU judicial standards. The CJEU based its reasoning not only on the principle of the primacy of EU law, but also on Articles 2 and 19 of the TEU and Decision 2006/928. This judgment was reconfirmed in relatively similar terms in another case that involved a lower court criminal judgment where the applicability of EU law was less directly implicated.[30]

This short overview of cases demonstrates that over recent years, the EC, EP, and CJEU have started monitoring and enforcing standards concerning the independence and impartiality of national courts, including constitutional ones, in a number of EU Member States. Initially, this review was timid and rather indirect, especially in the Hungarian cases. But recent Polish and Romanian cases indicate that the CJEU is adding more bite to its monitoring, in terms of both the substance of its judgments and its institutional priorities, considering the fact that many of these judgments are either Grand Chamber or Full Court cases.

Of course, all these cases relate to the application of EU law, and the applicability of accession documents, as well as the kind of monitoring that leads to such cases, does not apply to the constitutional courts analysed in this book. However, these judgments indicate that rule of law backsliding is taken seriously by the EU, and

[28] CJEU (GC), Joined Cases C-357/19, C-379/19, C-547/19, C-811/19, and C-840/19 *Euro Box Promotion and Others* ECLI:EU:C:2021:1034 (21 December 2021).
[29] ibid para 216.
[30] CJEU (GC), Case C-430/21 *RS* ECLI:EU:C:2022:99 (22 February 2022).

therefore that a politically captured and lopsided constitutional court which enters into a conflict with the CJEU or which needs to assess the constitutionality of legislation or actions that derive from EU law could potentially find itself falling foul of the standards elaborated under this case law and under Articles 2 and 19 of the TEU in particular. Constitutional courts that are either over-politicized or dominated by judges from one political party could be deemed to lack independence or impartiality under EU law.

This issue may manifest itself through questions about whether such constitutional courts can still be deemed courts or tribunals that are allowed to refer preliminary reference requests to the CJEU under Article 267 TFEU. One criterion is that such courts or tribunals must be deemed independent and impartial, a criterion that has been analysed extensively in CJEU case law. For instance, one case centred on the question of whether the Danish Telecommunications Complaint Board could be deemed a court or tribunal capable of making preliminary references, in response to which the CJEU explained that:

> the guarantees of independence and impartiality require rules, particularly as regards the composition of the body and the appointment, length of service and the grounds for abstention, rejection and dismissal of its members, in order to dismiss any reasonable doubt in the minds of individuals as to the imperviousness of that body to external factors and its neutrality with respect to the interests before it.[31]

Put briefly, under EU law, there are an increasing number of cases where the issue of independence and impartiality as regards the issue of (over- or mono-) politicization could become relevant. If constitutional courts become increasingly politicized in the way this book understands the term, the attendant risks to such politicization might be tempered or otherwise addressed through the emerging standards in EU law discussed above.

It is not only the EU that has become active in the field but also the other main regional supranational institution, the CoE, which through its bodies has intervened and set some standards and limits. I will discuss those developed by the ECtHR as well as by the European Commission for Democracy through Law (better known as, and hereinafter, 'Venice Commission').

[31] See eg: CJEU, Case C-222/13 *TDC A/S v Erhvervsstyrelsen* ECLI:EU:C:2014:2265 (9 October 2014) para 32.

5.1.2 Council of Europe bodies

Like the CJEU, the ECtHR has neither directly addressed the issue of over- politicization nor the even more extreme situation of mono-politicization of constitutional courts. This does not mean that the issue cannot arise in the future. The ECtHR has applied its vast and longstanding jurisprudence on the right to a fair trial and Article 6 of the ECHR to constitutional courts on several occasions, a point that will be discussed in more detail under subsection 5.2.2. In addition to its older case law on the right to a fair trial as well as the 'classical' issues concerning the judiciary's independence and impartiality and the separation of powers, in recent years the ECtHR has also become embroiled in cases that emerged from the aforementioned judicial reforms in the context of constitutional and democratic backsliding, especially in Poland.

As with CJEU case law, the ECtHR's control of internal judicial issues initially tended to be rather indirect. In the first case emerging from countries and reforms where rule of law backsliding is an issue, the ECtHR found a violation of Articles 6 and 10 of the ECHR when the President of the Hungarian Supreme Court was forcibly retired.[32]

The Polish judicial reforms have also found their way into the ECtHR's jurisprudence, leading to rulings which identify violations of the right to a fair trial (Article 6),[33] right to a private life (Article 8), and freedom of expression (Article 10) of individual judges,[34] or a combination of these provisions.[35] This increase in 'new' cases before the ECtHR—ie cases that deal with judicial reforms in certain Central and Eastern Europe (CEE) countries—has arguably also led to a qualitative (re-) assessment of the central role that the rule of law plays within the overall interpretation of many other rights under the ECHR, a role which is not limited to the rights embodied in Article 6.[36]

Interestingly, a case from an entirely different geopolitical area of Europe than the CEE triggered a jurisprudence that has since become relevant to one of this book's central themes relating to judicial appointments. In a case concerning the appointment of Icelandic judges, the Grand Chamber of the ECtHR found a violation under Article 6.[37] Iceland's Minister of Justice had breached national law by

[32] *Baka v Hungary* App no 20261/12 (ECtHR (GC), 23 June 2016).

[33] See eg: *Reczkowicz and two Others v Poland* App nos 43447/19, 49868/19 and 57511/19 (ECtHR, 5 June 2020); *Dolińska-Ficek and Ozimek v Poland* App nos 49868/19 and 57511/19 (8 November 2021); *Advance Pharma sp. z o.o v Poland* App no 1469/20 (3 February 2022); and *Grzęda v Poland* App no 43572/18 (ECtHR (GC) 15 March 2022).

[34] See eg: *Tuleya v Poland* App nos 21181/19 and 51751/20 (ECtHR, 6 July 2023).

[35] See eg: *Wałęsa v Poland* App no 50849/21 (ECtHR, 23 November 2023) (finding violations of both Arts 6 and 8 on top of applying the pilot judgment procedure).

[36] In this sense: Robert Spano, 'The Rule of Law as the Lodestar of the European Convention on Human Rights: The Strasbourg Court and the Independence of the Judiciary' (2021) 27 European LJ 211.

[37] *Guðmundur Andri Ástráðsson v Iceland* App no 26347/18, ECtHR (GC) (1 December 2020).

replacing some of the candidates for the newly created Court of Appeal who had been assessed to be most qualified by an evaluation committee, with candidates who were ranked lower on the list. All of this had been done without any independent evaluation and without parliament being given a chance to vote on each of the candidates. The ECtHR elaborated a three-step test to determine whether irregularities in the appointment process were serious enough to violate the fundamental right to a tribunal established by law. As to the first prong, there needs to be a manifest breach of domestic law and this breach can also occur if the appointment procedure is legal, but its outcome is incompatible with the rights enshrined in the ECHR. The second prong requires an assessment of whether the breach is serious enough to undermine the national court's judicial independence, whereas the third one needs to assess the breach's impact on the applicant's individual ECHR rights. As the appointment procedure patently breached Icelandic law (ie the first prong), the ECtHR had little difficulty in unanimously finding a violation.[38]

Bringing this logic to appointment procedures of constitutional courts and the possibility of ex-ministers or politicians being nominated to such courts, one can see how (over- or mono-) politicization could potentially fall foul of this three-step test. In a first judgment involving the Polish TK, the ECtHR did not accept the applicants' contention that the TK could still be considered an effective and impartial judicial body capable of fulfilling its constitutional duties but left the door open to doing so in future.[39]

And indeed, it did so in its *Xero Flor* judgment.[40] One of the elements of the Polish rule of law saga was that the Polish President had refused to swear in some constitutional judges elected by the previous parliament, and had instead received an oath of office from other constitutional judges elected by the new parliament under the PiS majority. The applicant company had both indirectly via ordinary courts and directly via a constitutional complaint procedure raised the issue of constitutionality of national hunting legislation which limited the compensation for damages to its turf business. These challenges failed internally also with regard to the applicant's argument that the TK was not a tribunal established by law because one of the judges deciding the constitutional complaint had not been elected legally. The ECtHR essentially agreed with that argument and additionally relied on the fact that the TK itself had held that the Polish President's refusal to swear in some judges and later to appoint others had been in violation of Polish law. Moreover, the Strasbourg judges also held that this breach of domestic law was so

[38] For a detailed analysis of this case, see: Robert Spano, 'The Rule of Law as the Lodestar of the European Convention on Human Rights: The Strasbourg Court and the Independence of the Judiciary' (2021) 27 European LJ 211, 220–22.

[39] *Solska and Rybicka v Poland* App nos 30491/17 and 31083/17 (ECtHR, 20 September 2018).

[40] *Xero Flor w Polsce sp. z o. o. v Poland* App no 4907/18 (ECtHR, 7 May 2021).

fundamental as to undermine the very essence of the right to a tribunal established by law.[41]

As evidenced by the preceding paragraphs, the control by the ECtHR becomes more substantial and may include in the future situations where appointments have been made in accordance with law, but where legitimate doubts about the independence and impartiality of the judges arise—not just as to form, but also as to substance due to their political closeness to the nominating authorities. The words of the former President of the ECtHR suggest that it might apply to such appointments thanks to the increased role that the rule of law has played in ECtHR jurisprudence of late:

> States are in principle free to choose the legislative framework for appointing judges on the basis of their legal traditions and constitutional structures. However, such rules and the procedures applied must always conform to the requirements flowing from the primordial principles of the rule of law as it finds its expression in the requirements of judicial independence and impartiality.[42]

A slightly different, yet related, question is whether the ECtHR would consider the kind of (over- or mono-)politicization that this book is concerned with also constitutes a violation of a *civil* right under Article 6. Failure to connect constitutional reforms of appointment procedures and the lengths of tenures at constitutional courts to an underlying civil right under Article 6 may essentially exclude the application of this provision. This occurred in a case brought by four sitting constitutional judges against a constitutional reform in Armenia which the ECtHR declared inadmissible.[43] The applicants had been nominated until they should reach retirement age under the previous constitutional system. When that system was changed through a constitutional reform, they were essentially forced off the Armenian Constitutional Court and could not challenge their 'dismissal' before any authority. This mechanism strongly resembles the above-mentioned 1929 Reform in Austria. The ECtHR held these complaints inadmissible essentially because they found the exclusion from access to a court justified under the unique conditions of the case, and that therefore Article 6 was not applicable *ratione materiae*.[44]

If instead, the ECtHR does find that such fact patterns fall within the scope of Article 6, then a substantive assessment of whether political capture of

[41] ibid, paras 255–91.

[42] Robert Spano, 'The Rule of Law as the Lodestar of the European Convention on Human Rights: The Strasbourg Court and the Independence of the Judiciary' (2021) 27 European LJ 211, 222.

[43] *Alvina Gyulumyan and Others v Armenia* App no 25240/20 (dec) (ECtHR, 21 November 2023) paras 68–85.

[44] See critically on this decision: Gertrude Lübbe-Wolff, 'One-sidedly Staffed Courts: A Problem of Impartiality – not only in Poland' (*VerfBlog*, 8 January 2024) <https://verfassungsblog.de/one-sidedly-staffed-courts/> accessed 9 January 2024.

constitutional courts threatens their independence and impartiality may be carried out. In such a scenario, the Strasbourg judges would be able to draw on a different line of cases. Indeed, there have been judgments involving public broadcasting monopolies that were de facto controlled by a single political party, in the sense that all their important managerial positions were occupied by individuals connected to that (usually governing) party. This led to challenges by journalists who alleged that such a concentration of control over national media violated their freedom of expression. In a 2009 judgment against Moldova, the ECtHR found a violation of Article 10 of the ECHR. Amongst other things, its decision stated that '[i]t takes as its starting point the fundamental truism: there can be no democracy without pluralism'.[45]

Two Austrian newspaper articles that discussed this case in relation to the presence of politicians on the governing bodies of public Austrian TV channels cited the current President of the VfGH, Christoph Grabenwarter. In an earlier publication he had written that 'if there is a too large representation of representatives of governing parties in such institutions, Article 10 [of the] ECHR may be violated.' Given that the ECHR has constitutional status in Austria, the question became whether the high number of government representatives in the Austrian public broadcasting governing body was constitutional.[46]

Grabenwarter later denied that the Moldovan case was directly analogous to the Austrian situation. Arguably, the direct transposition of the reasoning of a case concerning public media to a case concerning a constitutional court is even more hazardous, and such a transposition would face the additional difficulty of working out how Article 10 could be invoked in such a different institutional context. However, like certain forms of public media, constitutional courts have a monopoly. One could imagine that instead of journalists bringing a challenge based on an alleged violation of their freedom of expression, individual political parties to a constitutional procedure or individual judges might bring a challenge alleging the partiality of a constitutional court, and the latter scenario similarly justifies the invocation of the truism that 'there can be no democracy without pluralism'. Such statements must be taken seriously for constitutional courts too, and may prove useful in extreme situations of politically one-sided or captured constitutional courts and where there are legitimate doubts about their impartiality and independence.

[45] *Manole and Others v Moldova* App no 13936/02 (ECtHR, 17 September 2009) para 95.

[46] See on this: 'Armin Wolf über einen "offenkundig verfassungswidrig" besetzten ORF Stiftungsrat' *Der Standard* (Vienna, 13 March 2022) <https://www.derstandard.at/story/2000134060679/armin-wolf-ueber-einen-offenkundig-verfassungswidrig-besetzten-orf-stiftungsrat> accessed 16 February 2023; and Harald Fidler, 'Doskozil macht Verfassungsbeschwerde gegen Politeinfluss im ORF offiziell – und Armin Wolfs Anregung wahr' *Der Standard* (Vienna, 26 June 2022) <https://www.derstandard.at/story/2000136894772/doskozil-macht-verfassungsbeschwerde-gegen-politeinfluss-im-orf-offiziell-und-armin> accessed 16 February 2023.

As indicated above, another CoE institution, the Venice Commission, also became involved in these issues. This institution is an advisory body on constitutional matters, and it provides legal advice to its 61 predominantly European member states who wish to 'bring their legal and institutional structures into line with European standards and international experience in the fields of democracy, human rights and the rule of law'.[47] It is in connection with this function that it provides opinions upon request.

The Venice Commission's non-binding opinions have dealt head-on with the just-discussed controversial judicial reforms as well as other aspects that touch upon issues related to this book.[48] Its opinions on the deficits of Poland's reforms have been assessed positively due to their clear language and to the internal and international visibility that they have given to the issue, though their non-binding character means that they seldom have any significant (direct) effect on the ground.[49] The Venice Commission's Opinion on the judicial reforms in Armenia[50] has been received less positively,[51] and even served as justification for the above-mentioned admissibility decision in *Gyulumyan* by the ECtHR.[52]

[47] See the starting page of the Venice Commission: <https://www.venice.coe.int/WebForms/pages/?p=01_Presentation#:~:text=The%20role%20of%20the%20Venice,the%20rule%20of%20law1> accessed 28 September 2023.

[48] See eg the Venice Commission' opinions on Hungary <https://www.venice.coe.int/webforms/documents/by_opinion.aspx?country=17>; Venice Commission, *Opinion on the New Constitution of Hungary* adopted by the Venice Commission at its 87th Plenary Session (Venice, 17–18 June 2011), Opinion no 621/21, CDL-AD(2011)016; *Opinion on Act CLI of 2011 on the Constitutional Court of Hungary* adopted by the Venice Commission at its 91st Plenary Session (Venice, 15–16 June 2012), Opinion no 665/2021, CDL-AD(2012)009; *Opinion on the Amendment to the Act on the Organisation and Administration of the Courts and the Act on the Legal Status and Remuneration of Judges* adopted by the Venice Commission at its 128th Plenary Session (Venice and online, 15–16 October 2021), Opinion no 1050/2021, CDL-AD(2021)036; on Poland <https://www.venice.coe.int/webforms/documents/by_opinion.aspx?v=countries>: *Opinion on amendments to the Act of 25 June 2015 on the Constitutional Tribunal of Poland* adopted by the Venice Commission at its 106th Plenary Session (Venice, 11–12 March 2016), Opinion no 833/2015, CDL-AD(2016)001; *Opinion on the Act on the Constitutional Tribunal* adopted by the Venice Commission at its 108th Plenary Session (Venice, 14–15 October 2016), Opinion no 860/2016, CDL-AD(2016)026; and *Joint Urgent Opinion* endorsed by the Venice Commission on 18 June 2020 Opinion no 977/2020, CDL-AD(2020)017; and on Romania: *Opinion on the compatibility with Constitutional principles and the Rule of Law* adopted by the Venice Commission at its 93rd Plenary Session (Venice, 14–15 December 2012), Opinion no 685/2012, CDL-AD(2012)026; *Opinion on the draft Law for dismantling the Section for the Investigation of Offences committed within the Judiciary* adopted by the Venice Commission at its 127th Plenary Session (Venice and online, 2–3 July 2021), Opinion no 1036/2021, CDL-AD(2021)019; and *Urgent Opinion on three Laws concerning the Justice System* issued on 18 November 2022, pursuant to Article 14a of the Venice Commission's Rules of Procedure, Opinion no 1105/2022, CDL-PI(2022)047; and <https://www.venice.coe.int/webforms/documents/?country=25&year=all> all links in this footnote accessed 28 September 2023.

[49] Wojciech Sadurski, *Poland's Constitutional Breakdown* (OUP 2019) 193–96.

[50] Venice Commission, *Joint Opinion of the Venice Commission and the Directorate of Human Rights (DHR) of the Directorate General of Human Rights and Rule of Law (DGI, on the amendments to the Judicial Code and some other Laws,* adopted by the Venice Commission at its 120th Plenary Session (Venice, 11–12 October 2021), Opinion no CDL-AD(2019)024 <https://www.venice.coe.int/webforms/documents/?pdf=CDL-AD(2019)024-e> accessed 24 May 2024.

[51] Gertrude Lübbe-Wolff, 'One-sidedly Staffed Courts: A Problem of Impartiality – not only in Poland' (*VerfBlog*, 8 January 2024) <https://verfassungsblog.de/one-sidedly-staffed-courts/> accessed 9 January 2024.

[52] *Alvina Gyulumyan and Others v Armenia* (n 43) paras 74–77.

Beyond the specifics of Hungary, Poland, or Romania, the Venice Commission's compilation of opinions and studies on constitutional justice more broadly can assist in the task of assessing how or when the over-politicization of constitutional courts could be deemed problematic.[53] An analysis of the Venice Commission's compiled observations demonstrates that it favours a mixed-system of nominations—ie, a system like Italy's—where all branches of power are involved, which they seem to consider to be an expression of democratic legitimacy.[54] Moreover, it also takes into account the relevant jurisdiction's constitutional chronology, which means that a change from a system that is mostly executive- or parliament-led as regards appointments to a mixed one is generally welcomed. On the contrary, 'abandoning this system and moving to a combination of nomination of candidates by the President and their election by parliament is not welcome, although the proposed solution as such is acceptable and known in other countries'.[55] Most importantly, the Venice Commission has expressed concerns about systems 'in which all judges of the Court are elected by parliament on the proposal of the President', as such systems do 'not secure a balanced composition of the Court', especially when 'the President is ... from one of the majority parties', as in such situations 'it is ... likely that all judges of the Court will be favorable to the majority'.[56] This is clearly the case in the French situation.

Overall, the Venice Commission's opinions pay attention to context to a degree that the CJEU and the ECtHR could not manage in an analogous manner. It is therefore probable that if a constitutional court were (over- or mono-)politicized in the manner described or hypothesized in this book, the Venice Commission would notice it—based on its broad approach and existing set of opinions, reports, and studies –before any supranational European institution could make a ruling that gets to the heart of the issue.

5.2 Abstentions and Recusals

A second set of risks posed by former members of government acting as constitutional judges and the potential mechanisms to avert such risks—namely abstentions and recusals—has also been addressed supranationally. I will first look at the non-binding standards that have been developed internationally (subsection 5.2.1) before discussing the few binding cases that have been decided in this domain (subsection 5.2.2).

[53] Venice Commission, 'Compilation of Venice Commission Opinions, Reports and Studies on Constitutional Justice (Updated)', 7 December 2022, CDL-PI(2022)050 <https://www.venice.coe.int/webforms/documents/?pdf=CDL-PI(2022)050-e> accessed 28 September 2023.

[54] ibid 17 and 18, citing its opinions on Turkey and Ukraine.

[55] ibid 18, citing its opinion on Ukraine.

[56] ibid, citing its opinion on Montenegro.

5.2.1 Non-binding standards

With regard to non-binding standards, the Bangalore Principles of Judicial Conduct of 2002, developed within the UN framework, deserve mention.[57] These can be seen as a sort of international bill or consensus on—or perhaps a codification of—the universal principles that govern judicial behaviour.

The Bangalore Principles are organized around a set of guiding 'Values' that are complemented by a series of explanatory commentaries. Value 2 is dedicated to impartiality, and it provides that '[i]mpartiality is essential to the proper discharge of the judicial office. It applies not only to the decision itself but also to the process by which the decision is made.'[58] A series of applications and examples of the principle are then made, from points 2.1 to 2.5, which include that 'a judge shall ensure that his or her conduct, both in and out of court, maintains and enhances the confidence of the public, the legal profession and litigants in the impartiality of the judge and of the judiciary' (2.2); that 'a judge shall, so far as is reasonable, so conduct himself or herself as to minimize the occasions on which it will be necessary for the judge to be disqualified from hearing or deciding cases' (2.3); and that 'a judge shall not knowingly, while proceedings are before, or could come before, the judge, make any comment that might reasonably be expected to affect the outcome of such proceedings or impair the manifest fairness of the process. Nor shall the judge make any comment in public or otherwise that might affect the fair trial of any person or issue' (2.4).[59]

Most interestingly and relevant for the purposes of this book, point 2.5 provides that 'a judge shall disqualify himself or herself from participating in any proceedings in which the judge is unable to decide the matter impartially or *in which it may appear to a reasonable observer that the judge is unable to decide the matter impartially*.'[60] Several additional examples of bad practice accompany this last point, which relate to bias toward a party or personal knowledge of disputed facts in the proceedings (2.5.1), having previously served as a lawyer or material witness in the underlying proceedings (2.5.2), and having an economic interest in the outcome of the matter (2.5.3).

The Commentary specifies a series of questions that relate directly to various points discussed in previous chapters. First, it explains that the 'reasonable observer' is a 'fair-minded and informed' person.[61] Second, it refers to the principle that 'one may not be judge in one's own cause', clarifying that this principle may

[57] United Nations Office on Drugs and Crime (UNODC), *Commentary on the Bangalore Principles of Judicial Conduct*, 2007, <https://www.unodc.org/res/ji/import/international_standards/commentary_on_the_bangalore_principles_of_judicial_conduct/bangalore_principles_english.pdf> accessed 3 November 2022.

[58] ibid 43.

[59] ibid 44–52.

[60] ibid 53–58 (emphasis added).

[61] ibid 53.

apply outside of cases where a judge is a party or has an economic interest in its outcome but where their behaviour nonetheless may give rise to a suspicion that he or she is not impartial.[62] Third, it discusses the point from which a judge should make a disclosure on the record and invite comments from the parties, namely where there is a reasonable apprehension of bias. Such apprehension can be identified by a test, which the Bangalore Principles formulate as: 'what would such a person, viewing the matter realistically and practically—and having thought the matter through— conclude? Would such a person think that it is more likely than not that the judge, whether consciously or unconsciously, would not decide fairly?'[63] Fourth, it addresses the question of previous political affiliations and how they may enhance a judicial qualification rather than diminishing it, while stressing that judges are expected to abandon such affiliations and partisan interests upon taking up judicial office.[64] Fifth, as to offers of post-judicial employment, the commentary provides that they may disqualify judges, who would need to carefully consider whether such offers could raise debates about their impartiality.[65]

Some interesting points can also be noted regarding recusals. The commentary, on the one hand, explains that the possibility of recusals is supposed to 'protect the rights of litigants and preserve public confidence in the integrity of the judiciary'. On the other hand, 'frequent disqualification may bring public disfavour to the bench and to the judge personally, ... impose unreasonable burdens on the judge's colleagues, [and] [l]itigants may get the impression that they can pick and choose which judge will decide their case'.[66] In any case, judges ought not take recusal requests too personally when they are made.[67]

After these applications and explanations, the Bangalore Principles insert a proviso or exception which the commentary refers to as the 'Doctrine of necessity'. This doctrine establishes that the 'disqualification of a judge shall not be required if no other tribunal can be constituted to deal with the case or, because of urgent circumstances, failure to act could lead to a serious miscarriage of justice'.[68] The commentary further elaborates on this point and specifies that while such cases may be 'rare and special', they 'may arise from time to time in final courts that have few judges and important constitutional and appellate functions that cannot be delegated to another judge' and that '[t]his is certainly the case when there is only one court with constitutional jurisdiction and/or there are [a] limited number of judges and when disqualification may actually result in [a] denial of justice'.[69]

[62] ibid.
[63] ibid 54.
[64] ibid 56–57.
[65] ibid 58.
[66] ibid 49.
[67] ibid 56.
[68] ibid 61.
[69] ibid.

On the basis of the Bangalore Principles, it can be concluded that the mere fact that a judge has previously held governmental and political office does not alone—and certainly does not automatically—raise serious concerns. Nevertheless, judges and litigants alike need to tread carefully. Judges should consider if their former political actions and friendships could lead an outside observer to doubt their impartiality, and they should not take recusal requests as a personal affront. Litigants should in turn not use recusals to manipulate the bench to an excessive degree. Moreover, the doctrine of necessity seems to imply that even when a reasonable suspicion of bias arises because a constitutional judge is asked to decide on the constitutionality of a piece of legislation that they promoted or voted on as a member of government, these doubts may—and indeed must—be cast aside if a recusal on that basis is likely to result in denial of justice or if there is a suspicion that the recusal request is merely a tactical manoeuvre by the litigants to get rid of a judge they suspect may be less likely to rule in their favour.[70]

Moving from the global to the regional level, several opinions by the Venice Commission have also weighed in on issues relevant for the purposes of this book. Particularly interesting are its observations concerning the possibility of abstentions and recusals by constitutional court judges, found in a recent compilation of its opinions.[71] Overall, the Venice Commission's approach is rather cautious about abstention and recusal rules for constitutional court judges, again because they are concerned that automatic or mandatory mechanisms could grind constitutional courts to a halt, an idea that reflects the Bangalore Principles' 'Doctrine of necessity'. In this sense, the Venice Commission has stated that 'it must be ensured that the Constitutional Court as guarantor of the Constitution remains functioning as a democratic institution. The possibility of excluding judges must not result in the inability of the Court to take a decision.'[72] More specifically to the topic of this book, the Venice Commission also explained that 'the fact that a judge participated in [the] adoption of the law in Parliament should not be a valid reason for a recusal as this could easily lead to a *non liquet* because the number of remaining judges [then] drops below the quorum'.[73]

A concern related to the *non liquet* issue arose with regard to the 1992 reform of the CCR. The Venice Commission opined that the rules on withdrawal for ordinary civil judges could not apply to the constitutional court in the case of recusals,

[70] At the UN level, the UN Special Rapporteur on the independence of judges and lawyers also deserves mention, but it seems that neither their thematic reports nor their country visits deal directly with the issues discussed in this book. See: <https://www.ohchr.org/en/special-procedures/sr-independence-of-judges-and-lawyers> accessed 31 May 2023.

[71] Venice Commission, 'Compilation of Venice Commission Opinions, Reports and Studies on Constitutional Justice (Updated)' 14 April 2020, CDL-PI(2020)004 <https://www.venice.coe.int/webforms/documents/?pdf=CDL-PI(2020)004-e> accessed 3 November 2022.

[72] ibid 70.

[73] ibid 69.

because there would be no other judges available to step in. Hence, '[i]f rules for [the] challenging of a judge were deemed necessary in Romania they would have to apply specifically to the Constitutional Court and exclude the possibility [of] *non liquet* [in order to] apply . . . the fundamental principle of the Constitutional Court as a guarantor of the supremacy of the Constitution'.[74]

The Venice Commission has also made clear that a constitutional court needs to make a ruling even in matters 'in which some of its members may have, or [may] be perceived to have, an interest [in the case]'[75] in order to 'make sure that no law is exempt from constitutional review, including laws that relate to the position of judges'.[76] Another concern that arose with regard to abstention and recusal rules is that they could lead to external pressure on courts, as any external pressure from other branches of the state or the media which could lead judges to avoid delivering judgments must be avoided. Any such rules would therefore need to be 'defined narrowly and should be strictly limited'.[77]

Overall, from the various opinions adopted by the Venice Commission, it can fairly be stated that their approach is rather lenient and is intimately connected with the notion that constitutional courts must remain operative because the application of over-rigid recusal rules might prevent the reaching of the minimum quorum for making certain decisions. Moreover, such rules might lead to a general deadlock if reforms are made to constitutional courts themselves, because the application of generally applicable recusal rules to such a situation would require the recusal of the whole court.

In this sense, the non-binding standards at the international law level do not pose any fundamental issues as regards the current rules and practices of the four constitutional courts under analysis here.

5.2.2 Binding standards

This rather lenient approach is arguably not shared by the standards developed by the ECtHR through the binding judgments it has delivered, in particular with regard to the right to a fair trial enshrined under Article 6 of the ECHR. The relevant part of that provision reads as follows:

> In the determination of his civil rights and obligations or of any criminal charge against him, everyone is entitled to a fair and public hearing within a reasonable time by an independent and impartial tribunal established by law. Judgment shall

[74] ibid 68 and 70.
[75] ibid 69.
[76] ibid 70.
[77] ibid 69.

be pronounced publicly but the press and public may be excluded from all or part of the trial in the interests of morals, public order or national security in a democratic society, where the interests of juveniles or the protection of the private life of the parties so require, or to the extent strictly necessary in the opinion of the court in special circumstances where publicity would prejudice the interests of justice.[78]

In particular, with regard to violations of the impartiality requirement, the ECtHR's jurisprudence distinguishes between a subjective understanding (ie the personal conviction or specific interest of a given judge in a particular case) and an objective one (ie whether a specific judge, regardless of their specific conduct, may reasonably appear to be partial to an external observer).[79] The ECtHR summarizes this latter type of impartiality through the axiom that 'justice must not only be done, it must also be seen to be done'.[80] Most of the cases discussed here deal with the objective aspect of impartiality.

But before addressing that point, the ECtHR had to determine whether and how Article 6 applies to constitutional courts and proceedings before them. While its earlier case law on Article 6 mostly applied to ordinary courts, the ECtHR has since 1993 extended its fair trial jurisprudence to constitutional courts.[81] In that case, the applicants were the owners of a parent company that had been expropriated of their shares via legislation in the name of public interest and without compensation. They instituted civil proceedings against Spain. During those proceedings the constitutionality of the legislation was challenged via a preliminary reference to the Spanish TC, but, unlike the Spanish state, the applicants were not permitted to intervene and present oral or written observations before the TC. The ECtHR found violations of Article 6 relating to both the length of the overall proceedings (including those before the Spanish TC) and regarding the parties' inequality of arms before the TC. Important, however, was the question of whether constitutional court proceedings fell within the ambit of Article 6 at all, especially considering the legitimate doubts that were present concerning the extent to which the proceedings were in fact concerned with the determination of the applicant's civil rights and obligations or criminal liability.[82] Even though this case was not a constitutional complaint (*amparo*) procedure, but was instead an incidental constitutional proceeding, the ECtHR found Article 6 to be applicable.

[78] Art 6, para 1 ECHR.

[79] For an early application of this distinction, see: *Piersack v Belgium* App no 8692/79 (ECtHR, 1 October 1983) para 30.

[80] For an early invocation of this principle in their case law on Art 6 and the right to a fair trial: *Delcourt v Belgium* App no 2689/65 (17 January 1970) para 31; more recently, eg: *Harabin v Slovakia* App no 58688/11 (ECtHR, 20 November 2012) para 131.

[81] *Ruiz-Mateos v Spain* App no 12952/87 (ECtHR, 23 June 1993).

[82] ibid esp paras 55–60 and also in the partly dissenting opinion of Judge Pettiti, joined by Judges Lopes Rocha and Ruiz-Jarabo Colomer.

Based on the *Ruiz Mateos* judgment, if one refers back to Table 2.2 of this book, Article 6 undoubtedly applies to the constitutional complaint procedures that exist in Austria and Germany. It would also apply to presidential impeachment procedures in Austria, Germany, and Italy. To some extent—to precisely what extent would probably need to be determined on a case-by-case basis—it would also apply to preliminary references by courts, due to the legitimate fair trial concerns of those party to the underlying litigation, as it did in the *Ruiz Mateos* case.

With regard to other forms of litigation such as the abstract constitutionality review of legislation, institutional disputes around competences, electoral disputes, or referendum checks, the question becomes: to what extent does this litigation concern the underlying determination of the civil rights and obligations or the criminal liability of rights-holders? At least as far as electoral litigation is concerned, in the 1997 *Pierre Bloch v France* judgment, the ECtHR held that Article 6 does not apply because such disputes were dealing neither with civil rights nor with a criminal charge.[83] Whether this interpretation would still stand today is a different question. Indeed, there were two dissenters in that very case who criticized the ECtHR majority's formalistic approach which construed election issues as a political right, which therefore fell outside the ambit of civil rights, as well as considered the sanctions as so tenuous as to not deem them criminal, which would have resulted in such litigation falling under the scope of Article 6.[84] Things might be different had the ECtHR defined 'civil right' in a broader or more autonomous way (ie independent from national definitions or understandings), that would encompass the right to vote or to be elected, and this might have also led them to impose higher monetary or ineligibility sanctions for the violation of certain electoral campaign rules.

Since *Ruiz Mateos*, the ECtHR has applied Article 6 to various constitutional court proceedings if they concern the determination of civil rights and obligations or a criminal charge. While most of these cases dealt with unreasonably lengthy court proceedings,[85] *Juričić v Croatia*[86] is more directly relevant to the object of this book's study. In that case, the applicant claimed her right to fair trial had been violated in a constitutional complaint procedure before the Croatian Constitutional Court (the *Ustavni sud Republike Hrvatske*—CCC). The underlying litigation concerned the election of three new members to the CCC by the Croatian parliament. One of the three nominees brought a successful challenge in the administrative courts against one of the other candidates for not having the required years

[83] *Pierre Bloch v France* App no 120/1996/732/998 (ECtHR, 21 October 1997).

[84] ibid, dissenting opinions of Judges Meyer and Lõhmus.

[85] See eg: *Süssmann v Germany* App no 20024/92 (ECtHR, 16 September 1996); *Probstmeier v Germany* App no. 20950/92 (ECtHR, 1 July 1997); *Pammel v Germany* App no 17820/91 (ECtHR, 1 July 1997); *Faltejsek v Czech Republic* App no 24021/03 (ECtHR, 15 May 2008); and *Dos Santos Calado and Others v Portugal* App nos 55997/14, 68143/16, and 78841/16 (ECtHR, 31 March 2020).

[86] *Juričić v Croatia* App no 58222/09 (ECtHR, 26 July 2011).

of professional experience. As a result, the contested nominee brought a constitutional complaint against the applicant's successful challenge because that complaint had been decided behind closed doors, and the contested nominee had only been informed of the case's outcome when it was too late to appeal. Meanwhile, the two other nominees had testified to the regularity and lawfulness of the election in the original administrative procedure but had thereafter taken office and thus participated in the aforementioned closed-door judgment. The ECtHR found a violation only on the grounds of (in)equality of arms—ie the deficiency they identified was that the applicant was not afforded the opportunity to intervene in the latter procedure—but they emphatically did not impugn the CCC's impartiality nor did they consider the absence of a public hearing to be a violation of Article 6. To sum things up, under this aspect, the ECtHR has for years assessed procedures before constitutional courts under its right to a fair trial standard.

A second and more substantive question is whether the existence or non-existence of rules on abstentions and recusals before constitutional courts constitutes an issue from a fair trial rights perspective. Would, for example, the Austrian and Italian impossibility for parties to recuse a constitutional judge be considered a violation of Article 6?[87] So far, no cases have arisen that deal directly with this question. In the literature, however, the argument that such exclusions may violate constitutional and international human rights fair trial rights exists,[88] and is partly based on the ECtHR's case law. Indeed, in a judgment involving the Maltese Constitutional Court, the fact that Maltese law at the time did not establish an automatic obligation for judges to withdraw in cases where their impartiality could be disputed was seen as a violation of Article 6.[89] Automatic obligations to withdraw are linked with recusals in the sense that if judges fail to withdraw when they would have been legally obliged to do so, parties can request their recusal. For this reason, the Maltese judgment is important and of interest to this book's study because it makes the Austrian and Italian situations—where recusal of constitutional judges is not allowed—look especially problematic.

A similar argument could be derived from a more recent judgment that deals with the abstention and recusal rules of the Slovak Constitutional Court (*Ústavný súd Slovenskej republiky*—SCC).[90] The ECtHR identified a violation of Article 6 because the rules at the time did not stipulate that a certain relationship between a

[87] The French exclusion of recusal rules for electoral disputes, as things currently stand, would not fall under the scope of Art 6 ECHR.

[88] With regard to Austria, this argument was made years ago; see: Hans R Klecatsky, 'Über die Notwendigkeit einer grundlegenden Reform der österreichischen Verfassungsgerichtsbarkeit', in Gerhard Leibholz et al (eds) *Menschenwürde und freiheitliche Rechtsordnung. Festschrift für Willi Geiger zum 65. Geburtstag* (Mohr Siebeck 1974) 925, 941; for Italy, see: Veronica Magrini, 'L'astensione e la ricusazione quali strumenti per la realizzazione dell'imparzialità del giudice costituzionale' (DPhil, University of Pisa 2016) 58–68 and 119 <https://core.ac.uk/download/pdf/79621805.pdf> accessed 15 February 2023.

[89] *Micallef v Malta* App no 17056/06 (ECtHR (GC), 15 October 2009).

[90] *Petríková v Slovakia* App no 42149/17 (ECtHR, 25 November 2021).

judge and a party before the constitutional court could be grounds for a challenge due to bias. The SCC had accordingly rejected a recusal request on formalistic grounds, which led the ECtHR to find a violation of Article 6 generally and of the principle of objective impartiality in particular, a ruling which was also influenced by the SCC's failure to seriously analyse the practice when it was challenged.

A third question is whether the existing rules in France and Germany which stipulate that a minister, a high-level functionary in a ministry, or a member of legislature's participation in the elaboration of legislation is not a ground for recusal or exclusion[91] could be deemed a violation of Article 6 of the ECHR. The Austrian rules seem to be stricter and more in conformity with a robust interpretation of Article 6 on this point, as they stipulate that such participation is an automatic ground for exclusion.[92] A look at the practice and arguments raised in the French context may assist in getting a clearer view on—and perhaps an answer to—this question.

The first proposed rules for the recusal of CC members for various reasons in relation to the QPC (*question prioritaire de constitutionnalité*) procedures were presented in 2011.[93] The CC rejected these proposals inter alia by citing ECtHR case law. In particular, they relied on *Morel v France*, in which the ECtHR had found no violation of Article 6 in a case involving the participation of the same person in different stages of civil and then insolvency procedures in the same case, because inter alia, this could not 'by itself be regarded as justifying concerns about his impartiality'.[94]

By contrast, the parties proposing recusal rules relied on a different line of cases, namely *McGonnell v UK*[95] and its predecessor *Procola v Luxembourg*.[96] These two judgments are important for different reasons. *Procola* concerned judges on Luxembourg's Supreme Administrative Court who had played a legislative advisory function as part of the drafting process for a regulation about milk prices, and the same judges were later involved in deciding a case initiated by an applicant challenging that regulation. The ECtHR held that this combination of advisory

[91] As was already mentioned in Chapter 2, France enshrines this rule in Art 4, para 4 of the Règlement intérieur sur la procédure suivie devant le Conseil constitutionnel pour les questions prioritaires de constitutionnalité of 4 February 2010. Nothing is indicated specifically as to this hypothesis with regard to a priori procedures in the internal Decision no 2022-152 ORGA, 11 March 2022, even though in that context, the possibility that a former member of government or parliament would be sitting as a judge on legislation in whose elaboration they had participated is less likely due to timing. In Germany, a similar provision is found in Art 18, paras (2) and (3) BVerfGG. Belgium also has a similar rule in Art 101, para 2, loi spéciale sur la Cour constitutionnelle of 6 January 1989.

[92] Art 12, para 4 VfGG. The problem is then that it cannot be raised in the form of a recusal by parties to the procedure.

[93] A detailed summary of this can be found in: Nicoletta Perlo, 'Les premières récusations au Conseil constitutionnel: réponses et nouveaux questionnements sur un instrument à double tranchant' (2012) 27 *Annuaire international de justice constitutionnelle* 61, 65–67.

[94] *Morel v France* App no 34130/96 (ECtHR, 6 June 2000) para 45.

[95] *McGonnell v United Kingdom* App no 28488/95 (8 February 2000).

[96] *Procola v Luxembourg* App no 14570/89 (ECtHR, 28 September 1995).

and judicial functions was a violation of the objective impartiality required under Article 6.[97] In *McGonnell*, a bailiff who had presided over Guernsey's legislature when it approved a new zoning plan sat as a court member a few years later on a case that required the court to decide on an application requesting a modification of land use under that very same zoning plan. The ECtHR again held that this was a violation of Article 6 due to the absence of an appearance of independence, and thus due to a failure to fulfil the objective impartiality requirement. In so holding, the ECtHR reasoned that:

> any direct involvement in the passage of legislation, or of executive rules, is likely to be sufficient to cast doubt on the judicial impartiality of a person subsequently called on to determine a dispute over whether reasons exist to permit a variation from the wording of the legislation or rules at issue.[98]

Whether the ECtHR would ultimately apply the *Procola/McGonnell* or the *Morel* precedent to a hypothetical case involving the French, German, or Belgian provisions that explicitly stipulate that involvement in the passage of legislation is not a ground for recusal remains an open question. Nevertheless, it seems that, in principle, the *Procola/McGonnell* line of cases is more relevant to the issue than the more lenient *Morel v France* precedent that the CC invoked in response to the aforementioned proposal. Indeed, *Morel* deals with the intervention of a judge in different stages of the same *judicial* procedure, and thus only touches upon the question of subjective impartiality, while the questions raised in this book and in *Procola/McGonnell* both chiefly concern objective impartiality issues that arise from an individual's initial involvement in legislative/executive functions and subsequent involvement in judicial ones. The prevailing view in the relevant literature is that the rule developed by the CC on this issue is not in conformity with ECtHR case law.[99]

Whether the ECtHR will follow such views is a different question. It is one thing to declare a violation of the ECHR for the duration of proceedings before a constitutional court—as several of the cases cited above indeed have;[100] it is quite

[97] Mixing advisory and judicial functions has since been held not to be in violation of Art 6, see: *Kleyn and Others v Netherlands* App nos 39343/98, 39651/98, 46664/99 (ECtHR (GC), 6 May 2003).

[98] *McGonnell v United Kingdom* App no 28488/95 (ECtHR, 8 February 2000) para 55.

[99] For the argument that *Procola/McGonnell* are (more) applicable, see: Nicoletta Perlo, 'Les premières récusations au Conseil constitutionnel: réponses et nouveaux questionnements sur un instrument à double tranchant' (2012) 27 Annuaire international de justice constitutionnelle 61, 65–67; Alexia David, 'L'impartialité du Conseil constitutionnel' (DPhil thesis, Normandie Université 2021) 215–16 <https://normandie-univ.hal.science/tel-03331880v2/file/sygal_fusion_27488-david-alexia.pdf> accessed 12 October 2023; Jean-François Kerléo, 'Les conditions d'amélioration du régime du déport et de la récusation devant le Conseil constitutionnel' in Elina Lemaire and Thomas Perroud (eds), *Le Conseil constitutionnel à l'épreuve de la déontologie et de la transparence* (IFJD 2022) 233, 248–49; and Lauréline Fontaine, *La Constitution maltraitée* (Editions Amsterdam 2023) 42.

[100] See n 85.

another thing to declare that such courts' internal structural or organizational matters by themselves constitute a violation of the ECHR.[101]

A fourth question concerns the modalities and procedures that are adopted to deal with abstentions and recusals. The German practice is the most transparent. The BVerfG issues public and reasoned decisions which either accept or reject abstention or recusal requests.[102] In Austria, France—and in Italy in practice—things are essentially handled in-house with little transparency and/or no reasoned decisions that explain why a particular judge refrained from taking part in a case or why the constitutional court in question decided to accept or reject a requested recusal. Here again, some cases indicate that disclosures about potential conflicts and reasoned decisions in response to recusal requests may protect constitutional courts from an appearance of partiality.

In *Nicholas v Cyprus*,[103] the ECtHR held that a Supreme Court judge's failure to disclose that he was the father-in-law of one of the parties was a violation of Article 6, because this disclosure could have been an important procedural safeguard for guaranteeing objective impartiality.[104] This demonstrates that procedural transparency about disclosures and properly reasoned decisions can help constitutional courts ensure that they uphold their obligations under Article 6 of the ECHR.

Despite this potential for conflicts between the current national rules and practices of constitutional courts and the right to a fair trial as interpreted by the ECtHR, the latter institution has set certain limits to the applicability of Article 6 of the ECHR other than those relating to its scope. Just as the Bangalore Principles refer to the doctrine of necessity, the ECtHR has also indicated that in some cases, recusal requests may reach a dead-end. In two judgments involving Liechtenstein,[105] the applicants had requested the recusal of five judges of the Liechtenstein Constitutional Court (LCC). On the one hand, the ECtHR found no issues that raised questions of impartiality with regard to (a) some of the judges of the LCC having 'already dealt with different cases involving the applicant in which his claims were not allowed, even if there was a factual nexus between those cases',[106] (b) various judges' relationships—either as friends, family, or professional—with people involved in other proceedings involving the applicant,[107] or (c) the 'university lectures or legal opinions given by some of the judges or their membership in

[101] See in this sense: David Szymczak, *La Convention européenne des droits de l'homme et le juge constitutionnel national* (Bruylant 2006) 430.

[102] See: Art 19 BVerfGG.

[103] *Nicholas v Cyprus* App no 63246/10 (ECtHR, 9 April 2018).

[104] ibid 64–65.

[105] *AK v Liechtenstein* App no 38191/12 (ECtHR, 9 July 2015) and *AK v Liechtenstein (No 2)* App no 10722/13 (18 February 2016). For a commentary on the first judgment, see: Patricia Schiess Rütimann, 'Unparteilichkeit von Verfassungsrichtern und deren Ablehnung in grosser Zahl wegen Besorgnis der Befangenheit. Bemerkungen anlässlich von EGMR, A.K./Liechtenstein vom 9. Juli 2015' (2015) 42 Europäische Grundrechte-Zeitschrift (EuGRZ) 549.

[106] *AK v Liechtenstein* App no 38191/12 (ECtHR, 9 July 2015) para 74.

[107] ibid para 75.

the supervisory board of a state-owned company'.[108] On the other hand, it found fault with the LCC's procedure. While each of the challenged judges did not participate in their own recusal decision, they sat on those of the other four. Given the similarity of the claims brought against all five, this seemed to contradict the principle of *nemo iudex in causa sua,* and thus also of impartiality.[109] The ECtHR thus found a violation of Article 6 of the ECHR due to these procedural aspects, demonstrating these judgments' link with the previous point about the importance of procedure. Nevertheless, the Court also stressed that 'complaints alleging bias should not be capable of paralysing a defendant State's legal system and that in small jurisdictions, excessively strict standards in respect of such motions could unduly hamper the administration of justice'.[110]

The ECtHR is not the only body on the international level in which issues relating to abstentions and recusals can be raised. Indeed, there is an interesting pending case brought under the UNECE Convention on Access to Information, Public Participation in Decision-making, and Access to Justice in Environmental Matters (the Aarhus Convention),[111] in which the participation of two former French ministers in a judgment on the constitutionality of legislation that they had publicly supported during their political career is being challenged.[112] In fact, Article 15 of the Aarhus Convention provides for the elaboration of 'optional arrangements of a non-confrontational, non-judicial and consultative nature for reviewing compliance with the provisions of the Convention'. Eventually, four compliance mechanisms were established amongst which is also the possibility for members of the public to make communications to a committee (the 'Compliance Committee') which then makes findings. Admittedly, these are not binding and hence one might question this matter being discussed under this sub-heading. However, procedurally, the mechanism functions like a judicial proceeding, where the involved parties make their written arguments, including the possibility of *amicus curiae* briefs.

In the French matter, the applicants are three environmental NGOs, amongst which some university students at the *École Polytechnique* who were members of the *La Sphinx* association. This association had applied for the annulment of a construction permit granted to Total Energies for the development of a centre for research and innovation on their campus. The association's application was

[108] ibid para 76.

[109] ibid paras 77–85 and *AK v Liechtenstein (No 2)* App no 10722/13 (ECtHR, 18 February 2016) paras 66–68.

[110] *AK v Liechtenstein* App no 38191/12 (ECtHR, 9 July 2015) para 82.

[111] Convention on Access to Information, Public Participation in Decision-Making and Access to Justice in Environmental Matters. Aarhus, Denmark, 25 June 1998, United Nations, Treaty Series, vol 2161, 447 also available at: <https://unece.org/environment-policy/public-participation/aarhus-convention/text> accessed 15 June 2024.

[112] The relevant documentation on that case can be found at: <https://unece.org/env/pp/cc/accc.c.2022.197_france> accessed 15 June 2024.

denied by administrative courts for lack of standing because the association was less than a year old, a requirement that had been inserted into the French Urban Code via new legislation purportedly to avoid abusive and dilatory claims. The association challenged the constitutionality of this new requirement as a violation of their right to effective judicial recourse as well as to their freedom of association. The CC rejected their claims.[113]

The problem was that two members of the CC who took part in that rejection decision, Jacqueline Gourault and Jacques Mézard, had both supported the legislation in question which had the effect or purpose of limiting the opportunities available to NGOs to contest certain types of urban planning decisions, such as decisions which are likely to have environmental consequences. Hence, the challenge to the CC's decision and the composition of the bench in the case in question, as well as the French rule on recusal that allowed Jacqueline Gourault and Jacques Mézard to take part in the judgment despite their participation in the drafting process of the legislation under scrutiny. The applicants' argument was that that the two members should have abstained from participating in the judgment, that it was procedurally impossible to request the recusal of at least one of the two CC members due to timing issues—the official nomination of Ms Gourault occurred after the deadline to file a recusal request—and that due to the above, the CC was not an impartial tribunal insofar as their case was concerned. Though it is limited to environmental matters, Article 9 of the Aarhus Convention stipulates that:

> Each Party shall, within the framework of its national legislation, ensure that members of the public concerned (a) Having a sufficient interest or, alternatively, (b) Maintaining impairment of a right, where the administrative procedural law of a Party requires this as a precondition, have access to a review procedure before a court of law and/or another *independent and impartial body established by law*, to challenge the substantive and procedural legality of any decision, act or omission.[114]

The interviews conducted with some of the members of the CC provide a sense of the internal institutional perspective on this issue:

> We had a case where one of the two people involved in the recusal request felt that it was not justified. We examined this case of a former minister who was likely to

[113] Decision no 2022-986 QPC, 1 April 2022 (upholding the constitutionality of the provision). The two ministers involved were Jacqueline Gourault and Jacques Mézard. For a detailed analysis and critique of this issue, see: Jérôme Graefe and Thomas Perroud, 'L'impardonnable légèreté du Conseil constitutionnel avec l'impartialité' (2022) 18 Revue des droits et libertés fondamentaux (RDLF) <https://revuedlf.com/droit-constitutionnel/limpardonnable-legerete-du-conseil-constitutionnel-avec-limpartialite/> accessed 15 February 2023.

[114] Art 9, para 2 of the Convention on Access to Information, Public Participation in Decision-making and Access to Justice in Environmental Matters, 25 June 1998 (emphasis added).

> have been involved in drafting the text, and we found that this had not been the case. It was an error of analysis. The applicant requesting the recusal wrongly thought that this person had been directly involved. Had that person been *directly* involved then our internal practice of exclusion would have applied but the *indirect* involvement would be going too far.[115]

What is meant by direct and indirect involvement came up in another interview with regard to the same issue. Seemingly, the specific provision whose constitutionality was being challenged had been inserted at the parliamentary committee stage of the legislative process. The former minister and current CC member had thus not had any opportunity to intervene and had therefore not directly participated in the adoption of the relevant provision. The impartiality of the two members does not therefore seem to have been called into question.[116]

The French government's answer to the Compliance Committee contains, in essence, similar answers.[117] First, the government explains in general terms how and why Article 4 of the internal regulations on abstentions and recusals in the case of a posteriori constitutionality review conform to international standards, and in particular, to ECtHR case law and to Article 6 of the ECHR.[118] Second, it argues that the provision conforms to Article 9 of the Aarhus Convention in abstract terms, relying on the interpretation of the ECtHR's case law which they also seem to consider to be applicable to the interpretation of this provision.[119] Finally, it claims that neither Ms Gourault nor Mr Mézard had any direct role in the adoption of the challenged provisions, the former having become a minister after the law had been passed, while the latter had not been part of the parliamentary committee that inserted the challenged provision(s).[120]

Whether this challenge will prove successful remains to be seen, at the time of writing. Regardless of the outcome, the point here is that the ECtHR is not the only supranational venue in which certain rules concerning the participation of former ministers can be challenged from an objective impartiality point of view in both abstract and concrete terms.

Moving away from international instruments and institutions whose case law or opinions are directly applicable to the constitutional courts in question, there is one supranational body that has directly addressed the issue of former ministers acting as constitutional judges in its case law: the African Court on Human and

[115] Interviewee no 9, 21 March 2023.
[116] Interviewee no 8, 21 March 2023.
[117] Réponse de la France aux demandes d'informations du Comité de conformité concernant le respect par la France des dispositions de la Convention d'Aarhus relatives à l'accès à la justice (ACCC/C/2022/197), 12 June 2023, SEVS-SDPPD1-23-06-119 <https://unece.org/sites/default/files/2023-07/frPartyC197_21.07.2023_response_fre.pdf> accessed 10 September 2023.
[118] ibid Part C, points 1–2, 18–22.
[119] ibid Part C, point 3, 22–23.
[120] ibid 23–25.

People's Rights (ACtHR). In *Ajavon v Benin*,[121] the applicant challenged inter alia the impartiality of the Benin Constitutional Court (BCC) due to the participation of Benin's former Justice Minister, who had made public statements in favour of the prohibition of the right to strike, as well as presenting and preparing draft laws in this area of law. As President of the BCC, he then participated in a decision which declared the legislation in question to be constitutional. The ACtHR noted that '[i]t is undeniable that he had a preconceived opinion and should, for that reason, have recused himself' and that his '[n]ot doing so, is deeply troubling and demonstrates an attitude symptomatic of a disregard for the principles of proper administration of justice'.[122] Simultaneously however, it ultimately ruled that the principles of independence and impartiality were not violated simply because 'the remarks or opinion of a single judge out of a bench of seven (7) judges cannot, objectively, be considered sufficient to influence the entire Constitutional Court'.[123] So, at least as far as the African human rights system is concerned, the participation of an ex-minister as a constitutional judge and as President of a constitutional court in a case concerning legislation that he himself has made public statements in support of does not constitute a breach of the right to a fair trial.

To conclude this chapter, while the (binding) jurisprudence of international bodies does not forbid the participation of former members of government as constitutional court judges in absolute terms, it imposes certain limits on their participation in the name of the right to a fair trial, at least for the purposes of certain types of proceedings. First, it imposes minimal rules on abstentions and recusals. Secondly, it also seems to require that such rules should be procedurally clear and transparent. Thirdly, rules which stipulate that participation in the passage of legislation does not constitute cause for recusal in cases where the same legislation's constitutionality is being challenged are at least questionable in light of the ECtHR's jurisprudence on the right to a fair trial and also from the perspective of other international agreements such as the Aarhus Convention.

Finally and more generally, if the presence of former members of government on constitutional courts becomes majoritarian or controlling and said judges all hail from the same party or area of the political spectrum, this may also raise fair trial and rule of law questions under the standards elaborated by various bodies of the CoE as well as under EU law. Admittedly, the case law is—so far—rather inconclusive, but it is certainly dynamic and continuously evolving in line with societal and legal/constitutional changes currently taking place in the region and globally.

[121] ACtHR, *Ajavon v Benin* (judgment) (2020) 4 AfCLR 133.
[122] ibid para 297.
[123] ibid para 299.

6
Minimizing the Risks

Given the preceding chapters and in particular the risks identified in Chapter 4.2, as well as the potential insufficiencies from a supranational perspective of at least some mechanisms and set-ups of national constitutional courts, one could imagine various solutions that I will discuss here, ranging from the 'least extreme' to the 'most extreme' forms. If some of the risks described in the preceding chapters find the reader in agreement to a greater or lesser extent, here is how some aspects could be improved or addressed. I am aware the solutions proposed are mostly of legal(istic) nature and that I somehow fall into the trap of the *déformation professionnelle* of lawyers who focus on legal responses to sociological and political arguments, to paraphrase Martin Krygier,[1] especially as far as the issue of constitutional backsliding is concerned. The point is neither to disregard the underlying socio-political dynamics nor to completely eliminate the risks brought with such personalities joining constitutional courts—something that would, in any case, be impossible to do. Rather, the idea is to think of these suggestions or reform proposals as improvements and/or alarm systems against possible abuses. To remain with the metaphor of the thief, if someone intends to undermine or capture a constitutional court, nothing will prevent them from doing so. Until today, arguably the systems and constitutional courts analysed here have fared decently well and the participation of ex-ministers has not profoundly undermined their reputation. But the question is, what if the practices or the quality of nominees change? Could one build in some sort of alarm system, to avoid other types of former politicians than the ones who have joined so far joining constitutional courts unchecked? Of course, there is no perfect alarm system, with each having its downsides and shortcomings that will also be referred to in the proposals listed below.

Another proviso that should be added to the suggested improvements is the question of whether any or all of them could have a positive effect on the perception of independence and impartiality of these constitutional courts in the public eye? Probably it would improve such perception for the informed legal public from academics to practitioners or professionals working with and in constitutional courts and beyond. As limited as such informed or expert support may seem, I would argue that the support from the legal community is key to such institutions. This

[1] He refers to this professional bias with regard to anti-constitutionalism, which I partly address in the following sections. Martin Krygier, 'Introduction: Anti-Constitutional Populism' in Martin Krygier, Adam Czarnota, and Wojciech Sadurski (eds), *Anti-Constitutional Populism* (CUP 2022) 1, 21.

Ex-Ministers as Constitutional Judges. Mathias Möschel, Oxford University Press. © Mathias Möschel 2025.
DOI: 10.1093/9780198930228.003.0006

is the community with whom constitutional courts interact and talk directly on a daily basis. Getting their support and respect is therefore vital. It is also vital to become a place where the best lawyers aim to go.

How far the intricacies of nomination procedures, abstention and recusal rules, or the introduction of cooling-off periods could ultimately influence and strengthen the perception of constitutional courts by the broader and uninformed non-legal public is a different question. The polls and surveys presented for each country in Chapter 2 could reflect some of those changes.

6.1 Legal Education and Length of Professional Experience

The first point of intervention concerns criteria that could indirectly reduce the possibility of former politicians joining constitutional courts as judges. These would be related to the (professional) qualifications required to become a constitutional court judge. One first aspect is that in many, if not most, countries around the globe, some form of legal education is required to become a constitutional judge. A second aspect is that in some countries a certain duration of professional experience before becoming a constitutional judge is also required. The point here is that requiring either a legal education or a certain length of professional experience—or both—could indirectly reduce the probability of having former full-time politicians on a constitutional court for slightly different reasons.[2] In fact, they limit the pool of available candidates who are former politicians because either they are not lawyers, or because exercising a full-time profession and/or full-time political career simultaneously will not be sustainable over a long period of time.

Of the jurisdictions discussed here, the first suggestion is mostly relevant to the French context, but it could be extended to those few other constitutional or apex courts where a legal education, at least formally, is not required, like the United States, Switzerland, or Kazakhstan,[3] but also in Belgium for some constitutional judges.[4] This is clearly a minimum level intervention, which could prevent at least some politicians who do not have such an education from being nominated to a given constitutional court, despite being in very good standing with a given political regime or party. The Austrian history is interesting in this context, given that the 1929 Reform and its goal to 'de-politicize' the VfGH had introduced the

[2] Gertrude Lübbe-Wolff, *Beratungskulturen. Wie Verfassungsgerichte arbeiten, und wovon es abhängt, ob sie integrieren oder polarisieren* (Konrad-Adenauer-Stiftung 2022) 185–203 <https://www.kas.de/documents/252038/16166715/Beratungskulturen.+Wie + Verfassungsgerichte+arbeiten%2C + und+wovon + es+abh%C3%A4ngt%2C + ob+sie + integrieren+oder + polarisieren.pdf/a68323e0-dd86-6b7b-202e-bd4130edb511?version = 1.3&t = 1683291883575> accessed 25 September 2023.

[3] See on this overview: Guillaume Tusseau, *Contentieux constitutionnel comparé* (LGDJ 2021) 496.

[4] I am not entering into the debate as to whether the presence of non-lawyer or lay justices may have other benefits for such courts. On this aspect, see: Adrian Vermeule, *Law and the Limits of Reason* (OUP 2009) 123–62.

requirement of a legal education in order to prevent former politicians to sit on that body.

As to the second suggestion, this would again have an impact in France, where qualifications entry hurdles are very limited. But also in Germany, this could have some relevance given that—apart from the minimum age and the fact of having the formal qualifications to become a judge—there are no requirements for how long someone must have exercised a given profession. Such requirements exist to a limited extent in Italy for attorneys, who are required to have 20 years of experience. Only Austria requires ten years of professional experience for all the court members. This could (also) have contributed to the almost total absence of former politicians on the VfGH for a large part of its history.

Two observations should be made on the points raised above. Requiring a legal education as a minimum criterion is not to say that formally trained lawyers cannot and will not be politically malleable. To add to Gustavo Zagrebelsky's words described above under Chapter 4.1, what such courts need are strong personalities. Lawyers can be strong or weak personalities and in some of the systems described here, especially in Italy and Germany, history has shown that lawyers and judges have sometimes been good handmaids to certain regimes. The names and biographies of Azzariti, Lampis, Manca, and Geiger, all constitutional court judges with a legal education and for the three Italian ones, coming from the highest judicial bodies, are a reminder in this context. If someone wants to find a political friend to place on a constitutional court, there is plenty of choice. Nevertheless, the requirement of a legal education reduces the panoply of such choices.

A somewhat different observation concerns the possibility that the constitutional or legal requirements to become an eligible constitutional judge can be circumvented, even when some form of legal education or professional experience is required.

As to the issue of duration and experience, one could mention some examples from Italy. When Fernanda Contri was nominated, the question arose as to whether she had the required 20 years of practice as an attorney. At the time in Italy there existed two figures of practising attorneys, a lower level one called *procuratore*, and the fully qualified attorney, or *avvocato* that is also mentioned at Article 135 of the Constitution. In order to reach those 20 years, her years as *procuratore* were included. A related doubt as to the 20 years of exercise hovered over the already mentioned Luigi Mazzella, who had been nominated to the C cost in 2005. While he had become *avvocato di stato*, a sort of state legal advisor, in 1956, he had then had a mostly political career, which culminated in him becoming a minister. There were thus justified questions as to whether his 20 years of practice as an attorney existed in practice or only on paper.[5]

[5] Roberto Bin, 'Sull'imparzialità dei giudici costituzionali' (2009) LIV Giurisprudenza costituzionale 4015, 4028, fn 63.

Similarly, in Austria some reforms to the requirements in 1977 and 1999 were made to allow certain personalities to join the VfGH. For instance, prior to 1977 only law professors teaching in law faculties could become constitutional judges. That was changed to permit Karl Korinek, who was teaching law in a non-law faculty, to join the institution. For Gabriele Kucsko-Stadlmayer, a substitute member, the amendment was to strengthen her independence by exempting people in her position of civil servant from activities bound by instructions.[6] While such changes are done legally, they could set a precedent to be used to open the doors to less 'acceptable' and more politicized candidates in the future, especially in Austria, considering the relative ease with which the B-VG can be amended and legislative provisions declared to be of a constitutional nature.[7]

Having a legal education or some experience is neither an unrelated nor an unreasonable requirement for what judges need to do at constitutional courts. Whereas judicial review exercised by constitutional courts certainly is a type of political power exercised by non-elected judges, courts must exercise and legitimize that power through certain processes. This distinguishes judicial decision-making from a political one.[8] Such a distinction becomes more difficult to uphold if you have former politicians being part of your institution.

Possibly nowhere more than in Germany, out of the jurisdictions analysed here, is the requirement of a legal education and of a legalistic approach and understanding of this political power so visible. It has been argued that the BVerfG's value formalism and judicial style have contributed to its success and have functioned so as to somewhat insulate it from accusations of a certain politicization.[9] True, this has not prevented the BVerfG from seeing some former politicians joining the institution but, more often than not, they were also known for their legal skills. If (more) former non-lawyer politicians join constitutional courts, then there is a clear risk that such formalism might be undermined or not function as well as before.

From a slightly different angle, the importance of legal education as a unifying element is instead highlighted by another interviewee for the Italian system, with its mixed nomination arrangement:

[6] On these examples, see: Benjamin Kneihs, 'Constitutional Jurisdiction in Austria from 1918 to 2018: Continuities – Breaks – Compromises' (2020) 75 Zeitschrift für öffentliches Recht 885, 899–900.

[7] Heller critically notes that between 1977 and 2002, the B-VG was amended 47 times, or double the times that the US Constitution was amended in 200 years. Kurt Heller, *Der Verfassungsgerichtshof* (Verlag Österreich 2010) 414.

[8] Michel Rosenfeld, 'Judicial Politics versus Ordinary Politics. Is the Constitutional Judge Caught in the Middle?' in Christine Landfried (ed), *Judicial Power: How Constitutional Courts Affect Political Transformations* (CUP 2018) 36–65.

[9] Michaela Hailbronner, *Tradition and Transformations. The Rise of German Constitutionalism* (OUP 2015).

> This diverse background ensures a plurality of viewpoints, attitudes, people, cultures, ways of doing things, personal traditions that is truly fundamental. These three different backgrounds—you must have been a judge; you must have been a lawyer for twenty years; you must be a university professor in law—have common cultural roots.[10]

But even in the French system, where one might expect some reluctance to requiring a legal education for joining the CC, internal opinions seem to be less opposed than might have been expected, and even rather favourable for different reasons. One interviewee highlighted the technical dangers of having non-lawyers on the CC:

> There is a majority of non-lawyers who are unable to prepare both reports and draft decisions themselves. Thus, it is the legal services that do the work for them and even draft the decisions themselves, which are then put to the vote.[11]

In less decided ways another interviewee indicated that he could see no issues in requiring a legal education as a prerequisite, and that he had 'no religion on this point'.[12]

To sum up on this first point, legal education and requiring (a period of) professional experience of some constitutional judges will not directly exclude former politicians, but limit the number of those potentially available while being objective criteria for exercising this important function.

6.2 Nomination/Appointment Procedures and Practices

A second and more stringent level of intervention could be at the stage of the nomination/appointment procedure(s) and practices. There are different ways to think about how such procedures and practices can limit the excessive political exposure of constitutional courts and strengthen their judicial side.

One first and more general observation that has been made in the literature, is that whatever mechanism is considered in this domain, ideally its outcome should not be politically predictable. The argument has been made mostly for the situation where stalemates in the nomination/appointment procedure arise when certain majorities cannot be reached, regarding how to overcome them.[13] This

[10] Interviewee no 17, 9 June 2023.
[11] Interviewee no 1, 23 January 2023.
[12] Interviewee no 4, 8 March 2023.
[13] Gertrude Lübbe-Wolff, 'How to Prevent Blockage of Judicial Appointments' (*VerfBlog*, 7 October 2022) <https://verfassungsblog.de/how-to-prevent-blockage-of-judicial-appointments/> accessed 12 October 2023.

happens regularly in Italy for those elected by parliament, but also in Germany delays can occur.[14] Such arguments on the political (un)predictability of reforms to address deadlock concerns can be extended more broadly in this domain. For instance, when thinking about increasing the number of judges at the USSC to 13 in total by statutory amendment of the Judiciary Act,[15] a less partisan suggestion could be to have such a reform enter into force after the next elections or even in a more distant future, so that it would not be clear who would reap the political benefits of such a reform.

A second, rather obvious way to think about these nomination/appointment procedures and practices, is to require that a minimum number of judges sit on constitutional courts. As we have seen, in the four legal systems analysed, two (Germany and Italy) have the requirement that at least some of the members of the constitutional court need to be judges. Again, this is not a bullet-proof solution because it does not completely annul the 'risks' of politicians being nominated to a constitutional court, or that judges themselves may not come with their own baggage of problematic pasts and personalities, as already mentioned in the previous point.

Indeed, a look at the Italian reality demonstrates how one could 'circumvent' or 'bend' some of the existing rules to nominate politicians via the 'judge' category. For example, Gaetano Azzariti had indeed formally been a judge of Italy's supreme court, the Cass, but had for a large part of his career been on secondment in ministries or other legislative positions.[16] Similarly, Brunetto Bucciarelli-Ducci, a full-blood politician and parliamentarian who was nominated by parliament in 1977, had only formally been a judge at the Cass thanks to a system of automatic promotions without ever substantively exercising such a function.[17]

There is also another way for politicians to be nominated/appointed to the C cost without the substantial experience of having been a supreme court judge who decides cases. Another politician, Paolo Maria Napolitano, had been nominated

[14] In Spain, the blockage of nominations has been from the judicial side, demonstrating that it is not necessarily a political stalemate or majority in the traditional sense that can lead to institutional paralysis. On this, see: Sergio Martín Guardado, 'Polarización política y crisis en la renovación del Consejo General del Poder Judicial' (2023) 117 Revista de Derecho Político 131.

[15] See the two democratic bills introduced respectively in 2021 and 2023: Congressional Bills, 117th Congress, 1st Session, Bill S 1141, 'To amend title 28, United States Code, to allow for twelve associate justices of the Supreme Court of the United States' <https://www.govinfo.gov/content/pkg/BILLS-117s1141is/html/BILLS-117s1141is.htm> and Congressional Bills, 118th Congress, HR 3422, with the same title <https://www.congress.gov/bill/118th-congress/house-bill/3422/text?format = txt&q=%7B%22search%22%3A%5B%22California%22%5D%7D&r = 25&s = 1> both accessed 12 October 2023.

[16] Massimiliano Boni, *In questi tempi di fervore e di gloria* (Bollati Boringhieri 2022).

[17] Sergio Bartole, '"Cursus honorum" e Corte costituzionale' (1978) 101 Foro italiano, V, 89 and Alessandro Pizzorusso, 'Art 135' in Giuseppe Branca (ed), *Commentario della Costituzione: Garanzie costituzionali. Art 134–139* (Zanichelli Editore 1981) 144, 153, esp fn 12. On the constitutionality of this system of automatic promotions of judges to the Cass due to the implications this has in terms of qualifications of nominees to the C cost, see: Giuseppe Ferrari, 'Corte costituzionale e magistratura' (1976) XVI Rassegna dei magistrati 255.

by parliament in 2006. Formally, he had the title of being a member of the Cons St, thanks to a governmental nomination to the advisory (and not litigation) section of that institution. However, he continued on secondment in parliament and/or government until February 2006 prior to being elected to the C cost in July of that same year.[18]

One could argue that, at least formally, these individuals had the required qualifications and that, for this reason, there is nothing fundamentally wrong with such nominations/appointments and that the C cost simply tried to avoid direct conflicts with the nominating authorities. However, on the substance, the picture looks slightly different.

A comparative look to a contemporary and less democratic system demonstrates how tolerating such practices can backfire. The example comes from Turkey, where Mr İrfan Fidan, a former chief prosecutor, had just been elected to the Turkish Court of Cassation in November 2020, and only a week later announced he would be running to become a judge of the Turkish Constitutional Court under one of the quota seats allocated to the Cassation. According to Article 146 of the Turkish Constitution, the Cassation nominates three candidates, and the President then appoints one of them. Unsurprisingly, President Erdogan appointed the former prosecutor who became constitutional judge in January 2021. All was done in accordance with the constitutional and statutory letters, on paper. But in substance, this was interpreted as yet another example of abusive constitutionalism.[19]

Evidently, there are differences between these two stories as well as between Italy and Turkey. The point here is merely to indicate that even when judges are required to sit on constitutional courts, it does not eliminate the risk of political circumvention or use of the rules. In that sense, the Italian practice and its tolerance could easily take on a different tone. And under what basis could one then claim that something is wrong or off? That Italy has a longer-standing constitutional tradition?

A third way to consider nomination/appointment procedures and practices is to have a system of mixed nominations, like the one in Italy, where three different nomination authorities (parliament, President and judiciary) intervene and compose the C cost. Again, this mixed nomination/appointment system does not prevent the nomination/appointment of (former) politicians in absolute terms. However, it makes it less likely that one political party would have control over all three nominating authorities and thus most clearly would prevent or delay a mono-politicization.

[18] See: Roberto Bin, 'Sull'imparzialità dei giudici costituzionali' (2009) LIV Giurisprudenza costituzionale 4015, 4028, fn 63.

[19] See for the details on this story: Şen, İlker Gökhan, 'The Final Death Blow to the Turkish Constitutional Court: The Appointment of the Former Chief Prosecutor' (*VerfBlog*, 28 January 2021) <https://verfassungsblog.de/death-blow-tcc> accessed 10 May 2023.

This political compromise at the time of constitution-making has been described by the interviewees as one of the strengths and bulwarks against political capture of its constitutional court of any type. For instance, one of the interviewees stated that:

> In my opinion that is really a strength of the C cost, because any court packing or assault by one political force or by one political orientation is really complicated, also because its renewal takes place in different moments.[20]

Another interviewee confirmed with a similar emphasis:

> We have this real protection represented by the mixed nomination system which prevents from having a monolithic court. . . . Even if there is a majority that happens for whatever reason to appoint half of the C cost, there is still the other half that comes from somewhere else. In my opinion, this mixed nomination system is one of the major bulwarks.[21]

A third interviewee even saw this mixed nomination system as a generalizable rule:

> A general antidote [against political capture] for the C cost, which I think is fundamental is that of the three different origins, as well as the fact that one of the three is itself from three different backgrounds. In my opinion, that should be a general rule.[22]

As we can see, a mixed nomination/appointment procedure where at least some members need to be judges is seen as a good protection which somewhat reduces the possibility of a fully politically controlled body by former politicians.

A fourth thought concerning nomination/appointment procedures and practices is that of ensuring that they are constitutionalized in order to insulate them from future legislative changes. Systems where there exist very few formal rules or prerequisites for nomination to constitutional courts are most exposed to winds of political change. France is a perfect example of such a system. We have seen that there are very few formal requirements or rules on who can be nominated to the CC, even though some unwritten rules have been identified in the literature:

> Name at least one member of the opposition when the three [nominating] powers are in the hand of the same party; choose, at least once, a nomination based on pure competence; do not name one of your closest political friends but someone

[20] Interviewee no 7, 3 March 2023.
[21] Interviewee no 15, 7 June 2023.
[22] Interviewee no 17, 9 June 2023.

whose reputation of independence would increase the institution's prestige; above all, when nominating the President, keep in mind the general interest.[23]

But also in the other systems, certain (good) practices that have developed over the years would not suffer from being formalized or constitutionalized in order to better insulate constitutional courts from sudden political or regime changes. Just to cite one example that emerged from the interviews, the election of judges to the BVerfG is by a two-thirds majority in the Federal Council and by a three-quarters majority in the special committee of the Federal Assembly.[24] Given that these majorities are 'only' written in a legislative provision, they could be changed by a simple majority, thus taking away some of the safeguard that only candidates who are supported across the political spectrum are nominated.[25] Similarly in Italy, we have seen that the judges nominated by parliament in a joint session require a two-thirds majority, which is reduced to a three-fifths majority after two unsuccessful rounds of vote.[26] Here at least the rule is enshrined via a constitutional statute, but the worry is that the three-fifths majority may eventually be too low to avoid a sort of capture.[27]

In any case, nomination/appointment procedures and practices are another area in which some preventive mechanisms can be thought of.

6.3 Abstentions and Recusals

As we have seen, these previous solutions or thoughts would only constitute some minimal safeguards against ex-ministers on constitutional courts. If one sees benefits to them and does not want to miss their presence in such institutions, then one would at least need to make sure that rules that can effectively rein in some of the risks posed by such individuals to constitutional courts. One set of such rules are precisely those on abstention and recusal.

There exist three models on legislative regulation of abstention and recusal for constitutional or apex courts.[28] The first one consists in extending the general

23 Dominique Schnapper, *Une sociologue au Conseil constitutionnel* (Gallimard 2010) 199–200.

24 Arts 6 and 7 BVerfGG.

25 In this sense, interviewee no 19, 17 July 2023. See also the conversation published on Verfassungsblog where a similar issue is being discussed: Klaus Ferdinand Grätz and Maximilian Steinbeis, 'Die meisten Dinge, die in Polen und Ungarn gelaufen sind, könnten ohne weiteres auch hier passieren' (*VerfBlog*, 22 February 2022) <https://verfassungsblog.de/die-meisten-dinge-die-in-polen-und-ungarn-gelaufen-sind-koennten-ohne-weiteres-hier-auch-passieren/> accessed 12 October 2023.

26 Art 11, Legge costituzionale 22 November 1967, no 2.

27 In this sense, interviewee no 2, 1 February 2023.

28 See on this classification: Pierre Bon, 'Recuser un membre du Conseil constitutionnel' (2010) 186 Recueil Dalloz 2007, 2009–10.

rules applicable to other courts. Examples of this model are Spain[29] and Portugal. The second model is to design specific rules for such courts that take into account the reality and specificity of such institutions. Examples of this model are Austria, Germany, and France. The third model is to have very few or no rules at all, as is arguably the case in Italy and the United States,[30] but probably also the CJEU and the ECtHR.

The look at the four systems analysed in this book demonstrates that each of them poses some questions and room for improvement. I would classify them as follows in terms of urgency: (i) introduce explicit rules where none exist; (ii) improve existing rules; and (iii) improve or make publicly more visible existing (good) practice.

As to point (i), the Italian situation, the Austrian exclusion of recusal rules as well as the French silence on abstentions and recusals in electoral disputes before the CC look most problematic. That absence of abstention or recusal rules for electoral disputes was remarked upon as problematic even in the interviews, where one of the interviewees stated that '[i]n electoral matters, we should all have abstained. Well, there are some guys we did not know at all, but I knew some of them. Yes, we did not abstain.'[31] If one sides with the logic that former politicians bring more advantages than risks to constitutional courts, then at least certain rules on preventing or minimizing some of the risks mentioned above should be put in place. Moreover, as we have also already seen above, arguably international (human rights) law may require that some rules are devised from a right to fair trial perspective. Simply not having the possibility to recuse a constitutional judge at all in these situations seems to counter such right to fair trial, especially when they involve civil rights or criminal trials.

Despite or maybe precisely because of such lingering doubts from the international level and also for internal (constitutional) guarantees on the right to fair trial, the recommendations or actions that could be taken are to introduce at least some minimal rules on recusals for Austria, Italy, and France—in the last case for the electoral disputes—and for Italy also to allow and formalize abstentions.[32] Whether this takes the form of specific rules in the form of the second model, or of

[29] For an early overview of the Spanish experience with abstentions and recusals, see: Lorena Bachmaier Winter, *Imparcialidad judicial y libertad de expresión de jueces y magistrados—Las recusaciones de magistrados del Tribunal Constitucional* (Thomson Reuters Aranzadi 2008).

[30] On the critiques about few or no rules on abstentions and recusals before the USSC, see: Louis J Virelli III, *Disqualifying the High Court. Supreme Court Recusals and the Constitution* (Kansas University Press 2016). The recent introduction of a non-binding ethics code by the USSC in November 2023 does not change the overall picture.

[31] Interviewee no 5, 16 February 2023.

[32] With regard to Italy, also in the sense of introducing abstention and recusal rules: Alessandro Maionchi, 'Astensione e ricusazione tra processo comune e processo costituzionale. L'esperienza italiane e quella spagnola a confronto' in Elena Bindi, Mario Perini, and Andrea Pisaneschi (eds), *I principi generali del processo comune ed i loro adattamenti alle esperienza della giustizia costituzionale* (Giappichelli 2008) 369.

extending the ordinary rules to constitutional courts, is a different and more political discussion. Probably the jump from nothing to everything is asking too much and thus a shift to the second model looks more realistic.

One reason that such issues are not completely anodyne is that parties are trying to raise the issue of conflicts of interest by constitutional judges, even when the rules do not exist or do not allow it. In an Italian case dealing with the constitutionality of rules on mandatory anti-Covid vaccination for certain categories of people, the lawyers asked the recusal of a constitutional judge, Marco D'Alberti, who had allegedly participated in the drafting of these rules as the chief legal counsellor to the then Prime Minister.[33] A decision attached to the judgment simply mentioned that due to the internal rules, such recusal requests must be rejected.[34]

As to point (ii) and mostly for what concerns the second model, in which some specific rules on abstention and recusal have been put in place, one can also imagine that such rules should be improved, strengthened or rendered publicly more visible. We have already seen that France and Germany have specific rules providing that the mere participation in the elaboration of legislation does not constitute a cause for recusal.[35] If one sees an issue with former ministers (or high-level politicians) joining constitutional courts and to avoid any doubts as to the risks of infringing the principle of *nemo iudex causa sua*, of objective impartiality, and/or of public trust in such courts, this rule should (also) be amended and be nuanced.[36] For instance, one could imagine that active votes, direct involvement, or sponsorship of a legislative proposal should constitute a cause for mandatory abstention, exclusion, or recusal and/or that such former ministers or politicians should at least not become judge rapporteur on cases involving legislation.

The guiding logic or principle in any case is that in deciding whether abstaining from judging a case a constitutional judge should ask him or herself whether he/she 'should not anyhow always side with a stricter interpretation, if only to set the example?'[37] Similarly, one of the interviewees mentioned that, in view of the illiberal tendencies and attempts to control courts, the CC has the obligation of exemplarity.[38]

[33] See the recordings of the public debates that took place on 4 April 2023, under Point "Ruolo n.4", especially minutes 6.00–7.20 of the recordings <https://www.cortecostituzionale.it/actionUdienza.do> accessed 15 December 2023.

[34] C cost, sentenza no 156/2023, 5 April 2023, with the attached ordinanza which was read at the hearing of 4 April 2023, last paragraph.

[35] See: Art 4, para 4 of Règlement 2010 and Art 18, para 3 BVerfGG. The exclusion of members of parliament or of government who participated in the vote on legislation and then judging their constitutionality has also been argued early on in Italy before the C cost had started operating. At that point, theoretically the general rules on abstention and recusal before the Cons St were (still) to be applied. See: Ferruccio Pergolesi, 'In tema di ricusazione e di astensione dei giudici della Corte costituzionale' (1953) I Rivista di diritto processuale' 311.

[36] Favouring some nuance of the rule, see: interviewee no 19, 17 July 2023.

[37] In this sense: Sabino Cassese, *Dentro la Corte. Diario di un giudice costituzionale* (il Mulino 2015) 264.

[38] Interviewee no 8, 21 March 2023.

In any case, fears of too strict abstention and recusal rules leading to stalemate or limiting functioning of constitutional courts—especially in smaller countries—should be assuaged by several factors. From a more pragmatic point of view, the fact that abstentions and recusals could reduce judge numbers below the minimum quorum could be solved by having some substitute judges nominated, as is the case in Austria.[39] Germany's two-senate system is another practical solution to this theoretical argument.

There are other extra-legal reasons that reduce the risks related to parties abuse of recusal requests that then endanger constitutional courts' functioning. First, constitutional courts should or would still have control over the situation overall, presuming that they decide over abstentions and recusal requests.[40] Second, litigators themselves might have little interest in prolonging procedures and dragging things out even more. Third, litigators might want to avoid the risk of alienating the judges with such requests. With reference to Luhmann's *Gesetz des Wiedersehens* (translatable as the 'Law of Meeting Again') which highlights the role played by trust in repeated interactions and encounters in organizations, it has been written that 'recusal of judges is still a very difficult question [because] [b]arristers and judges will meet each other daily during more than 30 years and are not inclined to attack each other.'[41] Litigants who intend to recuse a judge might be perceived as challenging the judge's integrity and authority. Moreover, a similar difficulty might arise amongst constitutional judges who need to decide over such recusals in the absences of their colleagues and who might be rather suspicious of such requests from parties whom they may see only once during their mandate, whilst continuing to work on a regular basis with a disgruntled colleague whom one has declared partial.[42]

On a related note, one can also note some qualitative differences in how these rules are being operationalized. As we have already seen in Chapter 2.1, it is in Germany that abstentions, recusals and exclusions are handled publicly and in a transparent manner with a motivated decision from the BVerfG.[43] Initially, the BVerfG adopted a very strict standard—stricter than for ordinary judges—in

[39] On such a proposal in secondary literature for Italy, see: Giuliano Amato and Franco Bassanini, 'La Corte costituzionale, un istituto da riformare' (1972) III Politica del diritto 811, 818.

[40] In a rather critical sense about such an idea for the C cost, see: interviewee no 13, 28 April 2023.

[41] Marcel Storme, 'Reflections on Judicial Independence', in Shimon Shetreet and Wayne McCormack (eds) *The Culture of Judicial Independence in a Globalised World* (Brill 2016) 45, 47.

[42] In Germany such difficulties have partly been identified with the above-mentioned narrow standards developed by the BVerfG itself, but also due to the internal dynamics. For a critique in this sense, see: Rolf Lamprecht, 'Karlsruher Befangenheitslogik' (1999) Neue Juristische Wochenschrift (NJW) 2791. From an insider perspective by a former BVerfG judge: Ernst Benda, 'Befangenes zur Befangenheit' (2000) Neue Juristische Wochenschrift (NJW) 3620.

[43] The Spanish Constitutional Tribunal also decides recusal requests with publicly available decisions. See for one of the latest examples: Tribunal constitucional, Decision no 149/2022 of 15 November 2022, ECLI:ES:TC:2022:149A <http://hj.tribunalconstitucional.es/en-US/Resolucion/Show/29146> accessed 2 June 2023).

interpreting such cases, in the sense that rarely constitutional judges were held to be in a conflict of interest.[44] The justifications for those higher standards were and are the fear of manipulations of the composition via recusals leading even to a lack of a quorum, the special inner independence of constitutional judges due to their particular nomination and election mode, as well as the expectation of litigants in such important constitutional and state matters to have (more) faith in the constitutional judges.[45] At least the lack of a quorum argument had been addressed when a new provision about substituting a recused constitutional judge from the other senate had been introduced in the mid-1980s. That did not seem to immediately change the strict approach and justifications in a first case coming after this reform in 1986.[46] Since then, however, the standards seem to have loosened slightly, meaning that the BVerfG has lowered the interpretational hurdles to accept an abstention request or a recusal of one of their colleagues.[47] It would be fair to say that cases in which an abstention or a recusal are accepted in the BVerfG's jurisprudence are rare[48] and remain unclear even for former constitutional judges, especially with regard to public statements or publications made by constitutional judges.[49]

The BVerfG has also looked into situations that are relevant to this book, namely how the previous political positions or activities of constitutional judges may or may not be deemed to be an issue for the independence or impartiality of a constitutional court. As we have already seen, Article 18 BVerfGG establishes that participation in a legislative procedure that might be relevant in a pending case is not deemed to be a ground for exclusion. However, such a participation may still cause issues under Article 19 BVerfGG. In 1986, Herzog asked the question himself, regarding his participation as a state minister in a government decision for a site construction by Daimler-Benz against which a constitutional complaint had been lodged. The BVerfG held that indeed this was problematic, given that Herzog's participation in the decision might raise doubts as to his impartiality in

[44] For a critique on this approach, which could mean that constitutional judges can keep sitting on cases, even though they could have been recused as ordinary judges, see: Rudolf Wassermann, 'Richterlicher Selbstschutz bei der Ablehnung von Richtern des BVerfG? Zur Befangenheitsbesorgnis in verfassungsgerichtlichen Verfahren' (1987) Neue Juristische Wochenschrift (NJW) 418.

[45] On these points, see: Andreas Müller, 'Zur Ablehnung von Bundesverfassungsrichtern wegen Besorgnis der Befangenheit nach § 19 BVerfGG' (1993) Neue Zeitschrift für Verwaltungsrecht (NVwZ) 1167.

[46] BVerfG, 1 BvR713/83, 12 July 1986, as critically noted by Rudolf Wassermann, 'Richterlicher Selbstschutz bei der Ablehnung von Richtern des BVerfG? Zur Befangenheitsbesorgnis in verfassungsgerichtlichen Verfahren' (1987) Neue Juristische Wochenschrift (NJW) 418, 419.

[47] Welcoming this shift, see: Andreas Müller, 'Zur Ablehnung von Bundesverfassungsrichtern wegen Besorgnis der Befangenheit nach § 19 BVerfGG' (1993) Neue Zeitschrift für Verwaltungsrecht (NVwZ) 1167.

[48] See for an older overview of such cases: Hans Lechner and Rüdiger Zuck, *Bundesverfassungsgeri chtsgesetz. Kommentar* (5th edn, CH Beck 2006) 121–22. One of the recent successful recusal requests concerned an interview given by Astrid Wallrabenstein, BVerfG, 2 BvR 2006/15, 12 January 2021, ECLI :DE:BVerfG:2021:rs20210112.2bvr200615.

[49] See in this sense, interviewee no 20, 30 August 2023.

the eyes of the plaintiff.[50] Interestingly, in that decision the BVerfG did not enter the discussion whether it needed to loosen its standards or whether it was still applying the stricter standards of its early days.

A second decision of 1994 always concerned Herzog, but this time the issue was whether his (potential) political activities after his mandate as a constitutional judge could raise issues of impartiality. In fact, while he was still on the bench of the BVerfG, it became public that he was going to be a possible candidate for the Presidency of Germany. Again, he raised the question of his impartiality in that specific case as well as future ones, even though he himself did not believe there were any issues. The BVerfG agreed with him by arguing that neither the rules of incompatibilities for the President established at Article 55 of the GG nor those for constitutional judges at Article 94, para 1 mention the respective functions and therefore a candidacy could not be seen as problematic; nor would such a candidacy constitute a professional activity prohibited by Article 3, para 4 of the BVerfGG; nor was Herzog part of the Second Senate which deals predominantly with competence conflicts amongst state powers but of the First Senate that mostly deals with constitutional complaints and thus not with political conflicts.[51]

Two later cases revolved around a similar issue, namely the prohibition of the far-right party, the *Nationaldemokratische Partei Deutschlands* (NPD).[52] Two constitutional judges and ex-ministers, Peter Müller and Peter Huber, had made statements in favour of not providing state financing to the NPD, or of prohibiting them. Recusal requests were made against both. The BVerfG rejected them because in its opinion, the doubts concerning their impartiality were based on mere assumptions and that there were no factual indications that either had knowledge of or participated in some of the underlying procedures.[53] If one critique can be made for these two decisions it is that—while the rule that such decisions need to be taken in the absence of the concerned member was respected—Peter Huber took part in the decision against Peter Müller and vice-versa, when both were being recused by the same party for similar reasons. This casts a shadow of doubt over the absolute impartiality of the decisions and even of compatibility with the case law established by the ECtHR.[54]

The important takeaway from the German experience is that one can identify certain interpretive and jurisprudential standards which allow the public to follow and assess the BVerfG's reasoning.

[50] BVerfG, 1 BvR 1046/85, 4 June 1986.

[51] BVerfG, 1 BvR 1693/92, 27 January 1994. See the detailed commentary by Volker Epping, 'Die Selbstablehnung von Richtern am Bundesverfassungsgericht' (1994) 109 Deutsches Verwaltungsblatt (DVBl.) 449.

[52] The BVerfG ruled against such a prohibition due to a lack of evidence for the successful implementation of their anti-constitutional goals. BVerfG, 2 BvB1/13, 17 January 2017.

[53] BVerfG, decisions of the Second Senate of 1 March 2016, 2 BvB 1/13.

[54] See Chapter 5, n 105.

This is not the case in France, which has rather recent rules on abstentions and recusals. However, there used to be little or no visibility on how such abstentions and recusals are handled. Essentially, one needed to look at the names of those who took part in the decision and then second-guess from other sources or the official commentary of the decision issued by the CC itself why they had not been there.[55] In a July 2023 judgment, the CC indicated that it would henceforth indicate in the considerations (*visas*) inserted at the beginning of French judgments whether a member decided to abstain from participating in a case.[56] Moreover, in the commentary to that same judgment the CC specified that in its future decisions it would make decisions on recusals of one or more of its members public as soon as they are adopted and not only at the end of the procedure.[57] So, things are slowly changing in the right direction. This was also positively noted by one of the interviewees, who thought that 'this is an excellent development because so far we did not do this and it quells any discussions on such matters'.[58]

With regard to point (iii) (improving or making publicly more visible existing (good) practice), from the interviews a whole other set of good practices emerges that could be better institutionalized and rendered visible in order to strengthen the independence and impartiality of these constitutional courts toward the public and that could potentially have a bearing on the topics studied in this book. These existing practices could be helpful in devising or thinking about how to formalize them also toward the outside.

As already written above, in Italy abstentions are, at least formally, prohibited. In practice, however, judges who believe that there may be a conflict of interest do not show up at the deliberation and/or indicate internally that they have a legitimate reason (*legittimo impedimento*), such as (urgent) health or personal reasons or important institutional engagements for the President of the C cost, for being absent from the deliberations.[59] This covering up of an abstention with another excuse has been critiqued in literature because, in theory, such an excuse would extend to all activities and not simply one single case.[60] But it also seems to be below the honesty and image of constitutional judges who are nudged into unnecessary contortions of the truth, such as inventing medical appointments that, in reality, do not take place.[61] It would be easier and more consistent with the dignity and status of

[55] Probably the most consistent, painstaking, and recent work of this type has been made in the doctoral thesis by Alexia David, 'L'impartialité du Conseil constitutionnel' (DPhil thesis, Normandie Université 2021) <https://normandie-univ.hal.science/tel-03331880v2/file/sygal_fusion_27488-david-alexia.pdf> accessed 12 October 2023.

[56] CC, Decision no 2023-1058 QPC, 21 July 2023.

[57] Commentary on Decision no 2023-1058 QPC, 21 July 2023, note 1 <https://www.conseil-constitutionnel.fr/sites/default/files/as/root/bank_mm/decisions/20231058qpc/20231058qpc_ccc.pdf> accessed 15 December 2023.

[58] Interviewee no 31, 14 December 2023.

[59] See eg: interviewee no 11, 19 April 2023 or interviewee no 13, 28 April 2023.

[60] See on this: Alessio Rauti, 'Riflessioni in tema di imparzialità dei giudici costituzionali' (2009) LIV Giurisprudenza costituzionale 4029, 4030–32.

[61] Interviewee no 15, 7 June 2023.

judges to formalize abstentions. Moreover, abstentions exercised in this informal way are difficult to track from the outside because, as in the pre-July 2023 French situation, one can only glean from the names listed in a judgment if a certain judge was present or absent, but not necessarily why.

That there is an internal, albeit invisible, attention to impartiality at the C cost that may be relevant also for the issues discussed in this book, arose from another interview. Potential conflicts of interest are considered and avoided in the Italian C cost by the President when assigning a judge rapporteur for a given case if (s)he has the sense that there might be an issue of (objective) impartiality. This was expressed most clearly in one of the interviews in the following way:

> Perhaps one thing that may be useful to observe and which of course does not result from normative texts is that sometimes the President of the C cost who nominates the judge rapporteur takes these issues into account when cases are assigned. If a judge comes from the Cons St ... he is not assigned questions raised by that institution of which he might have been President, even when he was not a judge in that matter. It is not considered good to give a judge of the Cass, matters that have as their object conflicts of attribution at least during the first phase of the term of office. That is to say, in the choice of the judge rapporteur, the President makes considerations that somehow mitigate the direct contact, or the experience of the contact that may exist between a judge's previous professional experience and the underlying constitutional case. This is in the choice of the judge rapporteur. That judge, nevertheless, contributes to the decision. But, of course, the judge rapporteur is a figure of particular importance. Thus, the choice of the judge rapporteur is also made to try to achieve the highest degree of impartiality.[62]

From other interviews, it seems similar invisible and virtuous practices exist in Austria,[63] Germany,[64] and in France.[65]

Such practices could be made more visible and stable, for example, in internal rules of procedure and could thus strengthen the image of impartiality toward the public. At the moment, especially in Italy and France they depend heavily on the President in the allocation of cases to a judge rapporteur and thus on his/her sensitivity to the topic.[66]

[62] Interviewee no 6, 3 March 2023. Such an internal attention and practice was also confirmed by interviewee no 7, 3 March 2023.

[63] Interviewee no 22, 12 September 2023.

[64] Interviewee no 28, 16 November 2023.

[65] Interviewee no 30, 14 December 2023.

[66] In Germany, decisions on who is named judge rapporteur are taken by the respective senate. Interviewee no 28, 16 November 2023.

Austria also had to grapple with related issues. We have seen in Chapter 2.1 that in Austria abstentions and exclusions are essentially functioning based on a private communication between the concerned judge and the President of the VfGH. When Wolfgang Brandstetter joined the VfGH, that led to a new situation whereby internal rules and practices were adapted to make sure that no suspicion of bias caused by this former politician would arise. A judge of the VfGH described the practice as follows:

> We had the internal practice that we considered him to be biased for a certain time period—I think it was two or four years—for all provisions that he had co-decided as member of the federal government. That is relatively extensive because in our government the principle of unanimity applies. For instance, when the government passed the 17th VAT amendment, one could be relatively sure that he had nothing to do with it, was not interested in it, and had himself indicated that one could verify his absence of knowledge. We nevertheless considered him to be biased because he co-approved it. Moreover, we held him in any case biased for an even longer time period whenever his ministry had drafted legislative or other provisions. The question did not arise for much longer, because he soon left again. But we would have seen it very strictly.[67]

Hence as for France and Italy, in Austria—besides introducing rules and the possibility of recusal—abstentions could also be handled in more public ways alongside the practices that evidently exist.

It would also have the benefit of avoiding situations as they arose in a 2021 decision by the VfGH. In fact, in that case a claimant asked for the reopening of a procedure before the VfGH, inter alia for violation of the principle of objective impartiality after she had discovered that a judge from the VfGH had participated in a non-public decision on that judge's objective impartiality.[68] Regardless of whether the claimant was right or not, it shows how such behind-the-doors-decisions do not necessarily strengthen the image of impartiality and rather reinforce the fear in the general public that shady deals are being made behind closed doors.

Nevertheless, even here some caution in going too far with allowing recusals and their negative effect on constitutional judges was voiced during the interviews:

> If a party argues that something was only decided this way because judge X voted in favour of it, and I have reason to believe that he has always been biased in this matter, then you might have an initial reflex of thinking 'I don't need that' and withdraw, no matter how far-fetched the recusal is. But the VfGH cannot tolerate this. You cannot allow someone to take themselves out of the game, so to speak,

67 Interviewee no 14, 17 May 2023.
68 VfGH, E4483/2020, 30 November 2021, ECLI:AT:VFGH:2021:E4483.2020.

> unless there is a good reason. That should only be the case if there really is an appearance of partisanship.[69]

The internal practice at the French CC is (also) stricter than the rule. In fact, in one of the interviews the practice was described as follows:

> The CC checks whether any of its members have taken an active part in parliamentary debates by speaking out in favour or against a piece of legislation whose constitutionality is in question. If this is the case, attempts are made to speak informally with the member in question (if they have not spontaneously abstained) to see whether it would not be more appropriate for them to do so.[70]

This means that there is an internal control which is being performed behind the scenes and that goes beyond what the internal rules prescribe. However, this internal 'behind the scenes' control is more difficult and delicate to perform in the context for electoral litigation before the CC where, so far, no rules exist. The reason is that there are no parliamentary debates that can be checked to unveil possible biases which in this case are rather the personal or political closeness of the CC members with the candidate whose election is challenged or who challenges the election.[71]

Another difficulty is that these rules and practices are difficult to track and end up being invisible to the public. Transparent rules on abstentions and recusals should be introduced where they are lacking in order to limit some of the potential risks stemming from former members of government joining constitutional courts. This would not require complicated constitutional or legislative amendment procedures but simply a modification of internal rules, especially in France and Italy.

Based on these observations, reforms in the direction of introducing rules on abstentions and recusals where there are none, improving and rendering more transparent existing rules, and finally making existing informal abstention and recusal practices in the analysed constitutional courts more formal and visible, would probably not lead to the collapse of these institutions but rather strengthen them, eliminate doubts over their (im)partiality, and also protect them from some risks posed by former politicians joining these courts. As one author put it by commenting on the BVerfG's practice and standards in deciding on abstentions and recusals, 'one can only regret that the BVerfG is laxer here than the other [German] courts; for the constitutional jurisdiction is particularly dependent on trust in the

[69] Interviewee no 25, 20 September 2023.
[70] Interviewee no 8, 21 March 2023.
[71] In this sense, interviewee no 8, 21 March 2023.

impartiality of its judges'.[72] This statement sounds even more relevant for the other constitutional courts analysed here, where the standards are lower.

6.4 Cooling-Off Periods

Another mechanism that could provide a possible bulwark against some of the potential risks stemming from former ministers as guardians of the constitution would be to introduce a cooling-off period between the political position held by someone prior to becoming judge on a constitutional court. One could think about it as a sort of temporary incompatibility lasting for a given amount of time.

Pre-judgeship cooling-off periods would, most importantly, avoid the direct passage from the heat of politics to the 'cooler' and more hidden reality of independent and impartial judging. In this sense, it would certainly help avoid a highly visible and direct politicization of constitutional courts and the issues relating to separation of powers that would come with it.

A second risk which cooling-off periods would attenuate is related to the principle of *nemo iudex causa sua* and the possible doubts surrounding the objective impartiality of certain judges who might have contributed to the drafting of certain instruments whose constitutionality is being challenged as former politicians. It might also be helpful to curb other potential conflicts of interest like competence conflicts between state powers, electoral conflicts, or decisions on referenda where such former politicians may have been involved in or know people who are involved especially in electoral litigation due to previous party or political ties.

A third advantage of such cooling-off periods could be that it might prevent certain (former) politicians from joining constitutional courts with all the baggage and visibility that draws unnecessary attention and questions to constitutional courts. It may also have the benefit that some only 'use' constitutional court positions as merely one step on their political career ladder. Allowing time to settle things around a given personality can make their nomination publicly more acceptable.

A few questions arise with regard to such cooling-off periods. Mostly they relate to the length, and which previously held functions are identified as being temporarily incompatible in a given system. As to the first point of duration, one needs to strike a balance between having too long a period, which could mean that one forgoes potentially good candidates for a constitutional judgeship,[73] and too short

[72] Rudolf Wassermann, 'Richterlicher Selbstschutz bei der Ablehnung von Richtern des BVerfG?' (1987) Neue Juristische Wochenschrift (NJW) 418, 420.

[73] See on this argument with regard to a proposed cooling-off period for the judicial council in Montenegro the Venice Commission suggested to reduce a proposed ten-year cooling-off period to a five-year one: Venice Commission, *Opinion on the draft amendments to the Law on the Judicial Council and Judges* adopted by the Venice Commission at its 133rd Plenary Session (Venice, 16–17 December

a period, whereby some of the risks indicated above are not effectively addressed or limited.[74] As to the argument that cooling-off periods—like effective and strict abstention and recusal rules—may reduce the number of available and good candidates, one could mention that Austria has had such a rule since 1929 and despite being a fairly small country and thereby with a reduced pool of potential candidates, has not struggled with this issue. On the contrary, when a former politician was nominated after a long hiatus, it turned into something of a fiasco.

Differences and nuances might also be needed depending on the type of procedure and how long it takes for certain issues to reach constitutional courts. For instance, a priori decisions in France or competence conflicts in Italy probably reach the respective constitutional courts in shorter time than constitutional complaints in Germany or the type of indirect constitutionality review done by the C cost. Statistics probably provide indications on how long such procedures take to identify what could be the best length of time for the most efficient cooling-off period.

As to the second point, the variety also seems to stem from the fact that country- or system-specific events or past experiences have had as a consequence that certain previous political or non-political functions were perceived as more problematic than others and that such cooling-off periods are set only for certain judges and not for all.

A summary overview of existing or proposed cooling-off periods around the world shows the spectrum of possibilities. With regard to existing ones, as we have seen, Austria has a cooling-off period for the President and the Vice-President, if they were members of government or parliament, if they had an elected position at any level (federal, state, or European), or had been employees or officials of a political party in the five years prior to their nomination to the VfGH.[75] Hungary has a cooling-off period of four years for government members, leading officials in any political party or having held a leading state office or a senior political or professional office.[76] Mexico introduced a one-year cooling-off period for those who have been Secretary of State, Attorney General, Senator, Federal Representative, Governor or Head of the Federal District Government.[77] Colombia also has a one year cooling-off period for those who have been Cabinet minister or judges of the

2022), Opinion no 1110/2022, CDL-AD(2022)050, para 33 <https://www.venice.coe.int/webforms/documents/default.aspx?pdffile = CDL-AD(2022)050-e> accessed 9 June 2023.

[74] For a discussion on timing of a proposed post-judgeship cooling-off period in India and striking a balance between various interests involved, see: Arghya Sengupta, *Independence & Accountability of the Indian Higher Judiciary* (CUP 2019) 253–56.

[75] Combined reading of Art 147, para 4 B-VG and Art 147, para 5 B-VG.

[76] Art 6(4) of Act XXXII of 1989 on the Constitutional Court <https://hunconcourt.hu/act-on-the-cc/> accessed 28 April 2023).

[77] Art 95, para VI of the Mexican Constitution <https://www.scjn.gob.mx/constitucion-politica-de-los-estados-unidos-mexicanos/articulos/341> accessed 28 April 2023.

Supreme Court of Justice or of the Council of State.[78] Last but not least, in Albania a ten-year cooling-off-period exists for constitutional judges if they had political functions in the public administration or leadership positions in political parties.[79]

As to proposed cooling-off periods, the constituent assembly of Italy discussed one in 1947. Indeed, Giovanni Leone proposed a four-year cooling-off period for a series of governmental and political functions both at the state and regional levels which nevertheless did not make it into the final version.[80] The 2022 Chilean constitutional reform proposal included a cooling-off period of two years prior to joining the Constitutional Court for 'those who have served in positions of popular election, who have held the position of minister or minister of State or other positions of exclusive confidence of the Government'.[81] Also in 2022 there was a Polish constitutional reform proposal by civil society organizations for a four-year cooling-off period for Polish politicians (MPs, MEPs, members of the government such as ministers or vice-ministers as well as members of political parties) prior to joining the Polish TK.[82] In Germany, a 2023 reform proposal whose goal it is to depoliticize the BVerfG as well as to reinforce the acceptance of its decisions intends to change the BVerfGG by inserting a cooling-off period of six years for all members of parliament and government at both federal and state level.[83]

Two things can be noted: there is quite some variance in terms of timing and the sort of functions that are targeted by these cooling-off periods. Most of these, however, refer to political positions, including the ones discussed in this book. Moreover, there seems to be a growing use of this mechanism from the initial isolated adoption in Austria in 1929 to the various amendments and proposed cooling-off periods today.

Of the four jurisdictions analysed in this book, all have seen some discussion or proposal, either legislative or constitutional, to introduce some type of cooling-off period. Most interesting is possibly the recent 2023 proposal in France, given that this is where most former politicians have joined the CC and where such a

[78] Art 240 of the Colombian Constitution.

[79] Art 7/a, point c) of Statute no 8577 of 10 February 2000, as amended by Statute no 99/2016 of 17 October 2016 entitled 'On some additions and changes in Law no 8577, dated 10 02 2000 on organization and functioning of the Constitutional Court of the Republic of Albania' <https://rm.coe.int/law-99-2016-on-the-organization-and-functioning-of-the-constitutional-/16809eaed4> accessed 28 June 2023.

[80] See: Assemblea Costituente, Commissione per la Costituzione, Seconda Sottocommissione (Seconda Sezione) 23 January 1947, 167.

[81] Art 380, para 2 of the proposed Political Constitution of the Republic of Chile <https://constituteproject.org/constitution/Chile_2022D?lang = en> accessed 30 March 2023;

[82] Art 17 (2-3) <https://www.batory.org.pl/wp-content/uploads/2022/11/Spoleczny.projekt.ustawy.o.Trybunale.Konstytucyjnym.pdf> accessed 10 May 2023.

[83] Deutscher Bundestag, 20. Wahlperiode, 'Entwurf eines Gesetzes zur Entpolitisierung des Bundesverfassungsgerichts und Stärkung der Akzeptanz seiner Entscheidungen', Drucksache 20/6581, 27 April 2023.

cooling-off period could have the largest consequences and effect.[84] However, even in that country where nominations of former (prime) ministers to the CC are not rare, arguably there seems to be an unwritten practice or rule that a certain cooling-off period from active politics is at least wished for. Often the nomination comes as a reward—or more cynically as a consolation—at the end of a long political career when things have already calmed down around some personalities. One could cite Lionel Jospin or Alain Juppé as recent examples.

Instead, some of the more controversial or questioned nominations were those of people who went almost directly from a national government position to the CC. We have already mentioned the nomination of Robert Badinter, who was Justice Minister when François Mitterrand decided to nominate him to the Presidency of the CC. There were undoubtedly other elements that contributed to the controversy, and in particular the fact that in order for Badinter to become President, the actual President of the CC, Daniel Mayer, (was) stepped down from the Presidency via a resignation letter[85] to become 'only' an ordinary member of the CC for the remaining three years of his mandate. This was the first time such a thing happened in France, and it allowed Badinter to have a full nine-year mandate as President, rather than only six years.[86] But probably the direct nomination from a high political position to that of CC member was too much even for France. In a similar way, the recent nomination of Jacqueline Gourault from her ministerial position to that of judge at the CC did not go unnoticed, especially during the parliamentary hearings.[87]

The assessment of the literature of such cooling-off periods is scant but when there is such an assessment it is mildly critical for different reasons. As to Austria, Hans Kelsen in person commented on the 1929 Reform and the proposal of the cooling-off period. While agreeing with the requirement for a legal education, he thought the proposal to introduce a cooling-off period in the draft reform text went too far and wondered why such a period was being introduced only for the VfGH and the Austrian Administrative Supreme Court (VwGH), but not also for

[84] Proposition de loi constitutionnelle visant à garantir une meilleure impartialité et indépendance des membres du Conseil constitutionnel, no. 1107, lodged at the Présidence de l'Assemblée nationale on 20 April 2023
<https://www.assemblee-nationale.fr/dyn/16/textes/l16b1107_proposition-loi.pdf> accessed 4 September 2023.

[85] The resignation letter was published in Le Monde, 21 February 1986, 10.

[86] See against this: Maurice Duverger, 'Une fraude à la Constitution?' *Le Monde* (Paris, 22 February 1986) 7; rather in favour: Jean-Marie Colombani, 'L'opposition, à l'exception de M. Chirac, dénonce la nomination de M. Badinter' *Le Monde* (Paris, 21 February 1986) 1 and 10 ; and François Luchaire, 'La nomination de M. Badinter au Conseil constitutionnel. Réponse à Maurice Duverger' *Le Monde* (Paris, 26 February 1986) 9.

[87] Critically on those hearings, see: Eric Buge, 'Les auditions des candidats aux fonctions de membre du Conseil constitutionnel par les commissions parlementaires constituent-elles un filtre déontologique?' in Elina Lemaire and Thomas Perroud (eds), *Le Conseil constitutionnel à l'épreuve de la déontologie et de la transparence* (IFJD 2022) 83; more specifically on the hearing by Jacqueline Gourault: Lauréline Fontaine, *La Constitution maltraitée* (Editions Amsterdam 2023) 74–75.

the Austrian Supreme Court (OGH). In particular, he wondered why 'the rigour of the draft and its unflinching will to de-politicise stopped precisely before the OGH given that the current President of this institution would immediately lose his position if all three apex courts of the Republic had been measured by the same weight'.[88] What also emerges from Kelsen's commentary is that the draft 1929 Reform had intended to extend the cooling-off period to all VfGH judges and not only to the President and the Vice-President.[89]

For slightly different reasons and much later in time, Lauréline Fontaine wonders whether such a cooling-off period would indeed address some of these issues in France. In her recent critique of the CC, she states that:

> The law does not even provide for a cooling-off period (*'sas' temporel*) between the political work of future members and their entry into the CC. But the institution of a cooling-off period would certainly not be enough. Cases where former ministers or members of parliament have had to deal with a law as judges, even though they had been involved in drafting it years before, or on which they had expressed strong opinions, are not uncommon and are even more numerous.[90]

In a similarly doubtful way about whether such cooling-off periods would really achieve their goal, one could mention a recent study by former German constitutional court judge, Lübbe-Wolff, who rightfully observes that the presence of such a mechanism, for instance in Hungary, has not prevented constitutional courts from being staffed with former politicians or becoming captured by politics.[91]

Nevertheless, the reactions from the interviewees is overall less sceptical in those systems where a cooling-off period does not exist. Of course, there are those who doubt its usefulness[92] or question its feasibility in practice.[93] But overall, few objected to them in absolute terms[94] and the echo seemed to be fairly positive and overall interested. One of them stated that such cooling-off periods, both at the entry to and the exit from constitutional courts, could be useful instruments without being too rigid.[95] A second one thought that such periods have a certain

[88] Hans Kelsen, 'Die Verfassungsreform' (1929) 58 Juristische Blätter 445, 456.

[89] ibid.

[90] Lauréline Fontaine, *La Constitution maltraitée* (Editions Amsterdam 2023) 46.

[91] Gertrude Lübbe-Wolff, *Beratungskulturen. Wie Verfassungsgerichte arbeiten, und wovon es abhängt, ob sie integrieren oder polarisieren* (Konrad-Adenauer-Stiftung 2022) 198–203 <https://www.kas.de/documents/252038/16166715/Beratungskulturen.+Wie + Verfassungsgerichte+arbeiten%2C + und+wovon + es+abh%C3%A4ngt%2C + ob+sie + integrieren+oder + polarisieren.pdf/a68323e0-dd86-6b7b-202e-bd4130edb511?version = 1.3&t = 1683291883575> accessed on 25 September 2023.

[92] See eg interviewee no 12, 27 April 2023 and interviewee no 11, 19 April 2023.

[93] Interviewee no 2, 1 February 2023 who highlighted the difficulty that in Italy the President of the C cost is elected internally and thus a cooling-off period solely for that function would be difficult to put in place, and interviewee no 10, 19 April 2023, who did not think that the passage of time would really solve some issues.

[94] Interviewee no 17, 9 June 2023 did so, but linked it to the introduction of clear rules on abstentions and recusals. If those are put in place, then cooling-off periods would become moot.

[95] Interviewee no 7, 3 March 2023.

rationality.[96] A third one thought that such a period would be smart if it serves to provide extra guarantees with regard to public opinion, despite being somewhat a question of optics.[97] A fourth one indicated that, if introduced, it should apply to all constitutional judges, and not simply to some as is the case in Austria.[98] Whereas a fifth one indicated that it could constitute a break with the political past and nature of the CC and that French political parties might even be able to agree on such a rule at the constitutional level.[99]

As to Austria, where the mechanism exists, it is assessed positively and the proposed extension to all constitutional judges that will be discussed further below under Part 7.1 is seen as closing a legislative and constitutional gap that had become exposed with the latest events around Wolfgang Brandstetter.[100]

6.5 Prohibition or Limiting Numbers

The most extreme solution could be to simply prohibit certain personalities from becoming constitutional court judges or to insert a limitation in terms of how many judges of a given constitutional court are allowed to have political experience.

I am not aware of any system where this has actually happened. However, there may be situations in the future whereby a specific constitutional or historical experience leads to the necessity for such a rule to be put in place. And perceptions may change rapidly. It suffices that one or two personalities nominated to a constitutional court may end up discrediting it or involving it regularly in controversies or scandals and the damage is done, with calls for change becoming more insistent.

The Austrian example is again an interesting one from this perspective. After the 1929 Reform, with one exception in 1945, no more former politicians had joined the VfGH until 2018. The scandal(s) which then involved that judge accelerated the discussion of extending the cooling-off period to all judges at the VfGH. One bad experience could thus, in a given context, trigger a modification, in the sense of requiring a prohibition or making it seem more palatable.

Remaining with the Austrian context, we have already seen that Austria has some of the most rigid abstention rules and practices for what concerns the participation in the elaboration of legislation. Indeed, such stringent rules could all but prevent ex-ministers from becoming constitutional judges. In fact, the nominating authorities might be discouraged from proposing the name of someone who might be considered a lame duck for their first years on a given constitutional court

[96] Interviewee no 13, 28 April 2023.
[97] Interviewee no 4, 8 February 2023.
[98] Interviewee no 9, 22 March 2023.
[99] Interviewee no 8, 22 March 2023.
[100] In this sense: interviewee no 14, 17 May 2023.

because they must continuously abstain from judging, as has been the case with Brandstetter.

At the same time, despite all the benefits to constitutional and supreme courts of having political personalities on their bench, there are examples of courts which are composed only of professional judges not because of a prohibition but because one criterion for becoming a judge on a constitutional court is to be a professional judge. That is the case in Luxembourg, where since 1996 in conjunction with the reform triggered by the above-mentioned *Procola* judgment by the ECtHR, a constitutional court was created and constituted solely of professional judges.[101]

If one believes that the prohibition for all constitutional judges to have been ex-ministers goes too far, one could also imagine some nuances. For instance, one could provide that particularly visible or exposed positions, such as the President or Vice-President of a given constitutional court, need to be judges and cannot have held governmental or political positions before. Or that only a certain maximum number of former politicians can be nominated to a constitutional court.

To sum up, there is no one-size-fits-all solution, and the context will matter considerably. What this chapter set out to do is to highlight where and how one could intervene to minimize the risks, depending on the situation.

[101] On this see: <https://accf-francophonie.org/cour/cour-constitutionnelle-du-luxembourg/> accessed 21 June 2023.

7
Concluding Thoughts—Looking Back To Move Forward

This book has analysed what happens when former members of government become constitutional judges and thereby guardians of the constitution, to borrow the expression from the Kelsen-Schmitt debate of the 1920s and 1930s. By looking closely and comparatively at four established constitutional courts, one can note both commonalities and variations. Starting with the commonalities, arguably, in all four systems analysed, there is a constitutional court or institution that has the monopoly power to declare statutes unconstitutional, something that has become known as the European model of constitutionality review. Formal rules of independence are also guaranteed via long and non-renewable terms of the constitutional judges. Moreover, all four constitutional courts are inserted into a multilevel legal framework where especially the relationship with the CJEU and ECtHR plays an important role. Hence, from this perspective, the issue of former politicians becoming constitutional judges can have relatively similar effects.

With regard to the variations, it is fair to say that these emerge when one takes a closer look: no legal education required for constitutional judges (France), part-time constitutional judges (Austria), two-Senate structure (Germany), rotating presidencies (Italy), dissenting opinions (Germany), cooling-off period for some constitutional judges (Austria); prohibition of abstentions and recusals (Italy); many former politicians becoming constitutional judges (France). This means that, despite having a similar main task—namely the constitutionality control of legislation—they function (very) differently. Moreover, these variations exist not only comparatively, ie between the four systems, but also within one system, chronologically. So, the presence of former politicians in one constitutional system at a given time may change, depending on which system and at which moment that took place.

So far, this book has focused on the past and what has happened in each of the four systems. I posit that, comparatively, the risks which former politicians bring into constitutional courts outweigh the benefits. This assessment, however, is not necessarily shared by current and former constitutional judges. Apart from Austria, where it is fair to say that many of those I interviewed find that former politicians have little or no place in constitutional courts, in France, Italy and Germany their experience is assessed more positively. In France, it is almost seen as a prerequisite and a guarantee that such personalities have a sense of the state. For the latter two

Ex-Ministers as Constitutional Judges. Mathias Möschel, Oxford University Press. © Mathias Möschel 2025.
DOI: 10.1093/9780198930228.003.0007

systems, a proviso is added that not too many should join constitutional courts, because then indeed the risks might start outweighing the benefits.

Can we still remain so confident when looking ahead? I provided some forward-looking comments and thoughts when analysing the (potential) risks especially of (over- or mono-)politicization and how to address them in the two previous chapters. Further institutional changes for these constitutional courts are still taking place and are at the planning or proposal level. Thus, the role that former members of government play in such courts could shift (again) either because the texts governing them are amended or because the *con*texts within which they operate change. I will mention only some of the most relevant proposed *textual* reforms that are relevant for this book and that for the most part have not entered into force (yet) (section 7.1), before moving onto the *contextual* ones (section 7.2).

7.1 Textual Reform Proposals

In all four systems under consideration here, some relevant constitutional and/or legislative reform proposals have been made. I will briefly mention a few of them here to give the reader a sense of what is in the pipeline or under discussion.

As to Austria, in 2021 the Austrian government proposed a legislative reform on freedom of information (*Informationsfreiheitsgesetz*).[1] This reform would extend the cooling-off period of five years applicable so far only for the President and Vice-President of this institution to all judges and substitute judges at the VfGH, albeit limitedly to three years.[2] From the interviews, this part of the reform is the one encountering least opposition.[3] However, in that same reform proposal there is the discussion to introduce the possibility of dissenting opinions.[4] This aspect generated some misgivings within the VfGH, especially in view of the somewhat disguised way in which it was introduced in a legislation on transparency, thus raising the suspicion that it is a way to control and discipline the constitutional judges.[5] Last but not least, there is a constitutional reform proposal brought by a

[1] Bundesgesetz, mit dem das Bundes-Verfassungsgesetz, das Rechnungshofgesetz 1948 und das Verfassungsgerichtshofgesetz 1953 geändert und ein Informationsfreiheitsgesetz erlassen werden, 95/ME XXVII. GP—Ministerialentwurf—Gesetzestext, 22 February 2021 <https://www.parlament.gv.at/gegenstand/XXVII/ME/95> accessed 27 September 2023.

[2] ibid Art 1, para 10 which would add another sentence after Art 147, para 5 B-VG.

[3] See eg: interviewee no 14, 17 May 2023; interviewee no 24, 19 September 2023, who even described this reform as a necessity; and interviewee no 25, 20 September 2023, who found that an abolition of this rule would endanger the VfGH.

[4] ibid Art 4, para 4 which would add a para 3 to Art 26 of the VfGG.

[5] See eg: interviewee no 14, 17 May 2023; interviewee no 22, 12 September 2023; and interviewee no 24, 19 September 2023.

single parliamentarian, which would introduce a two-thirds majority requirement for electing constitutional judges similar to the one existing in Germany.[6]

In Italy, doctrinal reform proposals of the nomination procedure were already made in the 1970s.[7] More concrete, unsuccessful, textual proposals were then made in 1997, with the proposed introduction of a cooling-off period of five years for those who would like to take up governmental positions, publicly elected or government-nominated posts, or any role at independent administrative agencies *after* their mandate as a constitutional judge had already expired.[8] This period was then reduced essentially to three years in the constitutional reform proposal of 2005, which was rejected by a referendum in 2006.[9] The possible introduction of such a post-mandate cooling-off period was assessed positively by some of the interviewees[10] but not necessarily in the literature.[11] That same constitutional reform proposal would also have touched upon the nomination procedure by introducing a stronger regional involvement in the election of constitutional judges.[12] Less formally, one interviewee mentioned the possibility of reducing the three supreme court judges from the Cass to one and to substitute them with one first instance judge and an appeals court judge, thus guaranteeing an additional diversity of viewpoints at the C cost.[13]

For Germany, I would first mention the recent public and academic discussions concerning a possible constitutionalization of the two-thirds majority required to elect constitutional judges as well as other aspects concerning the functioning of the BVerfG.[14] As we have seen, the two-thirds majority is 'only' established

[6] Antrag der Abgeordneten Dr Nikolaus Scherak, MA, Kolleginnen und Kollegen betreffend ein Bundesgesetz, mit dem das Bundes-Verfassungsgesetz (B-VG) geändert wird, no 2919, 15 November 2022 <https://www.parlament.gv.at/gegenstand/XXVII/A/2919> accessed 27 September 2023.

[7] Giuliano Amato and Franco Bassanini, 'La Corte costituzionale, un istituto da riformare' (1972) III Politica del diritto 811.

[8] Commissione parlamentare per le riforme costituzionali, 'Progetto di legge costituzionale. Revisione della parte seconda della Costituzione', XIII Legislatura, Camera dei deputati no 3931-A and Senato no 2583-A, Art 135, para 4 <http://leg13.camera.it/_dati/leg13/lavori/stampati/pdf/39310A.pdf> accessed 11 October 2022.

[9] Art 51, para 4 of disegno di legge costituzionale no 2544-D, Senato della Repubblica, XIV Legislatura <https://www.senato.it/service/PDF/PDFServer/BGT/00149609.pdf> accessed 4 September 2023, which would have modified Art 135 of the Italian Constitution.

[10] See eg: interviewee no 2, 1 February 2023 and interviewee no 7, 3 March 2023.

[11] See Gustavo Zagrebelsky, *Principî e voti* (Einaudi 2005) 108–15.

[12] Art 51, para 1, of disegno di legge costituzionale no 2544-D, Senato della Repubblica, XIV Legislatura <https://www.senato.it/service/PDF/PDFServer/BGT/00149609.pdf> accessed 4 September 2023, which would have modified Art 135 of the Italian Constitution. The proposal would have kept the number of judges at 15, but only four would have been nominated by the President, four elected by the judges and seven by Parliament, of whom four by what was supposed to become the Federal Senate and three by the lower house.

[13] Interviewee no 17, 9 June 2023.

[14] Markus Sehl, 'Wie lässt sich das BVerfG vor Entmachtung schützen?' (*Legal Tribune Online*, 29 January 2024) <https://www.lto.de/recht/hintergruende/h/bverfg-gg-richter-demokratie-bundestag-rechtsstaat-verfassungsaenderung/> accessed 25 February 2024, and Michael Eichberger, 'Die erste von drei Säulen: Zum Arbeitsentwurf des BMJ zur Stärkung der Stellung des Bundesverfassungsgerichts' (*VerfBlog*, 16 April 2024) <https://verfassungsblog.de/die-erste-von-drei-saulen/> accessed 30 May 2024. For an earlier discussion in the literature on the various risks of hostile takeovers of the

statutorily by the BVerfGG. The idea here would be to insulate the BVerfG from a potential hostile takeover, especially by the far-right *Alternative für Deutschland* (AfD) party. In April 2024, the Ministry of Justice elaborated a draft for discussions that would need to involve a broad coalition to amend the relevant provisions of the GG.[15] On 23 July 2024, a common strategy agreed upon by a large spectrum of political parties to better protect the BVerfG was announced.[16]

Ironically, precisely that same party from whose influence the BVerfG is to be insulated, introduced its own bill in 2023 whereby it proposed to introduce a six-year cooling-off period for those who join the BVerfG as judges and who have been former members of parliament and government at both federal and state level.[17] This proposal was explicitly linked to the persona of the current President of the BVerfG, Stephan Harbarth, whose former political position but also activities as lawyer in a private law firm were identified as a problem for the independence (*sic*) of the BVerfG.[18] In a striking parallel to the Austrian 1929 Reform, this proposal also called for the de-politicization of the BVerfG and added the element of strengthening acceptance of its judgments by the introduction of such a cooling-off period. In its motivation, nevertheless, the proposal mostly zooms in on the private activities of Harbarth, rather than on the question of interest to this book, namely the fact that due to his political activities at the federal level, he is bound to have supported or opposed legislation whose constitutionality may be challenged later on before the BVerfG.

In France, there is a long-awaited and necessary constitutional reform to eliminate the ex officio membership of former Presidents of the Republic. Pursuant to the important 2008 constitutional reform and the introduction of an a posteriori constitutionality review, such members are by now an anachronism. While there seems to be an overall agreement on the need for such a reform[19] with suggestions

BVerfG: Konrad Duden, 'Richterwahl und parteipolitische Einflussnahme. Vergleichende Anregungen zum Schutz der Unabhängigkeit des Bundesverfassungsgerichts und der obersten Bundesgerichte' (2020) 84 Rabels Zeitschrift für ausländisches und internationales Privatrecht 637.

[15] Dr Felix W Zimmermann and Helen Schroeter, 'Bundesjustizministerium schlägt Grundgesetzänderung vor' (*Legal Tribune Online*, 28 March 2024) <https://www.lto.de/recht/nachrichten/n/resilienz-schutz-bverfg-gesetzesentwurf-bmj-grundgesetz-nderung-verfassung/> accessed 30 May 2024.

[16] For a first commentary on this draft, see: Markus Böckenförde, '"Resilience lite": Strengthening the constitutional protection of the German Federal Constitutional Court' (*ConstitutionNet*, International IDEA, 29 July 2024) <https://constitutionnet.org/news/voices/resilience-lite-german-federal-constitutional-court> accessed 21 August 2024.

[17] Deutscher Bundestag, 20 Wahlperiode, 'Entwurf eines Gesetzes zur Entpolitisierung des Bundesverfassungsgerichts und Stärkung der Akzeptanz seiner Entscheidungen', Drucksache 20/6581, 27 April 2023.

[18] ibid point A.

[19] See on a debate in favour of or against the presence of these former high-level politicians: Pascal Jan and Olivier Pluen, 'Les anciens présidents de la République, membres de droit du Conseil constitutionnel: un anachronisme bien vivant' (*Actu-Juridique*, 30 November 2016) <https://www.actu-juridique.fr/constitutionnel/les-anciens-presidents-de-la-republique-membres-de-droit-du-conseil-constitutionnel-un-anachronisme-bien-vivant/> accessed 4 September 2023.

to eliminate such a membership made by various officially mandated study committees for quite some time[20] and by concrete constitutional reform proposals,[21] little or nothing has happened so far.

Another constitutional reform proposal of 2023 coming from the left of the political spectrum intends to strengthen the impartiality and independence of the French constitutional judges and adds other interesting elements to the earlier proposals concerning the abolition of the ex officio membership of former Presidents. In particular, it would reform Articles 56 and 57 of the French Constitution by specifying that confirmation hearings are done by two parliamentary commissions that need to vote by a two-thirds majority; that the President is elected internally by the other members of the CC; and that of the nine members, only three can have exercised political or governmental functions during the ten years prior to their mandate as constitutional judges. The others six should be nominated due to their legal qualifications.[22] In essence, this proposal is the equivalent of a ten-year cooling-off period for six of the nine judges at the CC.

Last but not least, one could mention the 2017 proposal for a framework statute (*loi organique*) which was supposed to introduce some form of conflict of (economic) interest prevention of members of the CC with a goal of transparency and fight against corruption, which also has not been passed yet.[23]

It remains to be seen which, if any, of these proposals will enter into force and in what form they will do so. Clearly, they could affect some of the analyses made in this book.

[20] See eg the Vedel Committee of 1993: Comité consultatif pour une révision de la Constitution, présidé par le doyen Georges Vedel, 'Proposition pour une révision de la Constitution, 15 February 1993, esp ch I, point A. b) 3 <https://medias.vie-publique.fr/data_storage_s3/rapport/pdf/084000091.pdf>; the Balladur Committee of 2007: Comité de réflexion et de proposition sur la modernisation et le rééquilibrage des institutions de la Ve République, 'Une Ve République plus démocratique', 90 <https://medias.vie-publique.fr/data_storage_s3/rapport/pdf/074000697.pdf>; and the Jospin Committee of 2012: Commission de rénovation et de déontologie de la vie publique, 'Pour un renouveau démocratique', proposition n° 32, 102 <https://medias.vie-publique.fr/data_storage_s3/rapport/pdf/124000596.pdf> all accessed 27 September 2023.

[21] See most recently: Projet de loi constitutionnelle n° 814 relatif aux incompatibilités applicables à l'exercice de fonctions gouvernementales et à la composition du Conseil constitutionnel, lodged at the Présidence de l'Assemblée nationale on 14 March 2013 and the Projet de loi constitutionnelle n°911 pour une démocratie plus représentative, responsable et efficace, lodged at the Présidence de l'Assemblée nationale on 9 May 2018 <https://www.assemblee-nationale.fr/dyn/15/textes/l15b0911_projet-loi> accessed 27 September 2023.

[22] Proposition de loi constitutionnelle visant à garantir une meilleure impartialité et indépendance des membres du Conseil constitutionnel, no 1107, lodged at the Présidence de l'Assemblée nationale on 20 April 2023 <https://www.assemblee-nationale.fr/dyn/16/textes/l16b1107_proposition-loi.pdf> accessed 4 September 2023.

[23] Proposition de loi organique n° 359, relative aux obligations déontologiques applicables aux membres du Conseil constitutionnel, lodged at the Présidence du Sénat on 1 February 2017 <https://www.senat.fr/leg/ppl16-359.html> accessed 27 September 2023.

7.2 Contextual Changes

Apart from the *textual* reform proposals, *contextual* changes also may affect how to assess the role played by former politicians joining constitutional courts as judges. Despite this book arguing that the risks of such personalities becoming guardians of the constitution outweigh the benefits, *so far* in none of the four jurisdictions analysed here, has their presence led to unsurmountable problems for their respective constitutional courts and their legitimacy and impartiality in the public eye. The Austrian situation is where the issue is mostly seen in negative terms and the proposed extension of the cooling-off period to all constitutional judges goes in this direction.

But overall one can say that the observed judicialization of politics has not led to a 'politicization of the judiciary', in the understanding used for this book, and the risks have remained rather anecdotal than structural, even though they mount up, when looking at them comparatively and cumulatively.

However, it is not said that the contextual picture remains stable and that it is less the institutional modifications or amendments than the political-societal ones that will change the picture. The risks identified in this book could become greater as the rise of populism and illiberalism threaten to spread from less established constitutional democracies to more established ones. And this is not just a hypothetical situation and discussion. The attacks or proposed reforms of constitutional and supreme courts by leaders and politicians in Hungary or Poland have certainly come to the radar of constitutional judges in Western Europe, either via the case law of the CJEU and the ECtHR or via the opinions by the Venice Commission. What seems to spark even more urgency is that now threats to the independence and impartiality also hover over much more established Supreme Courts, like Israel's.[24]

In the interviews I conducted, the changing political context was worrying some interviewees. One of them indicated how the political changes had not been on his mind when joining the CC, but that it definitely was something that he closely looked at.[25] Another interviewee stated that 'it is not a good time at all to change anything about the way a constitutional court works, because things are far too volatile at the moment and the whole system is somewhat under pressure anyway'.[26] Apart from the overall context for institutional reforms, what is mostly on the minds of the interviewees is how internal political dynamics could affect

[24] See: Gabor Halmai, 'Is There a "Constitutional Moment" in Israel and Hungary?' (2023) 56 Israel L Rev 426. and other contributions in that same journal number.

[25] Interviewee no 4, 8 February 2023.

[26] Interviewee no 14, 17 May 2023.

future nomination procedures and practices, nominees, the quality and competences of such nominees and possible court capture by certain far-right political parties.

One first concern is that of the changed quality and institutional sense of the nomination authorities or political parties. One of the interviewees mentioned the following:

> When I was young and a university assistant, the individual political parties had a basic understanding of institutions, including the constitutional court. I think this has decreased drastically. This is a political issue, in general, and of course for right-wing parties.[27]

Another one went even further and highlighted a related point about nomination practices and the quality of candidates. Indeed, the worry is that nominations to constitutional courts are the result of a political give-and-take, rather than a search for the best possible and most qualified candidate.

> In principle, I fully support the fact that members of constitutional courts are appointed politically. What should not occur is that political favours are distributed. You choose people who have a certain ideological affinity, and they should of course be people who are highly qualified in their field. If it happens that people are chosen not because they are so good professionally, but because you want to thank them for something or some service rendered, then that is doubly dramatic. This may imply a real dependency in the sense of a tit-for-tat. But it can also be that you are looking for someone you know well, who is simply nice, and that is also bad if there are no professional qualifications. This does not necessarily only involve former politicians.[28]

Another concern is about existing nomination practices and how they could be influenced by certain political changes and ultimately also affect the quality and competence of the nominees:

> In the parliamentary election there is a practice that, due to the very high majority of votes required, one normally seeks an agreement. This is done not only to have the necessary electoral quorum but also to ensure that the elected judge is an expression of a cross-section of votes. The understanding is that such an agreement will be respected. We are trying to figure out what will happen now because at the moment the majority in Parliament is so high that there could be a sudden change in composition of the Constitutional Court. … Undoubtedly, a principle

[27] Interviewee no 24, 19 September 2023.
[28] Interviewee no 29, 5 December 2023.

> of competence must prevail—and I hope it will prevail. But I do not know if the parliamentarians will seek such a broad consensus, if they have such a broad majority in the united chambers. In little over a year, four parliamentary judges can be appointed which could completely change the situation today.[29]

Related to the quality of the nominees is the concern that future constitutional judges could feel less allegiance to their respective constitutional court than to external political forces and the consequences this could have on the internal culture of such institutions, especially when dissenting opinions are allowed:

> [T]he much greater danger is that there are people who feel connected to external political forces. And that then calls into question the secrecy of deliberations ... A potential breach of confidentiality goes straight to the heart of a court. ... And that is not something that can be absorbed by a majority decision. It is the destruction of a culture of consultation that cannot be restored in this form. The small destruction already takes place when someone always goes for separate opinions.[30]

One last concern that was cautiously voiced rather touches upon the judicial output and the implementation or lack thereof of constitutional judgments. The worry was not necessarily related to constitutional or democratic backsliding but a more generic loss of political culture.

> It is more about the implementation of case law and compliance with judgments. I have observed a certain self-assurance and complacency on the part of politicians—in the past this would have been called arrogance—who believe that they have everything under control, including the judicial power, and that they can ultimately cope with unpopular decisions. If I had to articulate my fears for the future of the BVerfG, my fear would be that politics will override case law. And there were certainly constellations during my time in office in which one could have the feeling, or at least imagine, that the GG was not at the forefront of a top German politician's thoughts, to put it kindly.[31]

Early American constitutional drafters devised checks and balances on a realistic notion that if men were angels, then no government would be necessary and by consequence also no external or internal controls on government would be needed.[32] Whether or not this development of the doctrine of separation of powers

[29] Interviewee no 13, 28 April 2023.

[30] Interviewee no 34, 22 February 2024.

[31] Interviewee no 21, 8 September 2023.

[32] James Madison, The Federalist No 51 (1788), reprinted in Geoffrey A Stone and others, *Constitutional Law* (6th edn, Aspen Publishers 2009) 22.

and checks and balances was based on a pessimistic vision of human nature or with the worst-case scenario in mind is discussed elsewhere.[33]

In a similarly realistic vein, I am trying to imagine how the current practices and rules at these constitutional courts would fare in the scenario of (hostile) take-over by political forces whose stated goal it is to undermine control institutions like courts or elites more broadly. Would the existing practices, traditions, interpretations, and constitutional culture on the issues discussed in this book still hold-up? One may wonder. Just because, so far and to a large extent, the kind of former politicians who joined the constitutional courts did not lead to institutional crises or larger public outcry or unrest does not mean this will remain the case.

One first observation to that open question is what kind of politicians get nominated. So far, the examples mentioned in this book are mostly established states(wo)men and—apart from France—also lawyers or law professors. Will we observe a change to this picture and the nominations of less politically visible personalities than the ones we have analysed here? Indeed, it might be wiser for an illiberal regime to nominate less visible and more controllable and malleable second-line politicians, attorneys or civil servants, than high-visibility personalities from government who attract too much attention from the larger public. Arguably, some of the greater dangers may indeed come from the hidden political links and the fact that minor personalities may be less resistant to pressures from authoritarian leaders than established political statesmen or stateswomen. Such pressures may be particularly present during a regime change towards an illiberal or autocratic regime.

A second observation links to the literature and some of the interviewees who mentioned that there is a certain 'peer pressure' to be competent, to be able to sustain one's case in hearings or when one is a judge rapporteur and that if one was suspected of any sort of political influence or argument, that person would be sidelined. Put more academically, many attested to the Becket effect, or something similar indeed existing. All this presumes that these issues matter to the newly nominated constitutional judges. What if they do not and new judges are nominated whose explicit or implicit goal is precisely to upset such a practice and pressure? The example of Wolfgang Brandstetter in Austria is a telling one. The point is not to claim that he was nominated to disrupt the VfGH or that he ever intended to do so. However, there was arguably on his side little wish to integrate the institution in a meaningful way and follow its rules and practices.

Hence, the attempt in the previous chapter to see where one could (preventively) insert some protective mechanisms to avoid a stronger and different kind of politicization of the judiciary and of such constitutional courts. Now, of course rules are written on paper and do not as such protect against anything. A dictatorship would

[33] James P Scanlan, '*The Federalist* and Human Nature' (1959) 21 The Review of Politics 657.

simply disregard such rules. But what may be even more dangerous is that illiberal regimes do not need to fully disregard rules but rather 'rule by cheating'[34] or use 'constitutional malice'.[35] Rules are thus formally kept in place, but they are circumvented, avoided, undermined or misused for a different purpose than the one originally planned for. Often, constitutional (or supreme) courts find themselves at the outset and core of such proposals and mechanisms in illiberal or autocratic legalist regimes. Examples abound and are part and parcel of illiberal governments' very creative rulebook.[36] Just to use Poland as a good example, the reforms tried to do all sorts of things, from requiring certain super-majorities in given cases, to limiting the publication of judgments.[37] But even in the past for the jurisdictions examined here, similarly creative examples can be found. Indeed, one of the interviewees mentioned the Austrian situation in the early 1930s when the government issued a decree stating that members of the VfGH who had been appointed by a specific institution, could only attend the sessions of the VfGH if all members having been appointed by that institution also attended. When two members of this category did not do so, the VfGH became unable to act.[38]

One could argue that whatever rule one devises to prevent mischief from happening, illiberalism will find a way to circumvent, undermine, or cheat that rule. Another reality is that even when rules exist or are put in place, constitutional courts function along informal rules and practices that may favour or hinder a given set of reforms.[39] The legal proposals suggested in the last chapter thus may fail or simply be dead letters, and it just may be that the ultimate solutions or answers to what is (also) a political issue should be political and not legal.

At the same time, as already stated above in Chapter 6, the logic of the proposed solutions discussed here is rather that of an alarm system. If one wants to prevent a thief from entering a house, one does not leave doors and windows open. Probably one would at least close them, lock them, and/or install an alarm system. Of course, if someone really wanted to break in, they would probably be able to do so. But it would become clear that they had to break in and could not simply walk in freely through open doors or windows. Using this metaphor and applying it to the object of this book, the solutions discussed in the previous chapter would represent the

[34] On this term and the related phenomena, see: András Sajó, *Ruling by Cheating. Governance in Illiberal Democracies* (CUP 2021).

[35] Kim Lane Scheppele, 'Autocratic Legalism' (2018) 85 The University of Chicago L Rev 545, 547.

[36] See globally on this point: Tom Ginsburg and Aziz Z Hug, *How to Save a Constitutional Democracy* (University of Chicago Press 2018).

[37] For an overview and critique of these, see the already mentioned the Venice Commission's opinion: *Opinion on the Act on the Constitutional Tribunal* adopted by the Venice Commission at its 108th Plenary Session (Venice, 14–15 October 2016), Opinion no 860/2016, CDL-AD(2016)026, esp paras 20–120 <https://www.venice.coe.int/webforms/documents/default.aspx?pdffile=CDL-AD(2016)026-e> accessed 25 July 2024.

[38] Interviewee no 23, 12 September 2023.

[39] On the issue of informality in courts more broadly, see: David Kosař, Katarína Šipulová and Marína Urbániková, 'Informality and Courts: Uneasy Partnership' (2023) 24 German LJ 1239.

closed/locked doors and windows, and/or the alarm system. Without any rules—as is mostly the case today—an illiberal ruler could, in theory, easily place their political cronies whether government members, parliamentarians, or party officials into such courts with few obstacles. Putting some rules into place now rather than when things are happening or have already happened might prevent the kind of possible politicization of courts that I have attempted to analyse here.

I hope to have provided some starting thoughts of what issues to look out for from a comparative perspective when former ministers join constitutional courts as judges and thereby become 'Guardians of the Constitution'. So far, I posit the phenomenon has received little attention in the literature, possibly because it has created few truly existential problems to such courts. As a first step, this book thus analyses what types of benefits and risks as well as legal rules regulate how such personalities operate on such courts. These analyses can be extended to other types of politicians, such as parliamentarians, as well as to other legal systems and supreme courts beyond the four systems analysed here and where arguably similar issues arise. If that should not be the case, then this study may serve as a basis for distinguishing from the points made here.

As a second step, this book also points to the risks associated with ex-ministers or other types of active politicians changing hats to become constitutional (or supreme court) judges. It may well be that such risks (or others that I have failed to identify) have already manifested themselves elsewhere in other legal systems. The open question is whether this practice could be seen in a different light also in chronological terms with the rise of constitutional and democratic backsliding. We have seen how courts in such systems are often amongst the first victims of attacks or capture. Nothing is easier than staffing constitutional courts with one's political friends, especially if existing rules put no or very few barriers in place. In such a scenario, judgeships would no longer be a question of selecting the most competent and widely reputed and accepted individuals, but might transform into just another position to be distributed to loyal political friends. Whether the Becket effect would then (still) function remains to be seen.

ANNEX 1

Survey Questions Sent to Potential Interviewees

Independence and Impartiality of European Constitutional Court Judges

The following survey deals with the independence and impartiality of European constitutional court judges in Austria, France, Germany, and Italy. As part of a research project funded by the Central European University (Vienna, Austria), I am looking at how qualifications, nomination processes, and/or prior personal, professional, and political experiences may affect independence and impartiality at constitutional courts, and what specific rules exist to strengthen such independence and impartiality from a comparative law perspective.

Please answer all mandatory questions marked with an exclamation mark (!) in full. It will take *no more than 5–10 minutes* to answer. By participating in this survey, you consent to the analysis and use of your answers in the context of the research project.

Note on privacy

The data collected through the survey will be anonymized and stored and analysed for research purposes in accordance with current data protection guidelines and in line with the principles of ethical research. After completion of your survey and preparation of the evaluation, your data will still be stored for archiving purposes and will be permanently deleted once the research project has ended.

In terms of data protection, you have the right to request information about the stored data and/or its deletion at any time, as well as to revoke your consent to the storage and processing of your answers. For this purpose, you can contact me by e-mail at any time. In addition, you will be given the opportunity to enter your e-mail address for the purpose of further contact.

Thank you in advance for your help!

Prof. Mathias Möschel
moschelm@ceu.edu
Head of the Department of Legal Studies
Central European University

----

1 What is your current function with regard to the constitutional court?
- Constitutional court judge
- Former constitutional court judge
- Staff at the constitutional court
- Other (please specify)

2 What are the rules for potential conflicts of interest?
- Incompatibilities with other functions or activities
- Abstention
- Recusal
- Cooling-off period (between previous position and function as constitutional judge)
- Other (please specify)

3 How satisfied are you with how these rules/practices function (Likert Scale) (5 points—satisfaction)?
- Incompatibilities with other functions or activities
- Abstention
- Recusal
- Cooling-off period (between previous position and function as constitutional judge)
- Other (please specify)

4 What was your profession before becoming a constitutional court judge?
- Academic
- Politician
- Attorney
- Judge
- Other (please specify)
- Not applicable

5 If your profession/activity was political, which of the following was your main one?
- Parliamentarian
- Minister
- (High) civil servant
- Other (please specify)
- Not applicable

6 In your opinion, what are the greatest risks to the *independence* of constitutional court judges?

7 In your opinion, what are the greatest risks to the *impartiality* of constitutional court judges?

ANNEX 2

Interview Questions

Question 1) In your opinion, what are the biggest risks for the independence and impartiality of your national constitutional court?

Question 2) Which role (if any) does the professional/political past of a constitutional judge play in their understanding of independence and impartiality of constitutional courts?

Question 3) (system specific):

Austria: As to the specific protection mechanisms, if I understood correctly, in Austria the recusal of a constitutional judge is prohibited or not possible. In your opinion, should this be changed? And how does the cooling-off period work? Should such a cooling-off period be also introduced after the mandate of constitutional judge?

Italy: As to the specific protection mechanisms, if I understood correctly, in Italy abstentions and recusals are prohibited in most procedures before the constitutional court due to an internal court rule. In your opinion, should this be changed? What do you think of a cooling-off period before or after the mandate of a constitutional court judge?

Germany: In your opinion, how do the rules on abstention and recusal of constitutional judges function in Germany? What do you think of a cooling-off period before or after the mandate of a constitutional court judge?

France: In your opinion, how do the recently introduced rules on abstention and recusal function in France? What do you think of a cooling-off period before or after the mandate of a constitutional court judge?

Question 4) As you probably know, our university was forced to move from Hungary to Austria for political reasons. How prepared do you think your national constitutional court is in terms of independence and impartiality for a similar political situation as the one we can observe in Central and Eastern Europe but also elsewhere? Are there any defence mechanisms?

Bibliography

Abeyratne, Rehan and Porat, Iddo (eds) *Towering Judges A Comparative Study of Constitutional Judges* (CUP 2021)

Abraham, Henry J, *Justices, Presidents and Senators* (5th edn, Rowman and Littlefield Publishers 2008)

Adamovich, Ludwig, 'Mein Vater Ludwig Adamovich (1890–1955)' in Häberle, Peter, Kilian, Michael, and Wolff, Heinrich A (eds), *Staatsrechtslehrer des 20 Jahrhunderts* (De Gruyter 2015) 371

Aders, Thomas, *Die Utopie vom Staat über den Parteien Biographische Annäherungen an Hermann Höpker Aschoff (1883–1954)* (Peter Lang 1999)

Agamben, Giorgio, *State of Exception* (transl by Attell, Kevin, University of Chicago Press 2005)

Alivizatos, Nicos C, 'Judges as Veto Players', in Döring, Herbert (ed) *Parliaments and Majority Rule in Western Europe* (Campus Verlag/Saint Martin's Press 1995) 566

Almeida Kato, Mariana, *La transparence de la justice constitutionnelle. Une étude de droit comparé (France, Brésil, États-Unis)* (Dalloz 2023)

Amato, Giuliano and Bassanini, Franco, 'La Corte costituzionale, un istituto da riformare' (1972) III Politica del diritto 811

Anders, Theodor and Schmidt, Fabian, 'MS vor Hausdurchsuchung Ex-Minister Brandstetter an Investor Tojner: "Wenn die heute kommen: ganz ruhig bleiben"', *Der Standard* (Vienna, 27 February 2021)

Aney, Madhav S, Dam, Shubhankar, and Ko, Giovanni, 'Jobs for Justice(s): Corruption in the Supreme Court of India' (2021) 64 Journal of Law and Economics 479

Avril, Pierre, 'Qui fait la loi?' (2005) 114 Pouvoirs 89

Balladur Committee of 2007: Comité de réflexion et de proposition sur la modernisation et le rééquilibrage des institutions de la Ve République, 'Une Ve République plus démocratique', 90

Bárd, Petra, 'In Courts We Trust, or Should We? Judicial Independence as the Precondition for the Effectiveness of EU Law' (2021) 27 European LJ 185

Bárd, Petra, *Rule of Law: Sustainability and Mutual Trust in a Transforming Europe* (Eleven 2023)

Bartole, Sergio, '"Cursus honorum" e Corte costituzionale' (1978) 101 Foro italiano, V, 89

Bau Nicolas and Israël, Liora, 'Quelques éclairages sociologiques sur la composition du Conseil constitutionnel', in Lemaire, Elina and Perroud, Thomas (eds), *Le Conseil constitutionnel à l'épreuve de la déontologie et de la transparence* (IFJD 2022)

Beauvois, Yves, *Léon Noël de Laval à de Gaulle via Pétain (1888–1987)* (Presses Universitaires du Septentrion 2001)

Becker, Theodore L, *Comparative Judicial Politics. The Political Functionings of Courts* (Rand McNally 1970)

Becker, Peter and Simon, Heike (eds), *Helmut Simon. Leben zwischen den Zeiten* (Nomos 2020)

Benda, Ernst, 'Befangenes zur Befangenheit' (2000) Neue Juristische Wochenschrift (NJW) 3620

Bickel, Alexander, *The Least Dangerous Branch. The Supreme Court at the Bar of Politics* (Yale University Press 1986)

Bierlein, Brigitte, 'Bundesrat und Verfassungsgerichtshof. Teil I', 18 December 2020

Bin, Roberto, 'Sull'imparzialità dei giudici costituzionali' (2009) LIV Giurisprudenza costituzionale 4015

Bingham, Tom, *The Business of Judging: Selected Essays and Speeches* (OUP 2000)

Blokker, Paul, 'Politics and the Political in Sociological Constitutionalism', in Blokker, Paul and Thornhill, Chris (eds), *Sociological Constitutionalism* (CUP 2017) 178

Blokker, Paul, 'Sociology of Constitutional Law and Politics', in Přibáň, Jiří (ed), *Research Handbook on Sociology of the Law* (Edward Elgar 2020) 230

Böckenförde, Ernst-Wolfgang, 'A Christian in the Office of Constitutional Judge [1999]', in Künkler, Mirjam and Stein, Tine (eds), *Religion, Law, and Democracy Selected Writings Ernst-Wolfgang Böckenförde* (OUP 2020) 280
Böckenförde, Markus, '"Resilience lite": Strengthening the Constitutional Protection of the German Federal Constitutional Court' (*ConstitutionNet*, International IDEA, 29 July 2024)
Boehme Nessler, Volker, 'Politiker als Richter?', *Die Zeit* (25 December 2018)
Bon, Pierre, 'Recuser un membre du Conseil constitutionnel' (2010) 186 Recueil Dalloz 2007
Bonelli, Matteo and Claes, Monica, 'Judicial Serendipity: How Portuguese Judges Came to the Rescue of the Polish Judiciary' (2018) 14 EU Cons L Rev 622
Boni, Massimiliano, *In questi tempi di fervore e di gloria* (Bollati Boringhieri 2022)
Boyron, Sophie, *The Constitution of France A Contextual Analysis* (Hart 2013)
Branca, Giuseppe, 'Collegialità nei giudizi della Corte costituzionale', in Corte costituzionale, *1956–2006: Cinquant'anni di Corte Costituzionale* (Corte Costituzionale 2006) 494
Brouard, Sylvain and Hönnige, Christoph, 'Constitutional Courts as Veto Players: Lessons from the United States, France and Germany' (2017) 56 European Journal of Political Research 529
Buge, Eric, 'Les auditions des candidats aux fonctions de membre du Conseil constitutionnel par les commissions parlementaires constituent-elles un filtre déontologique?' in Lemaire, Elina and Perroud, Thomas (eds), *Le Conseil constitutionnel à l'épreuve de la déontologie et de la transparence* (IFJD 2022)
Calamo Specchia, Marina (ed), *Le Corti costituzionali Composizione, Indipendenza, Legittimazione* (Giappichelli 2011)
Cassese, Sabino, *Dentro la Corte Diario di un giudice costituzionale* (il Mulino 2015)
Celotto, Alfonso and Olivetti, Marco (eds), *Commentario alla Costituzione Vol III* (UTET 2006)
Cheli, Enzo, *Il giudice delle leggi* (il Mulino 1996)
Chevallier, Jacques, 'Le juge constitutionnel et l'effet Becket' in *Renouveau du droit constitutionnel Mélanges en l'honneur de Louis Favoreu* (Dalloz 2007) 83
Chopplet, Antoine, 'Les membres de droit à vie du Conseil constitutionnel: inutile réforme ou abrogation nécessaire?' in Lemaire, Elina and Perroud, Thomas (eds), *Le Conseil constitutionnel à l'épreuve de la déontologie et de la transparence* (IFJD 2022) 123
Ciaudo, Alexandre, 'Un acteur spécifique du procès constitutionnel: le secrétaire général du Conseil constitutionnel' (2008) 73 Revue française de droit constitutionnel 17
Ciaudo, Alexandre, 'La place du secrétaire général du Conseil constitutionnel dans le procès constitutionnel', in Lemaire, Elina and Perroud, Thomas (eds), *Le Conseil constitutionnel à l'épreuve de la déontologie et de la transparence* (IFJD 2022)
Claes, Monica, 'Luxembourg, Here We Come? Constitutional Courts and the Preliminary Reference Procedure' (2015) 16 German LJ 1331
Cohen, Antonin, 'Legal Professionals or Political Entrepreneurs? Constitution Making as a Process of Social Construction and Political Mobilization' (2010) 4 International Political Sociology 107
Cole, Taylor, 'The West German Federal Constitutional Court: An Evaluation After Six Years' (1958) 20 The Journal of Politics 278
Cole, Taylor, 'Three Constitutional Courts: A Comparison' (1959) 53 The American Political Science Rev 963
Colombani, Jean-Marie, 'L'opposition, à l'exception de M Chirac, dénonce la nomination de M Badinter', Le Monde (21 February 1986) 10
Conti, Gian Luca, 'Art 135', in Bifulco, Raffaele, Celotto, Alfonso, and Olivetti, Marco (eds), *Commentario alla Costituzione. Vol. III* (UTET 2006)
Dam, Shubhankar, 'Active After Sunset: The Politics of Judicial Retirements in India' (2023) 51 Federal L Rev 31
David, Alexia, *L'impartialité du Conseil constitutionnel* (Droit Normandie Université 2021)
de Búrca, Gráinne, 'Poland and Hungary's EU Membership: On Not Confronting Authoritarian Governments' (2022) 20 ICON 13
de la Nuez, Elisa, 'Crisis constitucional' *El Mundo* (20 December 2022)

de Siervo, Ugo, 'Riflessioni su un'esperienza di lavoro alla Corte costituzionale' (2006) 11 Giornale di storia costituzionale 81
de Visser, Maartje, *Constitutional Review in Europe A Comparative Analysis* (Hart 2014)
Debré, Jean-Louis, *Ce que je ne pouvais pas dire* (Robert Laffont 2016)
Denizeau-Lahaye, Charlotte, 'La génèse du bloc de constitutionnalité', Titre VII [online], n° 8, Les catégories de normes constitutionnelles, avril 2022
D'Orazio, Giustino, *La genesi della Corte costituzionale: ideologia, politica, dibattito dottrinale, un saggio di storia delle istituzioni* (Edizioni comunità 1981)
Dieterich, Thomas, *Ein Richterleben im Arbeits- und Verfassungsrecht* (Berliner Wissenschaftsverlag 2016)
Dixon, Rosalind and Williams, George (eds) *The High Court, the Constitution and Australian Politics* (CUP 2015)
Drinóczi, Tímea and Bień-Kacała, Agnieszka, *Illiberal Constitutionalism in Poland and Hungary: The Deterioration of Democracy, Misuse of Human Rights and Abuse of the Rule of Law* (Routledge 2022)
Duden, Konrad, 'Richterwahl und parteipolitische Einflussnahme Vergleichende Anregungen zum Schutz der Unabhängigkeit des Bundesverfassungsgerichts und der obersten Bundesgerichte' (2020) 84 Rabels Zeitschrift für ausländisches und internationales Privatrecht 637
Duverger, Maurice, 'Une fraude à la Constitution?', *Le Monde* (22 February 1986) 7
Dyevre, Arthur, 'Unifying the Field of Comparative Judicial Politics: Towards a Theory of Judicial Behavior' (2010) 2 European Political Science Rev 297
Eichberger, Michael, 'Die erste von drei Säulen: Zum Arbeitsentwurf des BMJ zur Stärkung der Stellung des Bundesverfassungsgerichts', *VerfBlog*, 16 April 2024
Engst Benjamin G and others, 'Zum Einfluss der Parteinähe auf das Abstimmungsverhalten der Bundesverfassungsrichter – eine quantitative Untersuchung' (2017) 72 Juristen Zeitung 816
Epping, Volker, 'Die Selbstablehnung von Richtern am Bundesverfassungsgericht' (1994) 109 Deutsches Verwaltungsblatt (DVBl) 499
Epstein, Lee and others, *The Supreme Court Compendium* (6th edn, Sage 2015)
Escobar Lemmon, Maria C and others, *Reimagining the Judiciary: Women's Representation on High Courts Worldwide* (OUP 2021)
Fabiano, Laura, 'Legittimità e indipendenza della Corte suprema statunitense nella procedura di nomina dei suoi giudici', in Calamo Specchia, Marina (ed), *Le Corti costituzionali Composizione, Indipendenza, Legittimazione* (Giappichelli 2011) 63
Ferejohn, John, 'Judicializing Politics, Politicizing Law' (2002) 65 Law and Contemporary Problems 41
Fernández Segado, Francisco, *La justicia constitucional: una visión de derecho comparado*, Tomo III 'La justicia constitucional en América Latina y España' (Dykinson 2009)
Ferrari, Giuseppe, 'Corte costituzionale e magistratura' (1976) XVI Rassegna dei magistrati 255
Ferreres Comella, Victor, 'The European Model of Constitutional Review of Legislation: Toward Decentralization?' (2004) 2 ICON 461
Fessard de Foucault, Bertrand, 'Les ministres d'Etat' (1972) 22 Revue française de science politique 5
Flaherty, Martin S, 'The Most Dangerous Branch' (1996) 105 Yale LJ 1725
Fidler, Harald, 'Doskozil macht Verfassungsbeschwerde gegen Politeinfluss im ORF offiziell – und Armin Wolfs Anregung wahr', *Der Standard* (Vienna, 26 June 2022)
Fontaine, Lauréline, *La Constitution maltraitée* (Editions Amsterdam 2023)
Franck, Raphaël, 'Judicial Independence Under a Divided Polity: A Study of the Rulings of the French Constitutional Court, 1959–2006' (2009) 25 Journal of Law, Economics, and Organization 262
François, Bastien, 'Le juge, le droit et la politique: éléments d'une analyse politiste' (1990) 1 Revue française de droit constitutionnel 49
Fritz, Vera, 'Judge Biographies as a Methodology to Grasp the Dynamics inside the CJEU and its Relationship with EU Member States', in Rask, Madsen, Mikael, Nicola, Fernanda, and Vauchez, Antoine (eds), *Researching the European Court of Justice* (CUP 2022) 209

Fromme, Friedrich Karl, 'Ablehnung von Richtern im Kammer-Verfahren', in *Verantwortlichkeit und Freiheit Festschrift für Willi Geiger zum 80 Geburtstag* (Mohr 1989) 747
Geertz, Clifford, *The Interpretation of Cultures* (Basic Books 1973)
Gentile, Saverio, '"Le mani nella pasta, gli occhi al cielo" e la coscienza sporca: la magistratura e la legislazione antiebraica tra fascismo e Repubblica', in Meniconi, Antonella and Neppi Modona, Guido (eds), *L'epurazione mancata. La magistratura italiana tra fascismo e Repubblica* (il Mulino 2022) 115
Giannini, Amedeo, 'Ineleggibilità ed incompatibilità dei giudici costituzionali' (1956) 5–6 Il Consiglio di Stato 5
Ginsburg, Tom and Hug, Aziz Z, *How to Save a Constitutional Democracy* (University of Chicago Press 2018)
Glavina, Monika, 'From a Potentially Powerful to a Polarised Court: The Emergence of Dissenting Opinions on the Croatian Constitutional Court' (2024) 25 European Politics and Society 518
Grabenwarter, Christoph, 'The Austrian Constitutional Court', in von Bogdandy, Armin, Huber, Peter M, and Grabenwarter, Christoph (eds), *The Max Planck Handbooks in European Public Law*, vol 3 (OUP 2020) 19
Graber, Renate and Oswald, Günther. 'Brandstetter als Verfassungsrichter: "Von der Optik her ein Wahnsinn"' *Der Standard* (Vienna, 6 February 2018)
Graber, Renate and Schmidt, Fabian, 'Posten, Fouls und Verfassungsrichterinnen als Müllfrauen in Pilnaceks Chats', *Der Standard* (Vienna, 2 June 2021)
Graber, Renate and Schmidt, Fabian, 'Wolfgang Brandstetter zieht sich als Verfassungsrichter zurück', *Der Standard* (Vienna, 3 June 2021)
Graefe, Jérôme and Perroud, Thomas, 'L'impardonnable légèreté du Conseil constitutionnel avec l'impartialité' (2022) Revue des droits et libertés fondamentaux (RDLF), chron n°18
Grass, Nikolaus (ed), *Österreichische Rechts- und Staatswissenschaften der Gegenwart in Selbstdarstellungen* (Universitätsverlag Wagner 1952)
Grätz, Klaus Ferdinand and Steinbeis, Maximilian, 'Die meisten Dinge, die in Polen und Ungarn gelaufen sind, könnten ohne weiteres auch hier passieren', *VerfBlog*, 22 February 2018
Grimm, Dieter, *Verfassungsgerichtsbarkeit* (Suhrkamp 2021)
Grunert, Marlene, 'Ein Abendessen mit Nebenwirkungen', *Frankfurter Allgemeine Zeitung* (18 October 2021)
Guarnieri, Carlo and Pederzoli, Patrizia, *The Power of Judges A Comparative Study of Courts and Democracy* (OUP 2002)
Guéna, Yves, *Ecrits et discours III (1997–2007)* (La Lauze 2008)
Hailbronner, Michaela, *Tradition and Transformations The Rise of German Constitutionalism* (OUP 2015)
Haimbaugh Jr, George D, 'Was It France's Marbury v Madison?' (1974) 35 Ohio State LJ 910
Halmai, Gabor , 'Is There a "Constitutional Moment" in Israel and Hungary?' (2023) 56 Israel L Rev 426
Heller, Kurt, *Der Verfassungsgerichtshof* (Verlag Österreich 2010)
Herzog, Roman, *Jahre der Politik* (Siedler Verlag 2007)
Hirschl, Ran, *Towards Juristocracy The Origins and Consequences of the New Constitutionalism* (Harvard University Press 2004)
Hirschl, Ran, 'Judicialization of Politics', in Caldeira, Gregory A, Kelemen, R Daniel, and Whittington, Keith E (eds), *The Oxford Handbook of Law and Politics* (OUP 2008) 119
Hirschl, Ran, *Comparative Matters The Renaissance of Comparative Constitutional Law* (OUP 2014)
Holoubek, Michael and Wagrandl, Ulrich, 'A Model for the World: The Austrian Constitutional Court Turns 100' (2023) 17 ICLJ 251
Hönnige, Christoph, 'The Electoral Connection: How the Pivotal Judge Affects Oppositional Success at European Constitutional Courts' (2009) 32 West European Politics 963
Hönnige, Christoph, 'Beyond Judicialization: Why We Need More Comparative Research About Constitutional Courts' (2011) 10 European Political Science 346

Höreth, Markus, 'Sollen Politiker Verfassungsrichter werden?' (2011) 60 Gesellschaft, Wirtschaft, Politik 5

Horowitz, Donald, *Courts and Social Policy* (The Brooking Institution 1977)

Hourquebie, Fabrice, 'Les nominations au Conseil constitutionnel' Les Petites Affiches (31 May 2001) 79

Howard Jr, J Woodford, 'Judicial Biography and the Behavioral Persuasion' (1971) 65 American Political Science Rev 704

Jakab, András and Kochenov, Dimitry (eds) *The Enforcement of EU Law and Values* (OUP 2017)

Jan, Pascal and Pluen, Olivier, 'Les anciens présidents de la République, membres de droit du Conseil constitutionnel: un anachronisme bien vivant', Actu-Juridique, 30 November 2016

Jaremba, Urszula and Mak, Elaine, 'Interviewing Judges in the Transnational Context' (2014) 5 Law and Method

Jospin Committee of 2012, Commission de rénovation et de déontologie de la vie publique, 'Pour un renouveau démocratique', proposition n°32, 102

Joxe, Pierre, *Cas de conscience* (Labor et Fides 2010)

Juppé, Alain, *Une histoire française* (Tallandier 2023)

Kaplan, David A, *The Most Dangerous Branch: Inside the Supreme Court in the Age of Trump* (Crown 2018)

Kau, Marcel, *United States Supreme Court und Bundesverfassungsgericht: Die Bedeutung des United States Supreme Court für die Errichtung und Fortentwicklung des Bundesverfassungsgerichts* (Springer 2007)

Kelsen, Hans, 'Die Verfassungsreform' (1929) 58 Juristische Blätter 445

Kerléo, Jean-François, 'Les conditions d'amélioration du régime du déport et de la récusation devant le Conseil constitutionnel', in Lemaire, Elina and Perroud, Thomas (eds), *Le Conseil constitutionnel à l'épreuve de la déontologie et de la transparence* (IFJD 2022) 233

Klatt, Matthias K, 'Österreich auf dem Weg zum Sondervotum? Beobachtungen aus deutscher Perspektive', JuWiss-Blog, 21 April 2021

Klecatsky, Hans R, 'Über die Notwendigkeit einer grundlegenden Reform der österreichischen Verfassungsgerichtsbarkeit', in Leibholz, Gerhard and others (eds) *Menschenwürde und freiheitliche Rechtsordnung Festschrift für Willi Geiger zum 65 Geburtstag* (Mohr Siebeck 1974) 925

Kneihs, Benjamin, 'Constitutional Jurisdiction in Austria from 1918 to 2018: Continuities – Breaks – Compromises' (2020) 75 Zeitschrift für öffentliches Recht 885

Kommers, Donald P, *The Constitutional Jurisprudence of the Federal Republic of Germany* (Duke University Press 1989)

Kommers, Donald P and Miller, Russell A, *The Constitutional Jurisprudence of the Federal Republic of Germany* (3rd edn, Duke University Press 2012)

König, Thomas and Ehs, Tamara, 'Ludwig Adamovich Jurist, Minister, Rektor und Verfassungsrichter', in Ash, Mitchell G and Ehmer, Josef (eds), *Universität – Politik – Gesellschaft* (Vienna University Press 2015) 305

Korkea-aho, Hanna Emilia and Leino-Sandberg, Païvi Sirkku Maria, 'Interviewing Lawyers: A Critical Self-reflection on Expert Interviews as a Method of EU Legal Research' (2019) 12 European Journal of Legal Studies 17

Kosař, David, Šipulová, Katarína, and Urbániková, Marína, 'Informality and Courts: Uneasy Partnership' (2023) 24 German LJ 1239

Kramer, Helmut, *Willi Geiger Vom Antisemiten und Staatsanwalt am NS Sondergericht zum Richter am Bundesverfassungsgericht* (Kugelberg Verlag 2017)

Kramer, Larry D, *Popular Constitutionalism and Judicial Review* (OUP 2004)

Kranenpohl, Uwe, *Hinter dem Schleier des Beratungsgeheimnisses Der Willensbildungs- und Entscheidungsprozess beim BVerfG* (Verlag für Sozialwissenschaften 2010)

Krugman Ray, Laura, 'Lives of the Justices: Supreme Court Autobiographies' (2004) 37 Connecticut L Rev 233

Krygier, Martin, Czarnota, Adam, and Sadurski, Wojciech (eds), *Anti-Constitutional Populism* (CUP 2022)

Lamarque, Elisabetta, 'Chi sono gli assistenti di studio dei giudici costituzionali', in *Alle frontiere del diritto costituzionale Scritti in onore di Valerio Onida* (Giuffrè 2011) 1065
Lamarque, Elisabetta, *Corte costituzionale e giudici nell'Italia repubblicana* (Laterza 2017)
Lamprecht, Rolf, 'Karlsruher Befangenheitslogik' (1999) Neue Juristische Wochenschrift (NJW) 2791
Lamprecht, Rolf, *Ich gehe bis nach Karlsruhe Eine Geschichte des Bundesverfassungsgerichts* (Spiegel Buchverlag 2011)
Landfried, Christine, 'Die Wahl der Bundesverfassungsrichter und ihre Folgen für die Legitimität der Verfassungsgerichtsbarkeit' in Ooyen, Robert Chr van and Möllers, Martin HW, *Das Bundesverfassungsgericht im politischen System* (Verlag für Sozialwissenschaften 2006) 229
Landfried, Christine, 'The Selection Process of Constitutional Court Judges in Germany', in Malleson, Kate and Russell, Peter H, *Appointing Judges in an Age of Judicial Power* (University of Toronto Press 2007) 196
Lasser, Mitchell de SO-L'E, *Judicial Dis-Appointments: Judicial Appointments Reform and the Rise of European Judicial Independence* (OUP 2020)
Latour, Bruno, *The Making of Law An Ethnography of the Conseil d'Etat* (Polity Press 2010)
Lawson, Gary S, 'The Rise and Rise of the Administrative State' (1994) 107 Harvard L Rev 1231
Lechner, Hans and Zuck, Rüdiger, *Bundesverfassungsgerichtsgesetz Kommentar* (5th edn, CH Beck, 2006)
Le Gendre, Bertrand, 'Un homme de droit', Le Monde (Paris, 21 February 1986) 8
Lemaire, Elina and Perroud, Thomas (eds), *Le Conseil constitutionnel à l'épreuve de la déontologie et de la transparence* (IFJD 2022)
Lenoir, Noëlle, '1992–2001 Souvenirs d'une femme au Conseil constitutionnel' (2008) 25 Les cahiers du Conseil constitutionnel 15 <https://wwwconseil-constitutionnelfr/nouveaux-cahiers-du-conseil-constitutionnel/1992-2001-souvenirs-d-une-femme-au-conseil-constitutionnel#:~:text=La%20d%C3%A9cision%20du%20Conseil%20a,soit%20statu%C3%A9%20sur%20sa%20demande%20%C2%BB>
Ley, Richard, 'Die Wahl der Mitglieder des Bundesverfassungsgerichtes Eine Dokumentation anläßlich des 40jährigen Bestehens' (1991) 22 Zeitschrift für Parlamentsfragen 420
Lorenz, Astrid, 'Das Verfassungsgericht des Landes Brandenburg als politisiertes Organ? Möglichkeiten und Grenzen politischer Einflussnahme', in Reuter, Werner (ed), *Landesverfassungsgerichte Entwicklung – Aufbau – Funktionen* (Springer, 2017)
Lorenz, Astrid and Anders, Lisa H (eds), *Illiberal Trends and Anti-EU Politics in East Central Europe* (Palgrave Macmillan 2021)
Loughlin, Martin, *Against Constitutionalism* (Harvard University Press 2022)
Lübbe-Wolff, Gertrude, *Beratungskulturen Wie Verfassungsgerichte arbeiten, und wovon es abhängt, ob sie integrieren oder polarisieren* (Konrad-Adenauer-Stiftung 2022)
Lübbe-Wolff, Gertrude, 'How to Prevent Blockage of Judicial Appointments', *VerfBlog*, 7 October 2022
Lübbe-Wolff, Gertrude, 'One-sidedly Staffed Courts: A Problem of Impartiality – not only in Poland', *VerfBlog*, 8 January 2024
Luchaire, François, *Le Conseil constitutionnel* (Economica 1980)
Luchaire, François, 'La nomination de Robert Badinter au Conseil constitutionnel Réponse à Maurice Duverger', Le Monde (Paris, 26 February 1986) 9
MacDonald, Douglas, 'Worlds Apart. The Appointment of Former Politicians as Judges' (2016) 41 Alternative LJ 17
Madison, James, The Federalist No 51 (1788), reprinted in Geoffrey A Stone and others, *Constitutional Law* (6th edn, Aspen Publishers 2009)
Magrini, Veronica, 'L'astensione e la ricusazione quali strumenti per la realizzazione dell'imparzialità del giudice costituzionale', Doctoral thesis, University of Pisa, June 2016
Maionchi, Alessandro, 'Astensione e ricusazione tra processo comune e processo costituzionale L'esperienza italiane e quella spagnola a confronto', in Bindi, Elena, Perini, Mario, and Pisaneschi, Andrea (eds), *I principi generali del processo comune ed i loro adattamenti alle esperienza della giustizia costituzionale* (Giappichelli 2008) 369

Manaouil, Cécile, Gignon, Maxime, and Jardé, Olivier, '10 Years of Controversy, Twists and Turns in the Perruche Wrongful Life Claim: Compensation for Children Born with a Disability in France' (2012) 31 Medicine and Law 661

Martín Guardado, Sergio, 'Polarización política y crisis en la renovación del Consejo General del Poder Judicial' (2023) 117 Revista de Derecho Político 131

Massing, Otwin, 'Legal Assistants at the German Federal Constitutional Court A "Black Box" of Research?', in Rogowski, Ralf and Gavron, Thomas (eds), *Constitutional Courts in Comparison: The US Supreme Court and the German Federal Constitutional Court* (Berghahn Books 2002) 180

Menzel, Jörg and Müller Terpitz, Ralf (eds), *Verfassungsrechtsprechung* (3rd edn, Mohr Siebeck 2017)

Mitterrand, François, *Le coup d'État permanent* (Les Belles Lettres 2010 [1964])

Monnerville, Gaston, *Vingt-deux ans de présidence* (Le Cherche Midi 1980)

Moraru, Madalina and Bercea, Raluca, 'The First Episode in the Romanian Rule of Law Saga: Joined Cases C-83/19, C-127/19, C-195/19, C-291/19, C-355/19 and C-397/19, Asociaţia 'Forumul Judecătorilor din România, and Their Follow-up at the National Level' (2022) 18 European Constitutional L Rev 82

Morelli, Alessandro, 'La Corte imparziale e i suoi nemici L'inapplicabilità nei giudizi costituzionali delle norme sull'astensione e la ricusazione dei giudici' (2009) Forum dei quaderni costituzionali 1–2, <https://wwwforumcostituzionaleit/wordpress/images/stories/pdf/documenti_forum/temi_attualita/corte_costituzionale/0004_morellipdf>

Müller, Andreas, 'Zur Ablehnung von Bundesverfassungsrichtern wegen Besorgnis der Befangenheit nach § 19 BVerfGG' (1993) Neue Zeitschrift für Verwaltungsrecht (NVwZ) 1167

Nir, Esther, 'Approaching the Bench: Accessing Elites on the Judiciary for Qualitative Interviews' (2018) 21 International Journal of Social Research Methodology 77

Noël, Léon, *De Gaulle et les débuts de la Ve République* (Plon 1976)

Pace, Alessandro, 'La Corte costituzionale nell'esperienza di un avvocato' (2006) 11 Giornale di storia costituzionale 93

Palermo, Francesco, 'La giurisprudenza costituzionale tedesca nel biennio 2009–2010' (2011) LVI Giurisprudenza costituzionale 3921

Palewski, Gaston, *Mémoires d'action 1924–1974* (Plon 1988)

Passaglia, Paolo, 'La disciplina della composizione come primo cardine dell'indipendenza e della legittimazione dell'organo: il caso della Corte costituzionale italiana', in Calamo Specchia, Marina (ed), *Le Corti costituzionali Composizione, Indipendenza, Legittimazione* (Giappichelli 2011) 203

Pavone, Tommaso, 'Lawyers, Judges, and the Obstinate State: The French Case and an Agenda for Comparative Politics' (2020) 18 French Politics 416

Pech, Laurent and Platon, Sébastien, 'Judicial Independence Under Threat: The Court of Justice to the Rescue in the ASJP Case' (2018) CMLR 1827

Pederzoli, Patrizia, 'I giudici della Corte costituzionale', *disCrimen*, 23 November 2018, https://discrimenit/i-giudici-della-corte-costituzionale/

Pelletier, Monique, 'Quatre années trop courtes' (2008) 25 Les cahiers du Conseil constitutionnel 37, <https://wwwconseil-constitutionnelfr/nouveaux-cahiers-du-conseil-constitutionnel/quatre-annees-trop-courtes>

Pergolesi, Ferruccio, 'In tema di ricusazione e di astensione dei giudici della Corte costituzionale' (1953) I Rivista di diritto processuale' 311

Perlo, Nicoletta, 'Les premières récusations au Conseil constitutionnel: réponses et nouveaux questionnements sur un instrument à double tranchant' (2012) 27 Annuaire international de justice constitutionnelle 61

Pertici, Andrea, 'Astensione e ricusazione dei giudici costituzionali: ragioni e limiti della loro esclusione ed ipotesi di una loro introduzione' (2004) XLIX Giurisprudenza costituzionale 3105, 3127

Pfeiffer, Gerd, 'Die innere Unabhängigkeit des Richters', in Fürst, Walther, Herzog, Roman, and Umbach, Dieter C (eds), *Festschrift für Wolfgang Zeidler* vol 1 (Walter de Gruyter 1987) 67

Pizzorusso, Alessandro, 'Art 135', in Branca, Giuseppe (ed), *Commentario della Costituzione: Garanzie costituzionali Art 134–139* (Zanichelli Editore 1981) 144

Poli, Maria Daniela, 'Le Corti costituzionali dei *Länder* in Germania: assetti strutturali e problemi aperti', in Calamo Specchia, Marina (ed), *Le Corti costituzionali Composizione, Indipendenza, Legittimazione* (Giappichelli 2011) 23

Quinault-Maupoil, Tristan, 'Conseil constitutionnel: les nominations de la macronie font polémique', *Le Figaro* (Paris, 15 February 2022), <https://wwwlefigarofr/politique/emmanuel-macron-propose-de-nommer-jacqueline-gourault-au-conseil-constitutionnel-20220215>

Rauti, Alessio, 'Riflessioni in tema di imparzialità dei giudici costituzionali' (2009) LIV Giurisprudenza costituzionale 4029

Ritterspach, Theodor, 'Erinnerungen an die Anfänge des Bundesverfassungsgerichts', in Klein, Eckart (ed), *Grundrechte, soziale Ordnung und Verfassungsgerichtsbarkeit Festschrift für Ernst Benda zum 70 Geburtstag* (CF Müller 1995) 201

Robert, Jacques, *La garde de la République Le Conseil constitutionnel raconté par l'un de ses membres* (Plon 2000)

Rodotà, Carla, *Storia della Corte costituzionale* (Laterza 1999)

Rosenfeld, Michel, 'Judicial Politics versus Ordinary Politics Is the Constitutional Judge Caught in the Middle?', in Landfried, Christine (ed), *Judicial Power: How Constitutional Courts Affect Political Transformations* (CUP 2018) 36

Rousseau, Dominique, 'Le procès constitutionnel' (2011) 137 Pouvoirs 47

Ruggeri, Antonio and Spadaro, Antonino, *Lineamenti di giustizia costituzionale* (Giappichelli 2014)

Russell, Peter H, 'Toward a General Theory of Judicial Independence', in Russell, Peter H and O'Brien, David M (eds) *Judicial Independence in the Age of Democracy: Critical Perspectives From Around the World* (UVA Press 2001) 1

Sacco, Giovanni Andrea, 'I giudici emeriti e l'indipendenza della Corte costituzionale', in Costanzo, Pasquale (ed), *L'organizzazione e il funzionamento della Corte costituzionale* (Giappichelli 1996) 157

Sadurski, Wojciech, *Rights Before Courts* (Springer 2005)

Sadurski, Wojciech, *Poland's Constitutional Breakdown* (OUP 2019)

Sajó, András, *Ruling by Cheating. Governance in Illiberal Democracies* (CUP 2021)

Scanlan, James P, '*The Federalist* and Human Nature' (1959) 21 The Review of Politics 657

Scheppele, Kim Lane, 'Democracy by Judiciary (or why can courts be sometimes more democratic than Parliaments)', in Czarnota, Adam, Krygier, Martin, and Sadurski, Wojciech (eds), *Rethinking the Rule of Law in Post-Communist Europe* (CEU Press 2003) 25

Scheppele, Kim Lane, 'Constitutional Ethnography: An Introduction' (2004) 38 Law and Society Rev 389

Scheppele, Kim Lane, 'Autocratic Legalism' (2018) 85 The University of Chicago L Rev 545

Schiess Rütimann, Patricia, 'Unparteilichkeit von Verfassungsrichtern und deren Ablehnung in grosser Zahl wegen Besorgnis der Befangenheit Bemerkungen anlässlich von EGMR, AK/Liechtenstein vom 9 Juli 2015' (2015) 42 Europäische Grundrechte-Zeitschrift (EuGRZ) 549

Schmitt, Carl, in Vinx, Lars (ed), *The Guardian of the Constitution. Hans Kelsen and Carl Schmitt on the Limits of Constitutional Law* (CUP 2015)

Schnapper, Dominique, *Une sociologue au Conseil constitutionnel* (Gallimard 2010)

Schwarz, Hans-Peter, 'Memoirenfron und Memoirenlust, oder: Warum und wie schreiben unsere Spitzenpolitiker ihre Erinnerungen? Beobachtungen eines geneigten Lesers', in Herdegen, Mathias and others, *Festschrift für Roman Herzog zum 75 Geburtstag* (Beck 2009) 485

Sehl, Markus, 'Wie lässt sich das BVerfG vor Entmachtung schützen?', *Legal Tribune Online*, 29 January 2024, <https://wwwltode/recht/hintergruende/h/bverfg-gg-richter-demokratie-bundestag-rechtsstaat-verfassungsaenderung/>

Seibert-Fohr, Anja, 'Richterbestellung im Verfassungswandel: Der Einfluss des Individualrechtsschutzes auf Funktion und Auswahl oberster Richter in Europa' (2010) 49 Der Staat 130

Şen, İlker Gökhan, 'The Final Death Blow to the Turkish Constitutional Court: The Appointment of the Former Chief Prosecutor', *VerfBlog*, 28 January 2021
Sengupta, Arghya, *Independence and Accountability of the Indian Higher Judiciary* (CUP 2019)
Shapiro, Martin, *Courts A Comparative and Political Analysis* (Chicago University Press 1980)
Shapiro, Martin and Stone Sweet, Alec, *On Law, Politics, and Judicialization* (OUP 2002)
Somek, Alexander, 'Das Hohe und das Menschliche: eine Anmerkung zur Affäre Schnizer' *VerfBlog*, 3 October 2016
Spano, Robert, 'The Rule of Law as the Lodestar of the European Convention on Human Rights: The Strasbourg Court and the Independence of the Judiciary' (2021) 27 European LJ 211
Steinbeis, Maximilian, 'The Thuringia Project', *VerfBlog*, 16 June 2023
Steininger, Silvia, 'Talks, Dinners, and Envelopes at Nightfall: The Politicization of Informality at the Bundesverfassungsgericht' (2023) 24 German LJ 1300
Stone, Alec, *The Birth of Judicial Politics The Constitutional Council in Comparative Perspective* (OUP 1992)
Stone Sweet, Alec, *Governing with Judges Constitutional Politics in Europe* (OUP 2000)
Stone Sweet, Alec and della Cananea, Giacinto, 'Interview with Dieter Grimm' (2021) 21 German LJ 1541
Stone Sweet, Alec and della Cananea, Giacinto, 'Biographical Interview with Ernst-Wolfgang Böckenförde [2011]', in Künkler, Mirjam and Stein, Tine (eds), *Constitutional and Political Theory: Selected Writings Volume I* (OUP 2016)
Storme, Marcel, 'Reflections on Judicial Independence', in Shetreet, Shimon and McCormack, Wayne (eds) *The Culture of Judicial Independence in a Globalised World* (Brill 2016) 45
Szymczak, David, *La Convention européenne des droits de l'homme et le juge constitutionnel national* (Bruylant 2006)
Tamanaha, Brian Z, 'Understanding Legal Realism' (2009) 87 Texas L Rev 731
Thompson, Dennis F, 'Paradoxes of Government Ethics' (1992) 52 Public Administration Rev 254
Thompson, John B, *Political Scandal: Power and Visibility in the Media Age* (Polity Press 2000)
Tuleja, Piotr, 'Der polnische Verfassungsgerichtshof', in von Bogdandy, Armin, Grabenwarter, Christoph, and Huber, Peter (eds), *Handbuch Ius Publicum Europaeum Band VI, Verfassungsgerichtsbarkeit in Europa: Institutionen* (CF Müller 2016)
Tushnet, Mark, *Taking the Constitution Away from the Courts* (Princeton University Press 1999)
Tushnet, Mark, *The Constitution of the United States of America A Contextual Analysis* (Hart 2009)
Tusseau, Guillaume, *La déontologie publique: trajectoire et présence d'une notion ambiguë* (IFJD 2019)
Tusseau, Guillaume, *Contentieux constitutionnel comparé* (LGDJ 2021)
United Nations Office on Drugs and Crime (UNODC), *Commentary on the Bangalore Principles of Judicial Conduct*, 2007
Valdini, Melody E and Shortell, Christopher, 'Women's Representation in the Highest Court: A Comparative Analysis of the Appointment of Female Justices' (2016) 69 Political Research Quarterly 865
Vanberg, Georg, *The Politics of Constitutional Review in Germany* (CUP 2005)
Vanberg, Georg, *Constitutional Politics in Germany* (CUP 2005)
Van Dijk, Frans and Vos, Geoffrey, 'A Method for Assessment of the Independence and Accountability of the Judiciary' (2018) 9 International Journal for Court Administration 1
van Ooyen, Robert Chr (ed) and Kelsen, Hans, *Wer soll der Hüter der Verfassung sein?* (2nd edn, Mohr Siebeck 2019)
Vassalli, Giuliano, 'Testimonianza' (2006) 11 Giornale di storia costituzionale 55
Vauchez, Antoine, 'Judicialization: A Sociohistorical Perspective (Lessons and Questions from the French Fifth Republic)', in Madsen, Mikael Rask and Thornhill, Chris (eds), *Law and the Formation of Modern Europe Perspectives from the Historical Sociology of Law* (CUP 2014)
Vauchez, Antoine and De Witte, Bruno (eds), *Lawyering Europe: European Law as a Transnational Field* (Hart 2013)

Vedel, Georges, 'Neuf ans au Conseil constitutionnel' (1989) 55 Le Débat 48
Vermeule, Adrian, *Law and the Limits of Reason* (OUP 2009)
Vinx, Lars, *The Guardian of the Constitution Hans Kelsen and Carl Schmitt on the Limits of Constitutional Law* (CUP 2015)
Virelli III, Louis J, *Disqualifying the High Court Supreme Court Recusals and the Constitution* (Kansas University Press 2016)
Vogel, Wolfram, *Demokratie und Verfassung in der V Republik Frankreichs Weg zur Verfassungsstaatlichkeit* (Leske + Budrich 2001)
Volcansek, Mary, *Constitutional Politics in Italy* (Macmillan Press 2000)
Volcansek, Mary, *Comparative Judicial Politics* (Rowman 2019)
Wachsmann, Patrick, 'Sur la composition du Conseil constitutionnel' (2010) Jus Politicum 30–31
Wachsmann, Patrick, 'Les membres du Conseil au risque de la déontologie', in Lemaire, Elina and Perroud, Thomas (eds), *Le Conseil constitutionnel à l'épreuve de la déontologie et de la transparence* (IFJD 2022) 33
Waldron, Jeremy, *The Dignity of Legislation* (CUP 1999)
Waldron, Jeremy, 'The Core of the Case Against Judicial Review' (2006) 115 Yale LJ 1346
Wassermann, Rudolf, 'Richterlicher Selbstschutz bei der Ablehnung von Richtern des BVerfG? Zur Befangenheitsbesorgnis in verfassungsgerichtlichen Verfahren' (1987) Neue Juristische Wochenschrift (NJW) 418
Zagrebelsky, Gustavo, *Principî e voti La Corte costituzionale e la politica* (Einaudi 2005)
Zagrebelsky, Gustavo and Marcenò, Valeria, *Giustizia costituzionale, I Storia, principi, interpretazione* (2nd edn, il Mulino 2018)
Zagrebelsky, Gustavo and Marcenò, Valeria, *Giustizia costituzionale, II Oggetti, procedimenti, decisioni* (2nd edn, il Mulino 2018)
Zanon, Nicolò, *Le opinioni dissenzienti in Corte costituzionale* (Zanichelli Editore 2024)
Zimmermann, Felix W and Schroeter, Helen, 'Bundesjustizministerium schlägt Grundgesetzänderung vor', Legal Tribune Online, 28 March 2024
Zürn, Michael, 'The Politicisation of World Politics and its Effects: Eight Propositions' (2014) 6 European Political Science Rev 47

Index

For the benefit of digital users, indexed terms that span two pages (e.g., 52–53) may, on occasion, appear on only one of those pages.

Tables and figures are indicated by an italic *t* and *f* following the page number.